POSTCOMMUNISM AND
THE THEORY OF DEMOCRACY

POSTCOMMUNISM AND THE THEORY OF DEMOCRACY

Richard D. Anderson, Jr.

M. Steven Fish

Stephen E. Hanson

Philip G. Roeder

WITH AN INTRODUCTION BY
George W. Breslauer

PRINCETON UNIVERSITY PRESS

PRINCETON AND OXFORD

LIBRARY OF CONGRESS CATALOGING-IN-PUBLICATION DATA

POSTCOMMUNISM AND THE THEORY OF DEMOCRACY /
RICHARD D. ANDERSON, JR. . . . [et al.];
WITH AN INTRODUCTION BY GEORGE W. BRESLAUER.
P.   CM.
INCLUDES BIBLIOGRAPHICAL REFERENCES AND INDEX.
ISBN 0-691-08916-7 (ALK. PAPER)—ISBN 0-691-08917-5
1. FORMER SOVIET REPUBLICS—POLITICS AND GOVERNMENT. 2. DEMOCRATIZATION—
FORMER SOVIET REPUBLICS. 3. POST-COMMUNISM—FORMER SOVIET REPUBLICS.
4. EUROPE, EASTERN—POLITICS AND GOVERNMENT—1989–
5. DEMOCRATIZATION—EUROPE, EASTERN. 6. POST-COMMUNISM—
EUROPE, EASTERN. I. ANDERSON, RICHARD (RICHARD DAVIS), 1950–
JN6531 .P67 2001
320.947—dc21   20010322107

THIS BOOK HAS BEEN COMPOSED IN SABON TYPEFACE

PRINTED ON ACID-FREE PAPER. ∞

WWW.PUP.PRINCETON.EDU

PRINTED IN THE UNITED STATES OF AMERICA

1   3   5   7   9   10   8   6   4   2

1   3   5   7   9   10   8   6   4   2
(PBK.)

CONTENTS

CONTRIBUTORS

Richard D. Anderson, Jr., is Associate Professor of Political Science at the University of California, Los Angeles, where he is also active in Communication Studies. He is the author of *Public Politics in an Authoritarian State* (Cornell University Press 1993). His research interests concern the new field of political linguistics.

George W. Breslauer is Chancellor's Professor of Political Science and Dean of Social Sciences at the University of California, Berkeley. He is the author or editor of eleven books, including *Khrushchev and Brezhnev As Leaders: Building Authority in Soviet Politics* (Allen and Unwin, 1982), *Russia in the New Century* (coedited with Victoria Bonnell, Westview 2000), and the forthcoming *Gorbachev and Yeltsin As Leaders*. He is also editor of the journal *Post-Soviet Affairs*.

M. Steven Fish is Associate Professor of Political Science at the University of California, Berkeley. He is the author of *Democracy from Scratch: Opposition and Regime in the New Russian Revolution* (Princeton University Press 1995).

Stephen E. Hanson is Associate Professor of Political Science at the University of Washington and Director of the Russian, East European, and Central Asian Studies Program of the Jackson School of International Studies. He is the author of *Time and Revolution: Marxism and the Design of Soviet Institutions* (University of North Carolina Press, 1997) and coeditor (with Willfried Spohn) of *Can Europe Work?: Germany and the Reconstruction of Postcommunist Societies* (University of Washington Press 1995).

Philip G. Roeder is Associate Professor of Political Science at the University of California, San Diego. He is the author of *Red Sunset: The Failure of Soviet Politics* (Princeton University Press 1993) and articles that have appeared in the *American Political Science Review, International Studies Quarterly, World Politics*, and other professional journals.

LIST OF TABLES AND FIGURES

ACKNOWLEDGMENTS

THE AUTHORS are deeply grateful to the following friends and colleagues who provided advice, assistance in our research, and valuable comments on earlier drafts of one or more of the chapters: Vladislav Andriushenko, Kathleen Bawn, Victoria Bonnell, Valerie Bunce, Valery Chervyakov, Barbara Ann Chotiner, Al Cuzan, Keith Darden, Shanto Iyengar, Margarita Kitaigorodskaia, Jeffrey Kopstein, Natasha Laufer, Lena Morozova, Matthew Murphy, Pavel Parshin, Tatiana Rebetskaia, Sharon Werning Riviera, Richard Rose, Nina Rozanova, Anatolii Shaikevich, Sidney Tarrow, Edward Walker and members of the Program on New Approaches to Russian Security. We did not always have the wisdom to incorporate all of the many incisive suggestions we received, but we did accommodate many of them, and our book is better as a result. The shortcomings that remain, of course, are wholly our own responsibility. The authors also thank the following agencies that provided funding to us individually or as a group: Harvard University's Minda de Gunzburg Center for European Studies, the National Council for Central and East European Research, the UCLA Center for European and Russian Studies, the UCLA Academic Senate, the UCLA International Studies and Overseas Programs, and the University of California's Institute on Global Conflict and Cooperation.

POSTCOMMUNISM AND
THE THEORY OF DEMOCRACY

ONE

INTRODUCTION

George W. Breslauer

WHAT IS a democracy? How does it come into being? What variants of democracy exist in the contemporary world? How do those variants operate? How well do they govern? And what are their developmental trajectories? This cluster of questions about democracy has been perhaps the central concern of American political science throughout the discipline's history. There was a time, not too many years ago, when students of the Soviet Union and Eastern Europe did not have to address these questions. Their scholarship was focused on nondemocracies, whether they were called "authoritarian" or "totalitarian" dictatorships. These were "democracies" only by self-definition or by a definition that removed political freedom and electoral accountability from the meaning of the term.

All this has changed since the collapse of communism. The successor states of the Soviet Union and the postcommunist states of Eastern Europe have gone their own ways—some toward procedural democracy, some toward new variants of dictatorship, and some in directions that are difficult to define. This has meant that some scholars specializing on this part of the world have suddenly become students of democracy, asking many of the questions that have occupied a great deal of attention among comparativists, Americanists, and political theorists during this century. Do Russia, Ukraine, Georgia, and Romania qualify as democracies? If so, what types of democracy are they? How can we explain their progress toward democracy—or their movement away from it? And how likely are they to make further progress in building democracies? The present volume makes an important contribution to these debates. But given the recency of transitions to democracy in many postcommunist states, the contributors to this volume are most concerned with questions of definition (are these really democracies?),[1] origination, and prospects for democratic consolidation, rather than with questions central to studies of the operations and performance of established democracies. The main concern of contributors to this volume is to address the vast literature on successful and unsuccessful transitions to democracy that has become a veritable cottage industry within political science in recent decades.

Students of democracy have always had an urge to understand the processes by which democracies emerge in the first place. For decades, the focus of such research was on the social, cultural, and economic conditions that had made possible the emergence of liberal democracies in Western Europe. These provided templates for the enforced democratization of West Germany, Japan, and Italy under occupation regimes following World War II. Retrospective analyses of the emergence of European fascism in the 1920s and 1930s attempted to fathom the conditions that led to the breakdown of regimes that had already embarked on democratizing projects. Bursts of decolonization from the 1940s to the 1960s, in turn, led to a huge effort by scholars to analyze and propose strategies for economic and political development in the Third World that might create the socioeconomic conditions for the eventual creation of stable democracies. The surprising emergence of apparently stable democracies in parts of southern Europe, Latin America, and East Asia during the 1970s and 1980s—the so-called Third Wave of democratization—fostered a large and growing literature that sought to explain how this came about; or, in the cases of works still in progress, to describe, analyze, and track an ongoing process of liberalization and democratization.[2]

Explanatory debates within this community of scholars focused on the necessary and sufficient conditions for procedural democracy to emerge. These debates were informed by differences concerning the relative weights to be assigned to structure versus agency, determinism versus "voluntarism," inherited conditions versus creative leadership on the part of societal or political actors. Many students of the "Third Wave" contested the claim that procedural democracy is a product of cultural and socioeconomic conditions unique to Western Europe. They argued that, within very broad limits, democracy can be constructed in seemingly unpropitious (i.e., unprecedented) conditions. They specified the institutions that, if built, could provide the foundations for inducing democratic behavior even by actors of authoritarian inclination. They explored the international pressures and inducements that might offset unpropitious domestic conditions. They searched for functional substitutes for factors that were present in the history of Western Europe but not present in the Third Wave. They distinguished between the initial "transition from authoritarianism" or "democratic breakthrough" and the subsequent, longer period of "democratic consolidation," each of which was marked by its own mix of social conditions and political creativity, and by its own policy requirements. Epistemologically, many of these scholars argued for open-mindedness about the possibilities—what Hirschman (1970) had originally called "possibilism"—and open-endedness of conclusions.

This literature was already well developed when communism collapsed in Eastern Europe and the Soviet Union during 1989–91. Suddenly, the

Third Wave was enlarging, with close to thirty new countries providing sites for possible democratization. The literature on transitions to democracy expanded accordingly, with new journals, such as *Journal of Democracy, East European Constitutional Review*, and others being founded to track the latest developments. Naturally, optimism reigned among the "possibilists," even as skepticism remained among those committed to the notion that initial sociocultural conditions, not political creativity, determine whether democracy can take hold. Optimists preferred to compare the postcommunist world to the success stories of the Third Wave, in search of common features. Pessimists, though equally committed to the ideal of procedural democracy, compared the postcommunist world to authoritarian regimes in much of the Third World and found unsettling commonalities between what they referred to as the "East" and the "South." Most scholars, however, avoided these predictive debates and settled into a vast tracking exercise, exploring the construction and operations of democratic institutions in postcommunist countries, the development of popular and elite attitudes and behaviors, and the domestic and international factors influencing the trajectory of change.

Within a very few years, it became clear that the postcommunist world was not proceeding in just one direction, be it west or south. Instead, patterns of differentiation were emerging that included striking divergence across postcommunist countries. Gati (1996), based on a combination of political and economic observations, referred to "leaders," "laggards," and "losers." Other scholars discovered four or five distinct clusters or types (Roeder, 1994). Still others conducted quantitative analyses that scaled postcommunist systems and located them at numerous points on the continuum (Frye 1997; Easter 1997; Fish 1998a, b). These studies were both encouraged and facilitated by the ongoing efforts of international and nongovernmental organizations to track "progress" in the democratization of these regimes. Their databases—such as the annual Freedom House scores—provided the foundation for many of these scholarly exercises.

The immediate purposes of the scholarly and public-organizational exercises are somewhat different, even though most individuals in each sector share a normative commitment to procedural democracy. Public organizations are principally concerned with influencing public policy: both the activities of governments and social organizations in the region and the attitudes and actions of the rich democracies vis-à-vis states and societies in the region. Though political scientists may also seek to influence public policy, their concern *as scholars* is to discover patterns that teach us something deeper about historical causality more generally. They treat the postcommunist region as a "laboratory" in which to test propositions about political life, or as a virgin land in which entirely new forms of political organization may grow. In the case of postcommunist democratization (or its absence), they seek to draw lessons from the provisional "outcomes" they observe in that domain. Patterns of differentiation after a decade of postcommunist change become the basis for generalization about the conditions and policies that are most—and least—likely to foster democratization after communism. And those generalizations are in turn used to "test" the explanatory range of propositions derived from earlier literatures on the first, second, and third waves of democratization in modern world history.

This is the academic niche in which the present book is located. It is a contribution to "third wave" studies and it begins with the premise that the pessimism of first-wave theorists about the likelihood of democracy emerging in postcommunist states is misplaced. This basic premise is the product of several intellectual choices. One choice is definitional. Though their concrete definitions of democracy vary, three of the authors employ some variant of a more or less minimalist definition of "democracy," be it derived from Schumpeter or Dahl. This leads them, in turn, to categorize the majority of postcommunist states as ones that have effected an initial democratic breakthrough (or more). Only Roeder explicitly dissents from this definitional choice, but he shares with his coauthors a sense of pleasant surprise that, despite sociocultural conditions propitious to authoritarianism, many authoritarian regimes in the region have failed to consolidate their hold. Hence, all four authors are closer to the optimistic "possibilists" of third-wave studies than to those who argued that postcommunist democratization was likely to be a fiasco.

The second choice that informs this perspective is temporal: The authors are looking back over a landscape that is only one decade (or less) in the making. They therefore treat the situation today as, in some sense, an "outcome" to be explained. They are not primarily interested in predicting whether a similar pattern of results will be observable in five or ten years, though some of their findings are amenable to conversion into a statement of the conditions that would lead to one or the other future scenarios. They do not share the view of those who would argue that it is much too early to draw conclusions, a view that can be associated with either high optimists ("eventually they will all choose democracy") or abject pessimists ("just wait! even the alleged success stories are extremely fragile"). Instead, the contributors to this volume wish to provide broad theoretical grounding for understanding both progress and regression, democratic institution-building and institutional fragility since the collapse of communism. They search far and wide for theoretical understanding and, in the process, offer the reader a panoramic overview of both social theory and the variegated political landscape of postcommunist systems.

Thus, Professors Anderson, Fish, Hanson, and Roeder are concerned with the progress of democratization in the postcommunist region and the implications of that degree of progress (or shortfall, or regression) for our thinking about democratization more generally. Their chapters are products of an understanding of relevant theoretical and methodological literatures, detailed familiarity with the empirical realities of postcommunism, and powerful intellects. But the chapters are not strictly additive or cumulative. Instead, they employ diverse methodologies and even epistemologies for addressing varied aspects of the democratization of postcommunist states.

Hanson, for example, focuses principally on Russia as the empirical case, but mines several theoretical literatures in order to address the utility of the concept "democratic consolidation." Hanson's concern is to understand what it takes to consolidate a democratic breakthrough; his is a Weberian approach to the problem. Positing that Russia may indeed succeed in such an effort (shades of "possibilism"?), he asks us to consider what type of theory would be required to understand *both* the current fragility of Russian democracy *and* the hypothetical success of Russia's democratic consolidation. He finds a satisfying answer neither in the theoretical literature on socioeconomic modernization nor in that on rational-choice institutionalism. Instead, he offers a novel definition of consolidation as an exercise in regime and elite re-formation under conditions of widespread social turbulence. Hanson, then, looks prospectively at the Russian future in order to explore what it would take to create a context in which elite actors would share incentives, time horizons, and interpersonal affinities propitious for the long-term maintenance of democratic institutions.

Anderson is also principally concerned with the empirical case of Russia and, like Hanson, devotes the bulk of his chapter to discussion of theoretical issues. But Anderson is concerned to explain the success of Russia's initial democratic breakthrough, rather than the prospects for democratic consolidation. And Anderson is an antistructuralist who could not have reached the conclusions that Hanson does. Critiquing prevailing structural theories in the literature of political science, Anderson proposes instead that we focus on the language of political discourse in postcommunist countries. The driving force behind Russia's democratic breakthrough, he argues, was the emergence within the elite of actors disposed to employ a new, more-democratic political language with which to appeal to the masses for support against representatives of the old order. Their success in following this strategy, he finds, hinged on the degree to which that language was intelligible and appealing to the masses of the population. For, absent a sense of shared identity between new elites and would-be citizens, individual members of the population could not overcome their collective action problems and act upon newfound opportunities to involve themselves in politics. The discursive indicators of such identification, then, are Anderson's base of evidence for explaining Russia's success in effecting its democratic breakthrough.

Whereas Hanson and Anderson devote the bulk of their chapters to discussions of theory—and the shorter, empirical portions to the example of Russia—Roeder and Fish focus on a large number of countries and offer a balance of theoretical discussion and large-*n* empirical analysis. Roeder takes the fifteen states of the former Soviet Union as his empirical referents, while Fish looks at all twenty-eight postcommunist states. Both scholars begin by sorting the cases into categories reflecting degrees of democratization. They then employ the methods of "normal science" (including statistical methods) to test hypotheses about why the cases cluster as they do. But beyond that, they ask quite different questions about the progress of democratization.

Fish has elsewhere published statistical analyses specifying the factors that best explain progress toward democratization in the postcommunist world (Fish 1998a). In the present volume, he is concerned primarily with understanding why a certain subset of states in the region initially effected a democratic breakthrough, but later slid back toward regimes that were, marginally or substantially, more undemocratic. He finds that in contrast to the determinants of democratic erosion and reversal in other parts of the world, postcommunist reversals are best explained by their existence within the regressive subset of an institutional, societal, and international context that allowed chief executives to aggrandize and abuse their powers to an unusual (for the region) degree.

Roeder's chapter has a somewhat different emphasis. He had elsewhere published a seminal article on the early development of *authoritarian* patterns among postcommunist regimes (Roeder 1994). In the present volume, he notes the strength of a countertendency that has prevented the *consolidation of authoritarian regimes* in the region, despite propitious economic and cultural conditions, and he seeks to explain that anomaly. He finds the explanation in the divergent institutional legacies bequeathed by the communist regime to its successor. In contrast to those who posit a relatively uniform Leninist institutional legacy, Roeder argues that those regimes differed consequentially with respect to the degree of incipient fragmentation within the governing apparatus of the late–Communist Party and the degree of incipient autonomy of late–communist governmental bureaucracies from each other. Where fragmentation and autonomy were high by Leninist standards, efforts to consolidate authoritarian successors to communism have generally failed.

For Fish, the important outcome to be explained is democratic reversals; for Roeder, the outcome (indeed, for him, the anomaly) to be explained is the rejection of authoritarianism. For Fish, the danger in post-communist systems is overweening executives, while the hope is that social, institutional, and international forces can be mobilized to prevent chief executives from usurping power. For Roeder, the danger is also an excessive concentration of power. But the hope lies in the existence or development specifically of *institutional* pluralism *within* the authoritarian regime. For Fish, Ukraine and Russia are among the cases that have experienced democratic erosion or reversal. For Roeder, the same two countries are among the anomalies to be explained for having prevented the consolidation of stable authoritarianism. There are complementary and additive qualities to these two chapters, but readers will have to search beyond the definitional differences, and the differences in dependent variables, in order to find them.

In sum, Fish is concerned with explaining democratic regression, Roeder wishes to explain authoritarian failure, Anderson searches for ways to understand and measure democratic breakthroughs, and Hanson seeks theoretical understanding of the dilemmas of democratic consolidation. While they all share a commitment to treating degrees of progress (or lack thereof) during the 1990s as the outcome to be explained, they differ with respect to the specific patterns they treat as anomalous.

Thus, in the end, this book cannot be classified facilely as derivative of either the "pessimistic" or "optimist" approach to the emergence of democracy. In contrast to most pessimists, it employs a minimalist definition of democracy, is written in the spirit of "possibilism," and is impressed by how many postcommunist states have met that standard while lacking the structural or cultural preconditions enjoyed by the first wave of democratizers in Western Europe. But in contrast to most optimists, the authors in this volume are as impressed with the shortfalls as with the progress and seek frameworks that would help them explain both the scope and the limits of change. By focusing on backsliders, the (missing) requisites of democratic consolidation, and the failure of authoritarian regimes to consolidate themselves, Fish, Hanson, and Roeder come at the challenge of building (or explaining) democracy from diverse directions—and thereby broaden our ways of thinking about the problem. And by suggesting that we employ discourse analysis to get at presumably more enduring cultural indicators of change, Anderson reaches optimistic conclusions about progress in Russia to date, but sets a high (i.e., culturalist) standard for the evaluation of future progress and challenges the field to rethink structural explanations for changes taking place in turbulent environments.

Readers of this volume will learn a great deal about both social theory and the diversity of postcommunist politics. But they will also learn by inference about the trajectory of intellectual endeavor in this subfield of comparative politics. Before Gorbachev's reforms began the process of liberalization and democratization in the Soviet Union, leading eventually to the collapse of communism in both Eastern Europe and the Soviet Union, specialists on the region did not have to know much about democratic theory, the workings of democratic systems, or processes of democratic transition and consolidation. Only a narrow range of theoretical literature appeared to be relevant to the realities of established communist regimes. And an even narrower range was relevant to research topics that censors in those regimes allowed Western scholars to investigate empirically.

All this has changed with the collapse of communism. A much wider range of ideal-typical and real-world analogues or models, and a wide range of deductive and inductively derived theories, are now employed to fathom the complexities of postcommunism. With the collapse of communist censorship, many of these countries have come to be open for empirical research on the full range of topics normally studied in "open societies." Diverse research methodologies are now standard in the literature on postcommunism, including comparative case studies, survey research, elite interviewing, participant observation, the construction and statistical manipulation of large data sets, formal modeling, interpretivist analysis of texts, and more. Epistemological pluralism has also come to mark the subfield. Scientific methodologies are being challenged by postmodernist epistemologies, just as structural approaches of all sorts are being challenged by constructivist approaches. Such diversity is healthy; it is a reflection of the new openness of the societies we study and is a precondition for sustainable intellectual progress.

One of the interesting features of this volume is that it is written by a middle generation of scholars. All of them are tenured associate professors at major research universities. All of them were originally trained as political scientists while the Soviet Union was in existence. In all four cases, their first books were principally or exclusively focused on the Soviet Union in the communist era, though Fish's volume uniquely concentrated on the Gorbachev era (Anderson 1993; Fish 1995; Hanson 1997; Roeder 1993). And yet, they are all now among the leading researchers and interpreters of trends in postcommunist societies.

In fact, the seeds of such standing can also be found in their first books, all of which were steeped in, and informed by, social-theoretical concerns. None of them treated the Soviet Union as a "unique" case to be understood only on its own terms. All displayed skill in applying extant theory and in displaying both the extent and limits of its explanatory power. Several of the books went so far as to revise extant theory in order to incorporate the lessons of the communist or Gorbachev eras. All of them displayed an intellectual discipline that boded well for their embracing methodological pluralism once postcommunist societies created opportunities for systematic research employing diverse methodologies. And all of them combined theoretical sophistication with an intimate empirical knowledge of the cases being treated in their books.

Since the collapse of communism, these four scholars have displayed a formidable capacity for absorbing and applying additional theories and methodologies, and for grappling with the challenge of describing and explaining divergent trajectories among postcommunist societies. But what is most striking about the chapters in this book is that the authors are not simply consumers and appliers of received theoretical wisdom. They are specialists on a region who are equally adept at the development of social theory. They are capable of being critical of regnant assumptions within several bodies of theoretical literature and are eager to revise or improve existing theories in light of the empirical realities of postcommunism. Thus, their commitment to *improving* or even *inventing* theory contrasts with the earlier commitment—in the 1970s and 1980s—of most specialists on the Soviet Union and East Europe to *consuming* and *applying* received theory. It no longer matters whether we call these four scholars "theoretically sophisticated area specialists" or "social theorists with an area specialization." They do both equally well.

In these respects, the intellectual profiles of Anderson, Fish, Hanson, and Roeder are not atypical of other first-rate specialists on postcommunism who have been trained during the 1990s, or of veteran specialists who have successfully retooled, theoretically and/or methodologically, to address problems of postcommunism. The postcommunist subfield of comparative politics has matured to the point that it needs no special advice as to what constitutes "proper" theoretical or methodological standards, much less a single orthodoxy on either score. Rather, first-rate intellects are engaged in a joint exploration, through diverse methodologies and epistemologies, of the phenomenon of postcommunist change. Theirs is a joint effort to develop theory in ways that will account for the diversity in the postcommunist world and will explore the lessons of that diversity for our thinking about analogous phenomena in other regions of the world. The present volume is a significant contribution to that enterprise.

A Note on the Order of Chapters

The record of democracy in the postcommunist world is mixed. Some states never began the transition to democracy; others started and then turned backward; only a few can be counted as consolidated democracies a decade after the process began. The chapters in this book address the ability of existing theories of democratization to account for the patterns in these outcomes. Each author highlights a different aspect of this complex process of political transition for which existing theories fail to provide an entirely satisfactory explanation. The order of the chapters reflects the rough chronological order in which the respective topics occur—from the rejection of authoritarianism to the consolidation of democracy. Roeder examines the initiation of transitions from authoritarianism; Fish analyzes regime stability once democratization begins; Anderson considers changes in politician and citizen behaviors in the transition to democracy; and Hanson explains regime consolidation. In the second chapter Philip Roeder examines the initiation of transitions within existing authoritarian regimes and asks why authoritarian leaders come to reject authoritarianism and choose democracy. By examining the experience of the fifteen Soviet successor states, Roeder finds that elites were more likely to reject authoritarianism and choose democracy where intrastate pluralism prevented agreements that could resolve the inherent dilemmas of authoritarian constitutions. In the third chapter Steven Fish examines the failure of transitions to democracy and asks why countries that begin a democratic transition then slide back to authoritarianism. In a comprehensive survey of all twenty-eight postcommunist countries, Fish finds that the most important variable explaining democratic reversals—but not the only variable—is excessive concentration of executive power. In the fourth chapter Richard Anderson examines the Russian transition to democracy and asks why previously cohesive authoritarian rulers begin competing with one another for public support and previously quiescent subjects begin taking sides in this competition. Anderson attributes these behavioral changes to shifts in political discourse that dissolve the political identity that had united despotic rulers and separated them from the ruled and to shifts in political discourse that create partisan identities binding citizens to politicians and motivating the citizens to take costly action on behalf of individual politicians. In the fifth chapter Stephen Hanson examines the successful consolidation of democracy. By examining alternative concepts of democratic consolidation and their application to Russia and other postcommunist states, Hanson concludes that democracy consolidates with the emergence of a staff of officials who are dedicated to the enforcement of democratic rules. As I note here, the authors' approaches diverge; they ask different questions and offer different reasons for the failure or success of democracy in postcommunist countries. The authors, however, find that their views have much in common. In the conclusion they draw out common themes and complementarities that link their separate approaches. For the authors, the differences among them are the beginning points for a continuing, fruitful exchange of ideas.

TWO

THE REJECTION OF AUTHORITARIANISM

Philip G. Roeder

VISITORS to the Soviet Union prior to Mikhail Gorbachev's rise to leadership in 1985 were frequently impressed by the oppressive authoritarian order that had been perfected during nearly seventy years of Soviet power. In each of the fifteen union republics that constituted the Soviet Union, the Communist regime had isolated virtually all dissidents who might otherwise seek to challenge this order. Beginning in 1987, however, Mikhail Gorbachev delivered a series of shocks to this equilibrium under the slogan of *demokratizatsiia*. Ironically, these shocks brought down the Soviet regime and the Soviet Union, but they failed to create democracy in most of the union republics. Even after the breakup of the Soviet Union, in eleven of the fifteen successor states the authoritarian regimes of the Soviet period either survived virtually unchanged or transformed themselves into new types of nondemocracy. The survival of authoritarianism—that is, the ability of a constitutional equilibrium, whether it is authoritarian or democratic, to survive such shocks by making the most minimal adaptations—should not surprise us. The unexpected outcome in the Soviet cases is the failure of some equilibria to "right themselves" after the exogenous shocks delivered by Gorbachev. This poses a question that existing theories of democratization seem unable to answer—why did authoritarianism fail in some successor states? The Soviet and post-Soviet experience of the union republics sheds significant light on this part of the process of democratization.

This obviously turns the question usually asked by theories of democratization on its head, but it does more than simply rephrase a familiar question in a clever way that might offer new insights. Most important, it points to an important lacuna in existing theories of democratization: It underscores the fact that theories beginning with the premise that democracy represents a choice—as is standard in much of the literature on transitions to democracy (Collier and Mahoney 1997, 285)—must also account for the nondemocratic alternatives that can be chosen or rejected. In short, our theories of democratization must become more complete theories of regime choice. Moreover, since the choice to make the transition to democracy, by definition, is made in the context of nondemocracy, theories of democratization must provide an account of the politics of choice within authoritarianism that explains this decision. In short, the Soviet experience shows that an understanding of democratization requires that we explain why those who have the power in nondemocratic regimes to make or break constitutions find the nondemocratic alternatives unacceptable and turn to democracy.

The experience of the Soviet transition shows that the usual answers will not work. This experience, in fact, challenges theories that have long been used to identify conditions favorable for transitions from authoritarianism to democracy. All of the successor states contained powerful political forces seeking to preserve or create some form of authoritarian rule, yet not all of these succeeded. None of the venerable political-economic and political-cultural theories in their present incarnation is adequate to explain the failure of these politicians and their authoritarian projects. Indeed, according to many of these standard theories of democratization, the Soviet successor states represent extreme cases of the most favorable conditions for the survival of authoritarian regimes—particularly, when compared to the other countries of the world. Nevertheless, the absence of bourgeoisies, high incomes, economic growth, democratic traditions, rich associational life, and trust did not save or foster authoritarianism and prevent democratization in all successor states. We need an alternative explanation. In order to find this I look closely in this chapter at the choices available to the "founding parents" of the new regimes and the constraints that made one option preferable to the other. The working hypothesis of this chapter is that the least favorable condition for the authoritarian option and the most favorable for the democratic option has been institutional pluralism *within* the authoritarian state. In the Soviet successor states the extent of institutional pluralism or unity was initially a legacy of the Soviet past. In the 1990s authoritarian regimes and authoritarian projects failed when the governing bureaucracies were relatively autonomous from one another and created a form of checks and balances among themselves. Rather than finding the source for the failure of authoritarianism in the economies, political culture, or social life of the successor states, the explanation attributes the failure of some authoritarian projects to the political institutions of the existing authoritarian order itself. That is, the choice of constitution was constrained by the balance of power among elites empowered to sit at the bargaining table of constitutional politics, and this balance was created by the institutions of the late Soviet system.

In order to probe the tenability of this intrastate balance-of-power hypothesis, I offer three applications that use the fifteen union-republics-turned-successor-states as cases. These applications include the pattern of regime choices made in preparation for the 1990 union-republic elections, the types of constitutions adopted immediately after the dissolution of the Soviet Union in 1991, and the rejection of authoritarian regimes and projects—and the success of democratization—from 1992 to 2000. Throughout these three applications, the working hypothesis is that in each Soviet successor state the stability of authoritarianism, the success of authoritarian and democratic projects, and the design of constitutions were constrained by the power configuration among bureaucratic elites. This was initially defined by the union republic's governing structures on the eve of the 1990 legislative elections, which, in turn, affected the balance of power within the new supreme soviets and governments instituted by these elections.

This chapter is divided into four parts. The first identifies alternative types of regimes in the Soviet successor states in the decade that began with the elections of 1990. This defines the dependent variable. In the second part, I attempt to use existing theories of democratization to explain these patterns, but find the usual answers wanting. The third part presents a model of regime choice. Finally, three empirical applications of this model examine the ability of the intrastate balance-of-power hypothesis to explain systematically patterns of constitutional outcomes in the decade from early 1990 through early 2000. Because the Soviet successor states began with nearly identical institutions that were established in their common recent history, the successor states provide a "natural experiment" in which to study the stability, adaptation, and rejection of authoritarian constitutions.

The Dependent Variable—Post-Soviet Regimes

Having posed the question of regime choice, a first gap left by existing theories of democratization is terminology to account for the alternatives to democracy. Democracy is frequently defined, following the lead of Joseph Schumpeter (1975), as "that institutional arrangement for arriving at political decisions in which individuals acquire the power to decide by means of a competitive struggle for the people's vote." That is, democracy is a political system that approaches the ideal in which any 50 percent plus one of the population can remove or prevent the removal of the governors. Alternatively, authoritarianism or autocracy is commonly a rubric that is used to describe all nondemocratic regimes that fail to make government accountable to the public. Thus, authoritarianism is an institutional arrangement in which (1) minorities can remove the governors, and the popular majority is powerless to prevent this, and (2) the popular majority is unable to remove the governors. Closer examination of the varieties of nondemocracy reveals the limits of a simple dichotomy between democracy and authoritarianism, because the latter term brackets a number of arrangements in which the governors are accountable to someone other than the entire adult population (Roeder 1994). We obviously need a richer vocabulary to distinguish the ways in which regimes may diverge from the democratic ideal, according to which any 50 percent of the population can remove or prevent the removal of the government.

The distinction *among* regimes that I propose builds on answers to the question—to whom are the rulers, in fact, accountable? Or stated differently—who can remove the rulers? Alternative regime-types or "constitutions" are defined by the nature of this *selectorate*—the group that can pose a credible threat of removing the policy makers (or can defeat such an attempt) (Roeder 1993). In the typology that I employ here, constitutions differ to the extent that (1) the governors are accountable either to a selectorate inside the state apparatus or to a selectorate in society, and (2) this selectorate constitutes either a narrow or a broad segment of the state or the society. The first distinction corresponds to one found in the canon of political philosophy between republican forms of government and tyranny; in the former the state represents society, in the latter the state is autonomous from society. The second concerns the proportion of the state *or* the proportion of the society that participates in the removal of effective decision makers.

By treating these two dimensions, the locus and the relative restrictiveness of selectorates, as dichotomies, we can define four types of constitutions—autocracies, oligarchies, exclusive republics, and democracies. *Autocracy* is a political order in which the rulers are accountable to the small circle of central decision makers within the royal court, revolutionary council, politburo, or junta. Autocratic leaders are removed by intrigues within this inner circle of the central decision-making elite. That is, the selectorate is entirely within the state apparatus and constitutes a narrow segment of the state. *Oligarchy* defines a political order in which the selectorate consists of a broader group of bureaucrats within the state. The power to remove oligarchic rulers is limited to people occupying posts within the state, such as second-tier military officers, the intelligence apparatus, or regional governors, but these bureaucrats do not participate in the day-to-day decision making of the regime. *Exclusive republics* make the governors accountable to society, but to only a narrow segment of society. The rural landowners in some Latin American countries around the beginning of the twentieth century constituted the selectorate in these exclusive republics; similarly apartheid South Africa limited the franchise to a small racially defined segment of society. As an ideal, *democracy* is the fourth cell in which governors are accountable to a broad segment of society. Democracy is a constitution in which any majority of the population can pose a credible threat of removing the effective policy makers (or can defeat such a threat).[1]

In 1990 with elections to their supreme soviets (or Congress of Peoples Deputies in the Russian SFSR), the union republics began to diverge in the extent to which the leaders expanded the political process to incorporate members of the bureaucracy or of society into the selectorate. Where among the Soviet successor states did the leaders preserve the highly restrictive selectorates of autocracy? Where did the leaders transform autocratic selectorates into oligarchies or exclusive republics? Where did the leaders reject authoritarianism and choose to expand the selectorate to include the entire adult population? Table 2.1 summarizes evidence presented later in this chapter and shows that from January 1990 to December 2000 there were twenty-five different constitutional orders in the union-republics and successor states. Only four of these were democratizing regimes that survived throughout this period. Five Soviet successor states experienced brief periods of democratization that ended with backsliding toward some form of nondemocracy; two of these became exclusive republics. Alternatively, fourteen of the twenty-five constitutional orders have been either autocratic or oligarchic.

Table 2.1 shows that autocrats retained power in six of the successor states—although in three of these there was a temporary expansion of the selectorate. Alternatively, in only four successor states did authoritarian leaders fail to preserve some form of restrictive selectorate. Stated differently, table 2.1 shows that in the eleven years from January 1990 to December 2000 there were four major patterns.

1. *Consistent exclusion of society from the selectorate.* Kazakhstan, Tajikistan, Turkmenistan, and Uzbekistan have consistently denied the public control over the leadership. In all but Tajikistan, the same government remained in office throughout this period. In Tajikistan the first autocratic government fell to an oligarchic coup, but survivors from the first autocratic elite reestablished autocracy.

2. *Inconsistent inclusion of society in the selectorate.* In Armenia, Azerbaijan, Belarus, Georgia, and Kyrgyzstan, popular majorities cannot currently change control of either the legislature or the presidency, but all five of these countries have at various times taken steps toward expansion of the selectorate. Armenia began under Soviet rule with a more democratic constitution, but since independence, leaders have progressively restricted the electoral process so that it is the notables rather than the people who choose leaders. In Belarus an oligarchic regime at first appeared to take steps toward democratization, but since 1994 one element of the oligarchy has consolidated autocratic rule. In Azerbaijan the first autocratic regime fell to a coup that introduced a more open political regime, but survivors of the old regime seized power in a countercoup

TABLE 2.1
Constitutions of the Soviet Successor States, 1990-2000

	Autocracy	Oligarchy	Exclusive Republic	Democracy
Armenia		D/94–D/00		Ag/90–D/94
Azerbaijan	F/90–My/92 Je/93–D/00			My/92–Je/93
Belarus	N/96–D/00	My/90–N/96		
Estonia			Ag/91–D/00	Ap/90–Ag/91
Georgia		Ja/92–D/00		N/90–Ja/92
Kazakhstan	F/90–D/00			
Kyrgyzstan	Ap/90–O/90	O/90–D/00		
Latvia			Ag/91–D/00	My/90–Ag/91
Lithuania				Mr/90–D/00
Moldova				Ap/90–D/00
Russia				My/90–D/00
Tajikistan	Ap/90–S/92 N/94–D/00	S/92–N/94		
Turkmenistan	Ja/90–D/00			
Ukraine				Jl/90–D/00
Uzbekistan	Mr/90–D/00			

Classifications based on electoral regime; see table 2.5.

Sources of data: Election observer reports published by the United States Commission on Security and Cooperation in Europe (1993a, 1993b, 1994a, 1994b, 1994c, 1994d, 1995a, 1995b, 1995c, 1996a, 1996b, 1996c, 1998a, 1998b, 1998c, 1998d, 1999a, 1999b, 1999c, 1999d, 1999e, 2000a, 2000b) and all annual editions of *Freedom in the World* beginning with Freedom House (1991).

and restored autocracy. Kyrgyzstan initially took steps toward democracy after 1991, but stalled far short of this end. Georgia's early democracy fell to an oligarchic coup in January 1992, but the regime has slowly liberalized politics since then. In both of the latter two regimes, it is consensus among power holders rather than open public contestation that selects their leaders.

3. *Selective inclusion of society in the selectorate*. Estonia and Latvia have consistently conducted competitive elections, but since 1992 under exclusionary citizenship rules.

4. Broad inclusion of society in the selectorate. Lithuania, Moldova, Russia, and Ukraine currently hold elections that offer citizens the opportunity to remove the incumbents. All four extended citizenship to all legal residents in 1991. Lithuania has come closest to the ideal of democracy in that its elections have been consistently inclusive and competitive. Alternatively, in Moldova, Russia, and Ukraine enough fraud exists in individual races that it requires substantially more than half the voters to oust incumbents or defeat the incumbents' chosen candidate. Still, all three have conducted elections that the Organization for Security and Cooperation in Europe characterizes as fair and competitive. In both Moldova and Ukraine the first popularly elected president was subsequently voted from office. In Ukraine the legislative majority has changed hands; in Moldova this has happened twice.

This classification of patterns in post-Soviet constitutions corresponds closely to some measures of democratization commonly used in the literature. For example, Robert Dahl's (1971) index of democracy or polyarchy defines regimes by the extent of public contestation and popular inclusion in the electoral process. In figure 2.1 the fifteen Soviet successor states and the states of Europe are arrayed according to Dahl's two dimensions. The measure of political contestation is the average of the ratings of political liberties offered each year by Freedom House (1992–99). The estimate of political inclusion is based on data from the Institute for Democratic Electoral Assistance (1998) on electoral registration of the adult population. In this period, most of Europe fell into the category of inclusive and competitive politics indicated by the outlined box in figure 2.1. Most of the Soviet successor states did not. None of the European states excluded more than 20 percent of its adult population from the vote—mostly immigrants. Yet, the two Baltic states excluded over 30 percent of the adult population from citizenship and participation in national elections. Only two of the European states—Yugoslavia and Bosnia—restricted contestation so that elections might be called noncompetitive; fully nine of the Soviet successor states tended to have noncompetitive politics. The post-Soviet democracies fall inside the upper-right box in figure 2.1. The two exclusive republics cluster in the quadrant of high levels of public contestation but lower levels of inclusiveness. The three oligarchies cluster just below the democracies in levels of public contestation. The six autocracies cluster at the bottom of public contestation.[2]

This classification of constitutions defines our central empirical questions about regime choice in the following terms. First, in only three successor states did autocrats survive in power without at least temporary expansion of the selectorate. What makes Kazakhstan, Turkmenistan, and Uzbekistan different from the other successor states? Second, authoritarians have reversed steps toward democratization in three additional

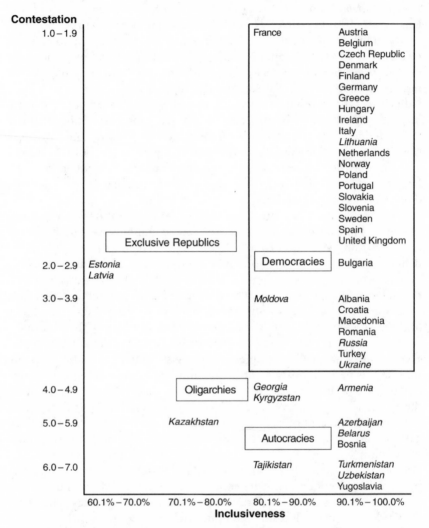

Contestation

	60.1%–70.0%	70.1%–80.0%	80.1%–90.0%	90.1%–100.0%
1.0–1.9			France	Austria Belgium Czech Republic Denmark Finland Germany Greece Hungary Ireland Italy *Lithuania* Netherlands Norway Poland Portugal Slovakia Slovenia Sweden Spain United Kingdom
2.0–2.9	*Estonia* *Latvia*		Democracies	Bulgaria
3.0–3.9			*Moldova*	Albania Croatia Macedonia Romania *Russia* Turkey *Ukraine*
4.0–4.9		Oligarchies	*Georgia* *Kyrgyzstan*	*Armenia*
5.0–5.9		*Kazakhstan*	Autocracies	*Azerbaijan* *Belarus* Bosnia
6.0–7.0			*Tajikistan*	*Turkmenistan* *Uzbekistan* Yugoslavia

Exclusive Republics

Inclusiveness

Figure 2.1. Contestation and inclusiveness in Europe and NIS,
January 1992 to January 1999.

states and established new autocracies. These countries differ from both the stable autocracies and the regimes that have maintained more inclusive selectorates. On one hand, what accounts for the instability of autocracy in Azerbaijan, Belarus, and Tajikistan and, thus, makes these countries different from the three stable authoritarian regimes? On the other hand, what accounts for the apparent success of new autocratic projects, which distinguishes these three from the successor states that have retained more inclusive selectorates? Third, four additional regimes have seen the expansion of the selectorate arrested (as in Kyrgyzstan) or reversed (as in Armenia, Estonia, Georgia, and Latvia) resulting in an oligarchy or exclusive republic. What makes the cases of transition to alternative forms of authoritarianism or nondemocracy different from the autocracies and different from the democracies? Fourth, four states have taken significant steps toward democratization of the selectorate. Why did the authoritarian regime choose to include the public in the selection process in Lithuania, Moldova, Russia, and Ukraine and why have new authoritarian projects so far failed to reverse this expansion?

Explanations That Fail

Existing theories of democratization are ill suited to explain the choices facing authoritarian leaders as they weigh democratization against authoritarian alternatives. Even on their own terms, these theories are unable to explain the success of democracy in some Soviet successor states. These theories might have led us to predict the failure of authoritarianism in Lithuania, but they would have led us to conclude that democracy was an improbable outcome in Moldova, Russia, or Ukraine following the collapse of the Soviet Union. In none of the latter three successor states should authoritarianism have failed and democracy survived for a decade after 1990.

For example, political-economic hypotheses have drawn a powerful connection between the economic conditions within a society and the likelihood its regime will be democratic. Yet, the usual economic hypotheses only serve to heighten the sense of the anomalous nature of Moldovan, Russian, and Ukrainian democracy. A sophisticated structural theory that sees an independent bourgeoisie that is not dependent on the state as a necessary condition for modern parliamentary democracy offers us little purchase on the failure of authoritarianism in these countries. If Barrington Moore's (1966, 418) hypothesis "no bourgeois, no democracy" is correct, then Moldovan, Russian, and Ukrainian democracy are an impossibility, and all should be authoritarian polities. As Moore notes (p. 481), prior to the 1917 revolutions, "[t]hough there had been flirtations with western constitutional notions, the Russian [Empire's] bourgeoisie was tied by many strings to the tsarist government." Seventy years of Soviet power that purged society of every last bourgeois down to his or her distant cousins among the kulaks did not improve the class conditions for bourgeois democracy.

Simpler economistic hypotheses do not do much better at unraveling the anomaly of Moldovan, Russian, and Ukrainian democracy. The Soviet

TABLE 2.2

Income Levels and Likelihood of Authoritarianism

Quintile	GNP (PPP) / capita	Authoritarian Regimes*	Odds of Authoritarianism	n
Upper	$16,501–	10%	1:9	20
Upper Middle	$6301–$16,500	33%	1:2	21
Middle	$2851–$6300	71%	2.4:1	21
Lower Middle	$1131–$2850	71%	2.4:1	21
Lower	$0–$1130	86%	6.1:1	21

*Authoritarian regimes are defined as countries scoring 4 or below in the Freedom House political liberties index. I use the Freedom House scores in this table so that there is less opportunity for me to bias the results by substituting my own codings. *Sources*: Freedom House 1997; World Bank 1998, table 1.1.

successor states are relatively poor, although not impoverished; but they also suffer under conditions of rapid economic decline. That is, by all odds they should be authoritarian. Samuel Huntington (1991, 62–63) identified states in the second-highest quintile of economic development (GNP between $1,000 and $3,000 in 1976 U.S. dollars) as those most likely to participate in the third wave of democratization. They were less likely to have democratized previously, but were most likely to liberalize after 1974. Adam Przeworski et al. (1996, 40–42) offer some hope to states further down the income ladder by adding that "democracies can survive in poorer countries, if they generate economic growth with a moderate rate of inflation." Yet Moldova, Russia, and Ukraine, like most other successor states, fall below Huntington's upper-middle income group and have suffered from disastrous economic decline. As table 2.2 shows, the odds that a country in Russia's income bracket (the third quintile, or $4,190 in 1996 dollars) will be authoritarian are better than two to one. The same is true for a state in Moldova's and Ukraine's bracket (the fourth quintile, or $1,440 and $2,230, respectively; World Bank 1998, table 1.1). Moreover, the fall in their economies should increase these odds still further. Among the successor states, Uzbekistan recorded the highest average annual growth rate in per capita gross national product from 1990 to 1996, but this was still negative at–3.5 percent. Russia reported an annual rate of–9.0 percent; Ukraine–13.6 percent; and Moldova–16.7 percent (World Bank 1998, table 4.1).

Political-sociological hypotheses, which draw a connection between political cultures and "congruent" regime types (Almond and Verba 1963), do no better. When compared to most other societies, the effect of seven hundred years of czarist autocracy and seventy years of Soviet

power created one of the most favorable cultural environments for authoritarianism. The cultural traditions of Moldova, Russia, and Ukraine,
like those of the other successor states of the Soviet Union and Russian
Empire, provide sterile soil for the seed of democracy.

The imperial regime championed a policy of "Orthodoxy-Autocracy-
Nationality." Neither its ideals nor practices cultivated the form of civic
community that Robert Putnam (1993) finds in successful democracies.
Even if such community had existed under the czars in such pockets as
the peasant commune (*obshchina*) and assembly (*skhod*), this was
crushed under the commissars by collectivization.[3] Moldova, Russia, and
Ukraine today lack the rich associational life, let alone bowling leagues,
that underpin community. Trust beyond the narrow circle of one's private
life, particularly trust in public associations or democratic political institutions, is alarmingly low. In a 1995 Russian survey, for example, only 4
percent reported trust in the parliament and 6 percent reported trust in
the government (White 1995). In Ukraine on the eve of parliamentary
elections, only 4 percent of respondents expressed trust in their president
and a mere 2 percent in the cabinet (Kuzio 1995, 336). The proportion
of Ukrainian respondents saying they would approve "if parliament was
suspended and parties abolished" rose from 42 percent in late 1992 to 61
percent in late 1995 (Rose and Haerpfer 1996, 34–37). The proportion
agreeing that "it is best to get rid of Parliament and elections and have a
strong leader who can quickly decide things" jumped from 53 to 67 percent in the same period.

The associational ties of civil society, and particularly political society
as Alfred Stepan (1988, 4) labels it, are extremely weak—far weaker than
in Latin America, let alone in advanced industrial societies (Linz and
Stepan 1996). In the space between the purely private lives of households
and the state, the policies of forced departicipation under the Leninist
regime left a nearly atomized public sphere (Roeder 1989). On the output
(implementation) side these may be weak states facing strong societies, to
use Joel Migdal's (1988) phrase; on the input side of the polity, however,
society is very weak. The associations that mediate relations between society and politics—that is, political parties—are strikingly weak. The description of Ukraine's party system in its 1998 legislative elections presented by the Commission on Security and Cooperation in Europe would
be equally appropriate for Russia:

> Most of the thirty parties registered for the elections were rather anemic,
> characterized by weak organizational bases and a lack of coherent plat-
> forms. . . . Only the Communist Party, and to a lesser extent, the Socialists
> and Rukh [nationalists], could rely on a broad network of party organiza-
> tions. Others were hastily convened blocs and lobbies for various interest
> groups—or, perhaps more succinctly, political clans vying for power and con-

trol of the wealth. Many parties were personality, rather than platform-driven, adding prominent Ukrainians from the cultural, entertainment and sports worlds to shore up support. (U.S. CSCE 1998d)

Moldova may have the most developed party system of the three states, yet only one of the political parties that won seats in the 1994 elections survived to win seats in the 1998 elections—the Party of Democratic Forces, which had won in 1994 under the label Congress of Peasants and Intellectuals. The largest party in 1994, the Agrarian Democrats, splintered before the next elections and its major successor, the Movement for a Democratic and Prosperous Moldova, came in third in 1998. The largest party in 1998, the Communist Party, was running for the first time since independence (U.S. CSCE 1998c).

Moreover, these political cultures are infused with a rejection of the current democratic order and a nostalgia for some earlier nondemocratic forms of governance. Russian respondents favor the communist order over the contemporary by at least a two-to-one margin (White, Rose, and McAllister 1997, 182). By autumn 1995 two-thirds of Russians and three-quarters of Ukrainians evaluated the former Communist regime positively (Rose and Haerpfer 1996, 85). Moreover, significant segments of elite opinion believed that authoritarianism is necessary during the transition period from totalitarianism (Sautman 1995). The strongest Russian parties in this decade, including the Communist Party of the Russian Federation, the Agrarian Party, and the Liberal Democratic Party of Russia, were antisystemic parties with a doubtful commitment to democracy. Indeed, the Russian party system, if it can be called that, was characterized throughout its first decade by extreme pluralism, multipolarity, polarization, and centrifugation—which Giovanni Sartori (1966) warns are the least favorable cultural conditions for democracy.

Despite these unfavorable economic and cultural conditions, Moldova, Russia, and Ukraine did break with their authoritarian past and have so far avoided the relapse that many have feared. Even if authoritarianism should triumph tomorrow, these three anomalies pose one inescapable question—why did the "founding parents" reject authoritarianism in these, but not in most other Soviet successor states?

Regime Choice in Authoritarian Polities

The anomalous failure of authoritarianism in Moldova, Russia, and Ukraine; the expansion of the selectorate to include selected members of society in Estonia and Latvia; and the instability of authoritarian constitutions in Armenia, Azerbaijan, Belarus, Georgia, and Kyrgyzstan require that we look more closely at the situations in which authoritarian leaders may choose to break with the constitutions of the past. In order to gain some purchase on the rejection of autocracy, the acceptance or rejection of alternative authoritarian projects, and the choice to democratize the selectorate, I propose a simple bargaining model of regime choice within authoritarian regimes. It assumes that constitutional politics is an ongoing aspect of politics; that is, the rules of the polity are constantly under negotiation, even though they may change only infrequently. This model describes in simplified form a bargaining process from which a decision to retain or change the constitutional rules emerges. In schematic form the model links the following elements:

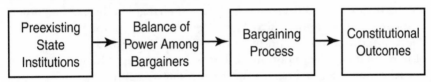

Figure 2.2 Schematic Representation of Model.

Constitutional outcomes result from a bargaining process that determines whether existing constitutional rules remain in place or change. In different countries at different times bargaining processes differ according to who is empowered to participate. Preexisting state institutions empower some political actors to participate and assign them advantages in the form of leverage over others in the bargaining process of constitutional politics. The element of human agency enters this process as strategically minded politicians seek to resolve dilemmas that inhere in different constitutional designs.

This model focuses on bargaining *within* authoritarian regimes. It does not address cases in which a coup or revolutionary seizure of power by the opposition simply replaces an authoritarian regime with another authoritarian regime or with a democracy. Nor does it address the bargaining—frequently stressed by theories of democratization—that begins once an authoritarian regime has decided to democratize. It seeks to explain the initiation of those processes that Samuel P. Huntington (1991) calls transformation and transplacements, which account for all but six of the thirty-five "third wave" democratizations that he analyzes. To initiate either transformation or transplacements, there must first of all be a change and choice within the authoritarian regime.

Institutional Constraints and Bargaining Outcomes

Constitutional outcomes that may initiate the transition to democracy result from agreements among authoritarian politicians. While it may be true, as Terry Karl and Philippe Schmitter (1991, 282) argue, that "transitions by pacts are the most likely to lead to political democracy," nevertheless, most pacts do not lead to democracy. Pacts as often create an autocracy, oligarchy, or exclusive republic. The participants in constitutional bargaining are politicians who seek to expand their own power (defined as influence over policy) and to increase their security in holding this power. By their success in the existing authoritarian regime, these politicians have demonstrated that they will embrace constitutional designs that produce these outcomes by denying significant parts of the public a say in politics. As a group, the constitutional designers who rose to prominence in the existing authoritarian order are more likely to settle among themselves on pacts that make fewer changes in the existing order.

What could possibly induce them to reach a compromise in which they reject authoritarianism and open the political process to a larger group of participants? The important difference among bargaining processes is not how much the politicians must compromise among themselves, but who can sit at the bargaining table and demand to be included in this compromise. Individual bargaining games differ from one another according to who sits at the table and the resources that each can use as leverage at the bargaining table. The primary working hypothesis of this model is that authoritarian regimes are more likely to change where there is institutional pluralism within the governing apparatus. That is, the more extreme this intrastate pluralism is, the more participants there will be in the bargaining process with more nearly equal power, and so the less likely it is that projects to create new authoritarian regimes will bring agreement.

The primary working hypothesis describes a general principle that can be applied to many countries, but the specific institutional arrangements that give rise to the intrastate pluralism, of course, vary among countries. In the specific context of the Soviet successor states this institutional pluralism was most likely to occur where (1) the Soviet agencies for mobilizing the population had been divided among urban institutions rather than unified in rural institutions and (2) significant parts of the union-republic elite—particularly its industrial elite—were subordinate to all-union agencies in Moscow and enjoyed greater autonomy from the union-republic's Communist Party indigenous leadership. In these specific conditions of intrastate pluralism, agreements to open the selectorate were more likely. Yet, this opening of the selectorate might stop short of democracy. First, elites of separate bureaucracies in some instances negotiated a pact to create oligarchic rule. Second, indigenous party and state leaders in other successor states isolated segments of the nonindigenous elite and mobilized an ethnic alliance to create an exclusive republic.

The Credible Commitment Problem in Authoritarian Constitutions

A second working hypothesis of this model is that the ability of authoritarian elites to agree on an authoritarian constitution is constrained by the difficulty in making credible commitments not to abuse the enormous powers that authoritarian constitutions assign to offices (Kiewiet and McCubbins 1991; Kubicek 1994). Authoritarian politicians deciding whether to retain an existing constitution or to design a new one may each want to be a god, but none wants simply to worship at the feet of another. In this lie two major dilemmas for constitutional designers—the dilemma of authority and the dilemma of accountability. During the process of designing political institutions, participants in constitutional bargaining may anticipate these dilemmas and the risks they pose to their own power. Yet, the problem the participants face is not simply "getting the institutions right," because, as dilemmas, each entails trade-offs, so that even as constitutional designers minimize some dangers to themselves, they increase others. As the participants in constitutional bargaining discover the types of rules likely to emerge from compromises, assess how these resolve the inherent dilemmas of authoritarian design, and weigh the payoffs and risks to their own power and security, individual bargainers may adjust their own preferences among the options on the table. In this way even authoritarians may come to appreciate democracy as a better guarantee of their power than authoritarian rules that leave them vulnerable to complete loss of power and total exclusion from politics.

THE DILEMMA OF AUTHORITY

The design of any regime, whether authoritarian or democratic, represents an attempt to find a mix between decisiveness and responsiveness in decision making (Shugart and Carey 1992). This dilemma is manifest principally in the design of the decision-making organs of the regime and the decision by constitutional designers to guarantee representation to all selectorate interests or only to some. Inclusive decision making may represent all interests, but it aggravates the collective action problems of the regime with the risk of stalemate and inaction. Restrictive decision making may create leadership that acts decisively, but it is more likely to ignore the preferences of many selectors. For the self-interested participant in constitutional bargaining, the potential payoffs and risks of delegating decision-making powers to decisive leadership are substantial. Decisive decision-making institutions represent a gamble that the decision makers will have a free hand to implement the participant's policy preferences. Yet, once these powers are in the hands of the decision makers, what then constrains the decision maker to select policies preferred by the participant? Without institutional guarantees, promises by a leader are unlikely to represent credible commitments. For this reason, individual constitutional designers who prefer decisive leadership that privileges their own preferences may, nevertheless, agree to more inclusive decision-making institutions, such as collective rather than autocratic leadership, if this is the only way to insure against the risks of decisive leadership.

THE DILEMMA OF ACCOUNTABILITY

One way to keep even decisive leadership responsive is through institutions of accountability. The design of any constitution, whether democratic or authoritarian, must designate a selectorate that can remove current leaders and choose their successors. Each participant in authoritarian constitutional politics seeks to tailor the selectorate by giving greater weight to his or her own supporters and less to opponents' supporters. This presents constitutional designers trying to reach agreement on an authoritarian constitution with a credible commitment problem—how does each assure the others that they will not change the selectorate (except in the most minimal ways)?[4] The choice of institutions to make such promises credible represents a dilemma because measures to prevent the expansion of the selectorate can create a power that is able to abridge the selectorate.

The dilemma of accountability in designing autocracies, oligarchies, and exclusive republics arises from the danger of competitive expansion of the selectorate through what has been labeled the oligarch's dilemma (Roeder 1993; Ramseyer and Rosenbluth 1996). In authoritarian regimes each leader is tempted—and knows others are tempted as well—to expand the political game by including his or her own allies or partisans in the selectorate (Rustow 1970, 360–61). For each leader, selective expansion of the selectorate will maximize the extent and duration of her or his power—as long as others do not also succeed at including their own partisans or allies. Alternatively, for each leader the worst outcome would result if other leaders mobilized their partisans while he or she does not. In the absence of guarantees that other leaders will not defect, all oligarchs feel a compulsion to defect in anticipation of others' defections. In their bargaining, self-interested authoritarian politicians may actually prefer democratization of the selectorate to weak authoritarian guarantees that leave them vulnerable to becoming the "sucker."

Institutions to prevent this competitive defection in the oligarch's dilemma may increase the opposite danger—the threat of further restriction of the selectorate. Institutions to preclude competitive expansion of the selectorate typically create monitoring and sanctioning agencies. Yet, monitoring and sanctioning agencies may also be used to abridge the se-lectorate—by excluding some of the current members. This was certainly one of the lessons from the creation of the Communist Party Secretariat and the post of general secretary in the early 1920s: By skillful exercise of the party's cadre policy, the general secretary changed the Congress and Central Committee that selected the party leadership.

As the previous paragraph underscores, the two dilemmas are inti-mately interlinked. Decisions concerning the design of decision-making organs can impinge on the stability of the selectorate and vice versa. For example, a strong leadership post not only provides decisive leadership, but also risks either abridgement of the selectorate under a leader with autocratic ambitions or expansion of the selectorate under a leader with populist or democratic ambitions. Conversely, monitors to guard the boundaries of the selectorate against expansion or contraction can use their powers to concentrate decision-making powers in their own hands and to tailor the selectorate.

THESE DILEMMAS IN SPECIFIC AUTHORITARIAN CONSTITUTIONS

Constitutional designers considering pacts to establish various forms of authoritarianism must anticipate the specific forms these dilemmas will take in the different authoritarian constitutions. Details of various author-itarian constitutions often represent an attempt to resolve these dilemmas with institutional guarantees of commitments. The failure to agree on such guarantees may make a specific authoritarian project less attractive than other authoritarian or democratic alternatives.

Autocracy depends on strong executive control not only over policy making, but also over the mechanisms by which decision makers are se-lected (Roeder 1993, 1994). In order to guard against competitive at-tempts to expand the selectorate, autocracies—such as the Soviet Polit-buro from 1953 to 1955—must prevent members from making intra-elite disputes public and from appealing outside the elite for support in these disputes.[5] Autocracies often designate one of their members leader and delegate to the leader extraordinary powers, but, since an autocratic leader may subsequently transform other members of the elite into depen-dent clients or dispense with them entirely, the designers of autocracies may seek to check the powers of their leader by sharing or parceling re-sponsibility for policy realms—such as the rules of collective decision making in the Soviet Politburo from 1953 to 1955. Yet, as the experience of the Soviet Politburo attests, this comes at a price in decisiveness, and, where such guarantees can be breeched, they may not even make commit-ments credible.

Oligarchy institutionalizes representation of separate bureaucratic interests, who delegate decision making to central leaders and retain the power to remove the leaders.[6] Yet, designers of oligarchies face acute dilemmas of authority and accountability. First, in order to solve its collective-action problem in decision making the oligarchy typically must delegate powers to agents (like a chief executive), but in doing so oligarchs give these agents powers that can be turned into autocracy. Designers of oligarchies may attempt to guard against this by dividing executive powers among separate posts or developing mechanisms for monitoring and controlling these executives. In Belarus the oligarchs initially selected Stanislau Shushkevich as chairman of the Supreme Soviet, so that they could avoid assigning the powers of the chairmanship to one bureaucratic faction. Yet, these institutional guarantees come at a cost in decisiveness. Second, a stable oligarchy must control the processes by which decision makers are selected and removed, preventing these selection processes from falling into the hands of the leader or devolving to popular control. Designers of oligarchy may adopt rules that define membership in the selectorate by ex officio representation of specific bureaucracies such as armed services, ministries, or regional administrations. Anticipating that competition among decision makers or interests in the selectorate may increase the temptation to expand the selectorate, designers of oligarchy may create a sanctioning agency to maintain discipline among members of the oligarchy, but this increases the threat of autocracy. The difficulty of agreeing on institutional guarantees to guard against these problems appears to make oligarchy a less attractive authoritarian alternative.

Exclusive republics make the state accountable to society, but limit the selectorate to some subset of social interests. Typically the designers of exclusive republics are politicians who find their greatest political advantage against other politicians outside the state itself, but fear that they will not survive in a democratic contest; they seek to establish or maintain their advantage in electoral politics by enfranchising some segments of the adult population, but not others. Since competitive defection from the exclusionary agreement can transform exclusive republics into democracies, institutional guarantees must check the temptation for parties to seek advantage by including excluded constituents. For example, a stable exclusive republic may depend on rules that require supermajorities to extend the franchise. Yet, creation of agencies to enforce the exclusionary rules can threaten the stability of exclusive republics as well. On one hand, leaders may seek to expand their powers by populist appeals to expand the franchise. On the other, the power to exclude can be used to narrow the franchise further. Those who join in the exclusion of segments of the population from the political process need assurances that they will not themselves become suckers who abide by the exclusionary agreement while others selectively expand the selectorate and that they will not themselves be excluded.

Rejection of Authoritarianism in 1990

Why did some union-republic Communist Party leaders reject authoritarianism in 1990 and expand the selectorate by permitting voters a real opportunity to influence the composition of the union republic's Supreme Soviet? The issue whether to expand the selectorate had been forced on each union republic by the democratization program of Mikhail Gorbachev. On the eve of the 1990 elections the leaders of each union-republic Communist Party organization had to devise a strategy for conducting those elections that was likely to maintain their own predominance within the union republic. If they failed to pack the new supreme soviets with their followers, they might lose control of the state organs such as the chairmanship (of the Presidium) of the Supreme Soviet. Moreover, Gorbachev had suggested that failure to gain a popular mandate in these elections would be a sign of unfitness to lead their union-republic party organizations.

In order to get out the vote in previous Soviet elections, union-republic party leaders had relied on the coordinated efforts of an enormous mobilizational machine that included governmental agencies, Communist Party organizations, so-called public organizations, the workplace, and their auxiliaries for agitation and propaganda (Friedgut 1979). The most important constraint on the leaders' choice of strategy in 1990 was their control over the elites that led these agencies within the union republic. In fourteen union republics a titular political elite—that is, an elite drawn from the ethnic group for which the union republic was named, such as the Armenians in the Armenian Soviet Socialist Republic—dominated the Communist Party leadership. The only exception was Russia, which had had no separate union-republic party organization for an extended period prior to the elections. Yet, each titular political leadership faced a different configuration of power within the authoritarian elite that had been the basis of Communist Party rule throughout the union republic. Each had to calculate how this would constrain their ability to maintain their own rule in the coming elections. Most important, the titular leaders had to decide whether to empower the new popular fronts as mobilizational agencies that could make an end run around those bureaucratic elites who sought to oppose their control of the union-republic Supreme Soviet.

The titular leaders were constrained by the extent to which these mobilizational agencies fell under their own control or under the control of all-union agencies in Moscow. In the specific context of late Soviet union-republic politics, three constraints were foremost in these choices of electoral strategy. First, control over the institutions of workplace, state, party, and public organizations that mobilized mass political activity differed in rural and in urban areas. In rural areas the titular elite atop the union-republic Communist Party organization had much firmer control and could count on the loyal following of party secretaries and the managers of collective and state farms. In rural areas institutions such as *sovkhozy, kolkhozy, raikomy,* and *raiispolkomy* were the dominant agencies of electoral mobilization; the union-republic leadership tightly controlled these; alternative mobilizational institutions under direct all-union control were less common in the countryside. As Harry Gelman (1990, 19) summarizes, "the main reason for the existence" of the party *raikomy* "has been to furnish local instructions and supervision over the collective and state farms and thus to dominate the life of the Soviet peasant" (Nove 1986, 124; Brovkin 1990, 16–17).[7] One manifestation of this control in all republics (except Armenia) was that the managers of collective farms constituted the single most "indigenized" elite of society. Alternatively, in urban areas a diverse set of institutions, not all of them under union-republic control, participated in the control and mobilization of mass political activity. Within workplaces such as factories and institutes the primary party organization and management played a major role. In residences, auxiliaries of the city government such as residence committees were also active. Public organizations such as *Znanie,* DOSAAF, and veterans' organizations supplemented these in mobilizing voters. Not all of these—particularly all-union enterprises and organizations—were subordinate to the union-republic leadership (Nove 1986, 54). In the impending elections, control over the countryside would be a decisive advantage in the union republics with a relatively large rural population. Yet, as table 2.3 shows, in only five union republics did more than 50 percent of the population live in the countryside. Alternatively, in five other union republics, voter mobilization was principally in the hands of various urban and industrial institutions; in these, more than 65 percent of the population lived in urban areas. The remaining four republics with Communist Party organizations had mixed structures of control and mobilization. (Russia, which had not had a separate Communist Party organization, fell into this last category.)

Second, the titular leadership of the union republics also had to consider whether elites from nontitular ethnic groups within the union republic would oppose an attempt to cement *titular* control over the soon-to-be-elected Supreme Soviet. Union republics differed in the extent to which other segments of the elite had been "indigenized" under the cadre policies of the titular leadership. Where union-republic leaders controlled appointments to posts, they were inclined to appoint loyalists from the titu-

TABLE 2.3

Configuration of Elites in the Union Republics prior to the 1990 Elections

Mobilizational Agencies*	Presence of Nontitular Elites**		Type of Election***
Rural-Agricultural Agencies Dominant	Indigenized Party	Tajikistan	Noncompetitive
		Turkmenistan	Noncompetitive
		Uzbekistan	Noncompetitive
	Nonindigenized Party	Kyrgyzstan	Noncompetitive
		Moldova	Mixed
Mixed Rural and Urban Agencies		Azerbaijan	Mixed
		Belarus	Mixed
		Georgia	Competitive
		Kazakhstan	Noncompetitive
Urban-Industrial Agencies Dominant	Indigenized Industrial Managers	Armenia	Mixed
		Lithuania	Competitive
		Russia	Mixed
		Ukraine	Mixed
	Nonindigenized Industrial Managers	Estonia	Competitive
		Latvia	Competitive

*Percentage of population mobilized by rural or urban agencies: Rural Dominant = 50% or more rural; Urban Dominant = 65% or more urban; Mixed = 50%–65% urban.

**Indigenized indicates more than half of party or managers drawn from titular ethnic group.

***Type of election refers to whether electoral blocs other than the Communist Party were permitted to offer candidates.

Sources: USSR 1990; USSR Facts and Figures Annual, various; Foreign Broadcast Information Service, Daily Report (Soviet Union) 1 February 1990, 43–44; 27 February 1990, 96; 6 April 1990, 105–107; 10 May 1990, 103–104; CSCE 1990, 128, 144.

lar nationality; where Moscow appointed elites, the all-union agencies were more likely to appoint nontitulars.[8] This had implications for the upcoming elections. Where members of nontitular ethnic groups constituted a larger share or even a majority of the elite within the union republic, the titular leaders could expect more extensive opposition to its electoral strategy for consolidating control over the new Supreme Soviet. Where these nontitular elites also controlled sizable blocs of votes, they could defeat this strategy; so, the titular leadership needed to reach outside the Communist Party to nonparty titular elites, particularly members of the indigenous intelligentsia, in order to win control of the Supreme Soviet. We can estimate the ethnic makeup of the elites by looking at the union-republic's Communist Party organization, for in every union republic the elite leading strategic institutions were gathered in the party organization. Table 2.3 shows that among the rural republics the titular ethnic groups constituted a solid majority of the Communist Party only in Tajikistan, Turkmenistan, and Uzbekistan. Alternatively, in Kyrgyzstan and Moldova significant segments of the Communist Party elites would resist any attempt to impose a titular autocracy at their expense.

Third, in the more industrialized union republics the titular leaders had to anticipate the reaction of industrial managers. The union republics varied in the extent to which the titular rulers directly controlled industrial management and had "indigenized" it. Titular elites had been most successful at "indigenizing" light industries that fell under republican control, but less successful in the heavy industries under all-union control. Where most industrial managers were drawn from nontitular groups—and particularly in industries under all-union subordination—the titular leadership could expect managers to oppose plans for titular domination of the new Supreme Soviet and to mobilize voters against this in the elections. In these circumstances the Communist Party leadership could mobilize titular supporters outside the party, but this alone might not be enough; where the nontitular industrial elite could mobilize significant numbers of voters, the titular leadership might have to neutralize the electoral power of these industrial managers by disfranchising their supporters. Of course, as long as the union republic remained within the Soviet Union, the all-union leadership would prevent the titular leaders from actually acting on this imperative. As table 2.3 shows, in the most industrialized union-republics, over half the industrial managers were drawn from the titular population in Armenia, Lithuania, and Ukraine but less than half in Estonia and Latvia.

Against the background of these specific institutional constraints and expectations about the reaction of members of the union-republic elite, the authoritarian leaders had to decide how far to democratize the selectorate. That is, in selecting electoral rules for the new legislature, the union-republic titular leaders had to decide whether to permit alternative electoral blocs to nominate candidates, with the possibility that these might win a majority in the Supreme Soviet and displace the Communist Party. This led to three different electoral strategies. First, in the rural republics with indigenized Communist Party, the leaders could retain Soviet-era electoral practices; authoritarianism would survive virtually unchanged. Indeed, as the final column in table 2.3 shows, in five union republics alternative electoral blocs were effectively excluded from offering candidates. These tended to be the most rural republics, where indigenous elites were certain of their control over republic institutions. In many of the other republics, titular leaders had to open the political process somewhat if they were to mobilize enough titular supporters against nontitular and all-union elites.

Second, where the combination of locked-in rural voters and nonparty urban voters could deliver a majority, the titular leadership might use a mixed strategy. That is, the leaders retained noncompetitive elections in the countryside where the titular party dominated, but encouraged competitive elections in the cities so as to permit titular popular fronts to challenge the nontitular party and industrial elites. Table 2.3 shows six union republics with "mixed" elections; in these union republics, electoral blocs were able to field or endorse candidates, although only in some districts, and these parties faced significant obstacles so that only a few contests offered voters a fair choice between parties. For example, in Azerbaijan, the opposition Azerbaijan Popular Front ran under serious handicaps, including a state of emergency and arrest or disqualification of many of its candidates, while Communist Party workers, who constituted the largest cadre of candidates, often ran for uncontested seats. In Belarus, the Popular Front could not register as a social organization and so could not nominate its own candidates; instead, it informally endorsed candidates who had been nominated by official organizations. In Ukraine the Communist Party–controlled electoral commissions registered opposition Democratic Bloc candidates in only 29 percent of the districts; the opposition bloc was able to find candidates it could endorse in less than half of all parliamentary contests (U.S. CSCE 1990).

Third, where the countryside could not deliver enough votes, the titular leaders might opt for competitive elections. Table 2.3 shows that in four union republics the elections to parliament were conducted on the basis of well-defined partisan groupings resembling parties, with almost all candidates carrying a partisan label and running on its platform. These tended to be the most urbanized republics where the leadership sought to counter the power of institutions led by nontitular and all-union elites within the union republic. In these circumstances the titular leaders had to devise electoral rules that would limit the expected gains to labor collectives and industrial managers that the titulars did not control. The titular leaders empowered the new popular fronts so as to take votes from the mobilizational agencies controlled by nontitular elites. Democratization was a strategy for authoritarian leaders seeking to protect themselves from the power of other bureaucrats.

In short, the titular leadership was more likely to permit alternative electoral blocs to run candidates in the 1990 elections where the union-republic elite was more diverse. First, the survival of the existing authoritarian order in 1990—specifically, the exclusion of the adult public from the selection of decision makers—depended on unity within the elite. The most unified governing elites (found in rural republics with indigenized Communist Parties) prevented alternative electoral blocs from contesting the elections. Second, rejection of authoritarianism resulted from intra-state pluralism. The most divided governing elites (found in urban republics with industrial managers who were nontitular and under all-union control) resulted in a strategy that permitted the popular fronts and other electoral blocs to contest seats. And third, as table 2.3 shows, between these two extremes, the proportion of noncompetitive elections declined and the proportion of competitive elections rose as the elite became more divided.

Creation of Independent Authoritarian Regimes, 1991–92

The August 1991 coup left the union-republic leaders to design new constitutions for newly independent states without the constraints of the all-union Soviet government. As table 2.1 shows, in the first two years after the breakup of the Soviet Union, the successor states adopted eighteen different constitutional orders. The initial balance of power within each union republic had significant impact on the types of authoritarian constitutions adopted immediately after the breakup of the Soviet Union. Moreover, many institutional details of the new authoritarian constitutions reflected the attempt of the elites to resolve the credible commitment problems associated with authoritarianism.

The survival of existing authoritarian constitutions and the creation of new ones were initially constrained by the configuration of power among elites elected to the legislatures and governments in 1990. Since this had itself been constrained by the configuration of power within the union republic on the eve of the 1990 legislative elections, subsequent constitutional development in each successor republic showed the imprint of the heavy hand of this institutional past. The figures in table 2.4 show the relationship between the configuration of power on the eve of the 1990 elections and the first constitutional order adopted in each successor state after the breakup of the Soviet Union. Although a longer (and potentially more attenuated) causal chain than that discussed in the previous section, the correlation is, nevertheless, strong. Four patterns emerged. In the first the parliamentary majority comprised bureaucrats that were united in a single chain of command. This majority backed the titular Communist Party leadership's consolidation of autocracy. This occurred everywhere that rural mobilizational structures were dominant and nontitular elites within the republic could not mobilize significant constituencies against the titular leadership (Tajikistan, Turkmenistan, and Uzbekistan). It also occurred less frequently under mixed-control structures (Azerbaijan and Kazakhstan), but these, and particularly Azerbaijan, were subsequently less stable autocracies.

TABLE 2.4
Influence of the Pre-1990 Power Configuration on the Initial
Postindependence Constitutional Order

Pre-1990 Power Configuration	Initial Postindependence Constitutional Order				
	Autocratic	Oligarchic	Exclusive-Republican	Democratic	n
Rural-Agricultural Dominant and Indigenized Party	100%	0%	0%	0%	3
Rural-Agricultural Dominant and Nonindigenized Party	0%	50%	0%	50%	2
Mixed Control Structure	50%	50%	0%	0%	4
Urban-Industrial Dominant and Nonindigenized Managerial Elite	0%	0%	100%	0%	2
Urban-Industrial Dominant and Indigenized Managerial Elite	0%	0%	0%	100%	4

In the second pattern the parliamentary majority comprised bureaucrats divided among separate chains of command. These separate bureaucratic factions negotiated forms of oligarchy. These more "autonomous"
bureaucrats feared a strong leader as a threat to their interests. At the
same time none could construct an alternative majority in parliament by
reaching out to a titular popular front. This occurred where many of the
bureaucrats had previously been subject to all-union rather than union-
republic control and where urban titular nonparty elites were weak as
well (Belarus and Kyrgyzstan). It also emerged in Georgia, and later in
Tajikistan, as a compromise among bureaucrats after they removed a
leader who had threatened to use an alliance with the popular front
against the bureaucrats' interests.

In the third pattern the parliamentary majority comprised an alliance
of titular Communist Party leaders with titular elites from outside the
Communist Party; they came to power by mobilizing the titular population against the nontitular (particularly managerial) elites. This parliamentary majority sought to maintain the involvement of its supporters,
but to disfranchise the supporters of the industrial managers. The result
was an exclusive republic. This occurred where urban and industrial mo-

bilizational institutions had been dominant and significant industrial institutions were under the control of nontitular elites (Estonia and Latvia).

In the fourth pattern the 1990 elections failed to produce a coherent majority on constitutional issues, but instead produced shifting temporary coalitions among titular party leaders, regional leaders, industrial elites, and popular front politicians. Here the compromise among elites rejected authoritarianism and accepted projects for democratization. This was the outcome in republics where urban mobilizational agencies had predominated and the industrial elite had been indigenized (Armenia, Lithuania, Russia, and Ukraine). Yet it also emerged in Moldova, where rural-agricultural institutions predominated and the party leadership was weakly indigenized. (I will discuss these cases in the section on the rejection of authoritarianism.)

AUTOCRACIES

In the newly independent states, the best foundation for creating autocracy was control of the Supreme Soviet by a unified bureaucratic hierarchy consisting of the former Communist Party apparatus and titular rural-agricultural managers. In Soviet political institutions, the executive had formally been the agent of parliament: The parliamentary majority delegated powers to a chairman (of the Presidium) of the Supreme Soviet, who served as chief of state, and to a council of ministers, which served as government. Where the union-republic Communist Party apparatus (plus the agencies it directly controlled) constituted a majority in the legislature, the parliamentary majority protected its special position within the successor state by backing the former first secretary of the Communist Party in the construction of autocracy (Kangas 1994; Nissman 1994; Nourzhanov and Saikal 1994).

The special position of the hierarchy depended on avoiding democratic elections. Thus, the autocracies tended to stage uncontested elections for a presidency that would assume the powers of the former first secretary. In Azerbaijan, Kazakhstan, and Turkmenistan the first presidential elections were uncontested. In Uzbekistan the president selected one party to challenge his candidacy, yet Muhammad Salih of the Erk Democratic Party posed little threat to an overwhelming majority for President Karimov. Alternatively, the two groups that could pose a more effective threat in the election were barred: The Islamic Renaissance party was banned altogether and the Uzbek Popular Front (*Birlik*) was permitted to register as a political movement, but not as a party that could legally field candidates (Brown 1992a, 24).

The unified-bureaucratic majorities gave the presidents control over the mechanisms by which the legislature was elected, since this was the best way to perpetuate the bureaucracy's dominance within the supreme soviets. In the modern variant of the circular flow of power, many of these legislatures gave the president power to appoint regional and local governments and gave to these governments power to conduct the elections to the legislature and presidency. In Uzbekistan, for example, a special session of the Supreme Soviet called on 4 January 1992, just after President Karimov's popular election, created the new post of governor (*hakim*) at the provincial (*oblast'*), district (*raion*), and town levels of government. Each governor headed both the executive and legislative organs of provincial and local government; but the governor was directly appointed by and answerable to the president rather than local interests. The Uzbekistan constitution adopted on 8 December 1992 enshrined this. These governors, of course, oversaw the local commissions that conducted presidential and legislative elections (Brown 1993; Fuller 1992b).

To limit challenges to the leader from outside the inner circle of the autocracy the regime stripped all other political forces of resources that could be used to mobilize political action. The Democratic Party of Turkmenistan, founded in December 1991, was monopolistic, serving as the "mother party" for all other political organizations, including the very loyal opposition. In Uzbekistan, after the fall of the leader in neighboring Tajikistan, the autocracy abandoned its limited toleration of opposition groups. In summer 1992 the regime tightened censorship, prohibited opposition demonstrations, and increased penalties for antigovernment activity. The following winter, Uzbek authorities arrested the leaders of the Democratic and Islamic Renaissance parties, suspended the popular front's activities, shut down its office, proscribed its newspaper, and fired popular front members from their jobs (Roeder 1994; Karpov 1992; Orlik 1992; Lebedeva 1993).

OLIGARCHIES

Where bureaucrats held the majority of seats in supreme soviets, but many of these bureaucrats were independent of the union-republic's leadership at the moment of independence, the compromise among the leaders of the different bureaucratic empires was likely to lead to oligarchy. The bureaucrats dominated the legislatures, but no one bureaucracy could muster a legislative majority. In order to maintain their autonomy the oligarchs adopted rules to block the emergence of another autocrat and to establish stronger accountability controls over the executive. Thus, oligarchies divided executive powers among agents that the parliament would hold directly accountable to itself and placed the electoral mechanism more directly under parliamentary control. In Belarus the coalition of bureaucracies that dominated the parliament initially resisted the creation of a presidency. The bureaucrats divided executive powers between the chairman of the Supreme Soviet and the chairman of the Council of Ministers; both of these were elected and removed by the Supreme Soviet. The Council of Ministers headed by Vyacheslau Kebich emerged as the executive committee of an oligarchy of regional administrative apparatus, Ministry of Defense, and military-industrial complex (Mihalisko 1993, 24–25). As noted, in order to prevent the power of the chairman of the Supreme Soviet from falling under control of any one bureaucracy, the leaders elected an intellectual without bureaucratic ties—Stanislau Shush-kevich. In Georgia, following the ouster of President Gamsakhurdia, the oligarchy that invited Eduard Shevardnadze to serve as leader placed limitations on his power. The parliament adopted a new law that made its chairman like a president, including popular election in October 1992, but denied him the power to dissolve parliament or to dismiss leading officials without parliamentary approval (Fuller 1992d). In August 1993 the oligarchy demonstrated its power against the executive by forcing the cabinet to resign, leading Shevardnadze to protest in exasperation, "whomever the head of state is, his word must be law for bodies subordinate to him" (ITAR-TASS, 5 August 1993).

In order to prevent expansion of the political process the post-Soviet oligarchies were almost as vigilant as the autocracies in suppressing political forces outside government. In Belarus, the Council of Ministers owned all radio and television broadcasting, 80 percent of the print media, as well as the ten largest publishing houses, and maintained a monopoly over all newspaper distribution (Lukashuk 1992, 18–21). In Georgia the oligarchy that seized control from Gamsakhurdia simply closed all opposition newspapers in June 1992 (Fuller 1992e, 74–76). Yet, as shown by the political liberty scores cited previously, the oligarchies tended to be somewhat less oppressive than the autocracies.

EXCLUSIVE REPUBLICS

Where the titular leadership could not rely on agrarian control structures, because the republic was urbanized, and where it also faced a strong non-titular counterelite in the industrial sector that could mobilize many votes, the titular leadership could only hold on by disfranchising these counterelites and their followers. In Estonia and Latvia, the Communist Party fragmented internally between titular and all-union parties during perestroika; competitive appeals to the public by these expanded the political process (Ishiyama 1993; Nelson and Amonashvili 1992). This permitted a coalition of titular Communist Party leaders and nonparty intelligentsia in the popular front to establish its dominance within the Supreme Soviet during the 1990 elections. This coalition did not rush to establish democ-

racy, but sought to cement its future electoral fortunes against the nontitulars by excluding segments of that population from politics.

In Estonia and Latvia electoral exclusion took place through restrictive
definitions of citizenship, which was granted only to those who were residents or descendants of residents in the republics prior to incorporation
in the Soviet Union in 1940. These laws had the predictable effect of
reducing the electorate and hit hardest those constituencies in the all-
union institutions established since the imposition of Soviet rule in 1940
(Barrington 1995). In Estonia the new law initially disfranchised about
45 percent of the electorate, which declined from 1.14 million to about
625,000. In Latvia the disfranchised accounted for about one-third of the
adult population.[9] In order to consolidate this new exclusionary order
after the breakup of the Soviet Union, Estonia and Latvia held parliamentary elections as soon as the new electoral rules and parliamentary institutions were in place. In Estonia it is estimated that more than 90 percent
of those permitted to vote were ethnic Estonians, and more than 90 percent of the disfranchised were non-Estonians. Moreover, following the
1992 elections, all 101 members of the first postbreakup parliament were
ethnic Estonians (Levitskii 1992; Hanson 1993, 18). In Latvia's first postindependence election, although ethnic Latvians constituted barely half
the population, they constituted about 70 percent of the eligible voters
(Bungs 1993, 48–49).

To guard against expansion of the political process the titular leadership sought to prevent ambivalent or less resolute members of its coalition
from seeking electoral advantage by appeals to the disfranchised. In Estonia, for example, as long as the 1990 Supreme Soviet remained in session,
the exclusionist majority delegated constitutional issues to more resolute
agents. Thus, they delegated the tasks of constitution writing to a constituent assembly that was purer than the parliament elected in 1990. The
constituent assembly was comprised equally of deputies from parliament
and the Congress of Estonia, a nonofficial organ elected only by voters
who qualified under the exclusive definition of citizenship. When the more
inclusive parliament sought to circumvent the Constituent Assembly on
the issue of the franchise by having the issue submitted to a popular vote,
the exclusionists who dominated the Constituent Assembly agreed to the
vote only as long as the electorate for this vote was limited to the restricted
body of Estonian citizens (Kionka 1992, 15–17).

In order to guard against the emergence of a populist leader who might
appeal beyond the franchised population, the exclusionists decided
against creating a strong, popularly elected presidency. Both Estonia and
Latvia chose parliamentary forms of government. In Estonia the exclusionists rejected calls for a strong presidency, fearing that the more concil-
iatory Arnold Ruutel would win the post (Kionka 1992, 31–34).

The Rejection of Authoritarianism, 1992–2000

The third application of the model of regime choice in authoritarianism examines the rejection of the existing authoritarian regime and new authoritarian projects and the agreement to expand the selectorate—even if only briefly—during the first nine years of independence. The evidence confirms the primary working hypothesis—where multiple centers of power contended with one another from within the state and no one coalition was able to establish its hegemony, projects to maintain authoritarianism or establish new authoritarian constitutions failed. Divided participants in the constitutional bargaining were more likely to opt for a more democratic alternative. This "pluralism within the state" prevailed after 1991 in all those successor states where indigenized urban and industrial agencies of mobilization had been predominant prior to the 1990 elections. All four of these successor states initially rejected authoritarian constitutions after 1991 (Armenia, Lithuania, Russia, and Ukraine) and only Armenia subsequently took steps backward toward authoritarianism (Dudwick, 1997).

The evidence also confirms the second working hypothesis—the inability to solve the dilemmas of authority and accountability contributed to the instability of many authoritarian projects. Thus, the probability of authoritarian failure was lower, but still significant, in two other groups of union republics with intermediate levels of institutional pluralism, because elites could not find institutional solutions to these dilemmas. First, the probability of authoritarian instability was significant where mixed control structures had prevailed prior to the 1990 elections. Thus, Azerbaijan, Belarus, and Kazakhstan experienced some institutional instability after 1991. Second, the probability of authoritarian instability was significant where a titular leadership relying on indigenized rural mobilization agencies prior to 1990 confronted a nontitular majority within the Communist Party elite. In Moldova leaders democratized the selectorate and in Kyrgyzstan they took tentative steps toward greater democracy.

FALL OF AN AUTHORITARIAN REGIME

Only one authoritarian regime fell in the nine years after 1991 to be replaced by a democratizing regime, and even this failure of authoritarianism was only temporary. In Azerbaijan at first the autocratic regime succumbed to a coup that promised democracy, but then the Communist-era bureaucrats regained power a year later and established a new autocracy. The instability resulted from divisions within the ruling elite. Following the failed August 1991 coup in Moscow, the willingness of President Mutalibov to compromise with the Azerbaijan Popular Front (AzPF) led the Supreme Soviet to remove him. Yet, the contending bureaucratic interests within the elite could not surrender this post to one bureaucratic interest and so transferred presidential powers to a relatively weak leader without significant bureaucratic ties—Etibar Mamedov, rector of the Baku Medical Institute. In a coup on 14–15 May 1992 the Popular Front seized power from the divided bureaucrats, named its own interim president, dissolved the *nomenklatura*-dominated parliament, and transferred legislative powers to a fifty-person National Council. Three weeks later, on 7 June, the Popular Front held presidential elections in which their candidate triumphed (Fuller 1992b, 1992c). Yet, one year after the first coup an armed insurrection forced the new president to flee. Behind this countercoup was reportedly "the former Party nomenklatura, whose goal is the convening of an emergency session of the Supreme Soviet, which had suspended its activities on May 15, 1992" (Mekhtiyev 1993). The segment of the bureaucratic elite that controlled the localities maintained its posts even during the one-year interregnum of democratization and drew together against their common enemy to back a return to autocracy. On 24 June 1993 the bureaucratic faction stripped the president of his powers and vested these in its new chair, Azerbaijan's former Communist Party first secretary and former chairman of the KGB, Geidar Aliev (Kechichian and Karasik 1995).

Constitutional Instability within Authoritarian Regimes

A number of authoritarian regimes have experienced institutional instability, particularly as a consequence of conflicts between oligarchic interests and leaders with autocratic ambitions. This conflict was moderate in Kazakhstan and Kyrgyzstan in the years after 1991, but became significant in Belarus and Tajikistan. In both of the latter, because the separate bureaucracies that dominated the supreme soviets in 1990 could not reach a stable agreement on an authoritarian constitution for an independent state, the oligarchies gave way to greater autocracy.

From the start the Belarusian oligarchy was buffeted by competing pressures for autocracy and democracy, but finally succumbed to the former. In order to stave off both autocracy and democracy the oligarchy initially refused to create a strong presidency. Many bureaucrats feared that in alliance with the popular front, Stanislau Shushkevich might use a presidency to consolidate his leadership and expand the selectorate at their expense. Following the removal of Shushkevich as chairman of the Supreme Soviet, however, many of these same bureaucrats shifted their stance and supported the project of Prime Minister Kebich to create a popularly elected presidency. They expected their bureaucratic "boss" to win handily, and, indeed, two-thirds of the Supreme Soviet deputies endorsed Kebich's candidacy. Ironically, because the bureaucracies had failed to establish centralized control over the electoral process, victory went to another bureaucrat Aleksandr Lukashenko (Zhdanko 1994a). President Lukashenko began to use his post to unseat his opponents and consolidate an autocracy. One segment of the bureaucracy, constituting a narrow majority in the Supreme Soviet, broke with the oligarchy and supported the efforts of President Lukashenko. They amended the law on local government in order to permit Lukashenko to abolish local soviets and appoint local heads of administration (Zhdanko 1994b). They endorsed the president's referendum that would ask citizens whether the president should be empowered to dissolve parliament (Natalyin 1995; Karmanov 1995). And by a bare majority in the Supreme Soviet they endorsed the president's call for a referendum on a new constitution (Starikevich and Urigashvili 1996). This constitution, which was adopted in the 24 November 1996 referendum, enabled Lukashenko to reconstitute the legislature with 110 loyalists (from the 199 delegates of the incumbent Supreme Soviet) (Lukashuk 1998; Mihalisko 1997).

In Tajikistan the Communist Party elite openly fragmented among regional subgroups—particularly, Leninabaders from the north and Kulyabis from the south (Martin 1993). This division had been kept just below the surface during the Soviet period by Moscow's patronage of the faction from Leninabad, but after the collapse of the Soviet Union this division in the governing elite kept Tajikistan's authoritarian regime in turmoil. Following the August 1991 coup attempt in Moscow, opposition demonstrations in Dushanbe brought these differences to the surface, and the governing elite forced President Makhkamov to resign. The Supreme Soviet appointed Rakhmon Nabiev to serve as acting president until elections could be held on 24 November 1991. Less than a year later, however, President Nabiev began to reach out to popular constituencies in order to strengthen his hand against the other members of the elite. The Supreme Soviet struck back by abolishing the presidency altogether (Brown 1992b, 1993). Yet, by November 1994, seeking to strengthen the central government in the face of protracted civil war, the Supreme Soviet created a presidency once again. The Supreme Soviet chairman, Imomali Rakhmonov, won the post in controlled elections.

REJECTION OF AUTHORITARIANISM

Lithuania, Moldova, Russia, and Ukraine stand apart from the other Soviet successor states in the first decade since Gorbachev first called for democratization of elections in 1990: They rejected both the existing authoritarian constitutions of their union republics and alternative authoritarian projects for their successor states; they expanded their selectorates to include society at large. From the perspective of existing theories of democratization the failure of authoritarianism in Lithuania is in many ways explicable (Clark 1995), but its failure in the other three successor states is anomalous. Our working hypotheses give us leverage.

The uniqueness of these four successor states is shown in a comparison of the competitiveness and openness of presidential and legislative elections in the first decade after 1990. Table 2.5 lists all presidential and legislative elections held between January 1990 and December 2000 and categorizes each by the extent to which it offered the whole adult population an opportunity to hold incumbents accountable. Reports of international observers provide estimates of (1) the proportion of the adult population enfranchised in the election, (2) the presence of alternative candidates, and (3) the extent to which the election was free of fraud that could distort the popular will. These are summarized in an answer to the question—could 51 percent of the adult population have removed the incumbent president or majority in parliament? At one extreme, the probability of this is low (p→0) because voters were given no choice in the elections. These are unambiguously nondemocratic elections. At the other extreme the probability is high (p→1) that the will of a slim majority would prevail against incumbents. Among these elections, more than half (seven of twelve elections) actually resulted in a turnover in party control of the legislature or defeat of an incumbent president. Where elections were competitive but the incumbents engaged in widespread fraud and threatened that they would not step down even if they failed to win voter approval, the ability of a majority to remove the incumbents becomes more uncertain. Where there is greatest uncertainty, it is as if the elections were followed by a coin toss to determine whether the will of a majority will be enforced (p→.5). Only four countries have conducted elections that approach the democratic standard.

In Moldova, Russia, and Ukraine the 1990 elections failed to produce a coherent majority. Coalitions among titular party leaders, regional leaders, industrial elites, and popular-front politicians were often temporary and fluid. A form of checking and balancing emerged within the legislature, between the legislative and the executive branches, and between the central and regional governments. Majorities to exclude one group of elites were difficult to construct; attempts were likely to produce defensive reactions from unbeatable countercoalitions. This balance emerged within the states of these three union republics because on the eve of the 1990 elections Soviet-era elites had been divided among bureaucracies that were relatively autonomous from one another. In Russia, and to some extent in Ukraine, *oblast'* leaders reported directly to the all-union leader-

TABLE 2.5
Accountability of Incumbents to Popular Majorities in Elections, 1990–2000*
(Probability That 51 Percent of Adult Population Could Remove Incumbent)

	Accountability Low (p→0)		Uncertain (p→.5)		Accountability High (p→1)	
	Parliament	President	Parliament	President	Parliament	President
Armenia			1995 2000	1996 1998		1991
Azerbaijan	1995 2000	1991 1993 1998		1992		
Belarus	1995 2000			1994		
Estonia			1992 1995 1999	1992		
Georgia		1992	1992 1995 1999	1991 1995 2000		
Kazakhstan	1994 1995 1999	1991 1995 1999				
Kyrgyzstan		1991 2000	1995 2000	1995		
Latvia			1993 1995 1998			
Lithuania					1992 1996 2000	1993 1997/98
Moldova		1991	1994		1998	1996
Russia				1996 2000	1993 1995 1999	1991
Tajikistan	1995 2000	1991 1994 1999				
Turkmenistan	1994 1999	1990 1992 1994				
Ukraine			1994	1991	1998	1994 1999
Uzbekistan	1994 1999	1991 1995 2000				

*Missing is Moldovan legislative election, 3 December 2000.

Method of coding: Single-candidate elections were coded as $p \to 0$, as were elections in which the only alternative candidates were offered by parties controlled by the regime. Uncertainty in accountability ($p \to .5$) was introduced into competitive elections when at least a third of the adult population was denied the vote, when international observers reported significant unfairness, coercion, and intimidation, fraud, or other voting irregularities, or when incumbents threatened that they would not relinquish power even if they lost the vote.

Sources of data: Election observer reports published by the United States Commission on Security and Cooperation in Europe (1993a, 1993b, 1994a, 1994b, 1994c, 1994d, 1995a, 1995b, 1995c, 1996a, 1996b, 1996c, 1998a, 1998b, 1998c, 1998d, 1999a, 1999b, 1999c, 1999d, 1999e, 2000a, 2000b) and all annual editions of *Freedom in the World* beginning with Freedom House (1991).

ship. Many enterprises were under all-union subordination. When the Soviet government ceased to exist, the new successor governments found these hard to control. Alternatively, the union-republic governments controlled enterprises of republic subordination and the rural-agrarian control institutions. In Moldova, Russia, and Ukraine the Communist Party apparatus itself was divided over the issue of independence—often along the lines of ethnicity. In Russia the absence of a union-republic Communist Party leadership left the separate organizations of the party to fragment along regional and sectoral lines.

The political balance that blocked authoritarian projects in Moldova, Russia, and Ukraine after the 1990 elections differed in one important way from the balance among coalitions that negotiated an oligarchic constitution in Belarus. In the Moldova, Russia, and Ukraine the fragmentation of bureaucratic interests and the alliances of some of these with popular fronts made it difficult to form a majority of bureaucrats that could exclude political parties. The mixed elections in 1990 had allowed bureaucrats with locked-in constituencies to mobilize their supporters and popular fronts to seek votes outside these locked-in constituencies. The initial majority coalition that elected the new presidents included a titular mass movement, such as the Popular Front of Moldova and Democratic Russia, that relied on expansion of the selectorate to mobilize voters outside the locked-in constituencies of the bureaucrats (Bojcun 1995; Crowther 1994; Kubicek 1994; Rutland 1994; Sakwa 1993). Alternatively, in Belarus a solid majority in the Supreme Soviet relied on locked-in voters and saw competitive politics that empowered the public as a threat.

The conditions that led to democratization of the selectorate also differed from the conditions leading to exclusive-republican constitutions. In Moldova, Russia, and Ukraine a titular alliance to exclude other ethnic groups was blocked by the internal divisions within the titular elites. In the Russian conflicts of President Yeltsin with the Congress of People's Deputies from 1992 to 1993 and the State Duma after 1993, both president and legislative leaders found the leaders of ethnic homelands to be too valuable as allies to disfranchise. In Ukraine industrial managers who were ethnically Ukrainian were also often Russian speakers and were unwilling to join Ukrainian nationalists to disfranchise Russian managers and their employees in heavy industry. In Moldova exclusionists at first had the upper hand, but the coalition quickly fragmented over the issue of reunification with Romania.

In Ukraine balancing between president and legislature and between central and regional governments blocked anyone from establishing authoritarian rule. Regional and cultural divisions overlay the bureaucratic divisions among state administrators, industrial managers, and farm directors, so that even the so-called party of power was internally divided in this period (Bojcun 1995; Craumer and Clem 1999; Karatnycky 1995; Kubicek 1994; Wilson and Birch 1999). Soviet-era bureaucracies commanding cohesive locked-in constituencies, such as the collective and state farm managers, remained (Gorchinskaya 1998, 61). Yet, these elites fragmented among regions and along the cultural divide among Ukrainian-speaking Ukrainians, Russian-speaking Russians, and a very large "swing" group of Russian-speaking Ukrainians who supported one or the other side tactically. Each group included partisans of various authoritarian projects, but no one of these could command a majority (U.S. CSCE 1998d, Gorchinskaya 1998, Kuzio 1995). For example, a proposal by the incumbent Leonid Kravchuk to postpone the presidential elections won support from his nationalist allies, but garnered only a quarter of the votes cast in the Verkhovna Rada (Kuzio 1996, 120–22).

In Moldova balancing among the presidential bureaucracy, the parliamentary Popular Front faction, and the parliamentary rural-bureaucratic faction prevented anyone from establishing an autocracy, exclusive republic, or oligarchy. The danger that the president and one faction would form an alliance to exclude the third faction was blocked by the multiple crosscutting cleavages among the three power centers. In the initial press for independence Mercea Snegur and his Popular Front allies in the parliament were victorious over the so-called *nomenklatura* faction. Snegur consolidated his presidency in an uncontested popular election, and the Popular Front consolidated its leadership in the parliament by winning the chair and a majority of seats on the Supreme Soviet Presidium. This presidential-nationalist coalition did not cohere on constitutional issues, however, and the president and the Popular Front increasingly opposed one another over the issue of reunification with Romania. The president turned to the Agrarian Democrats, who drew much of their strength from the rural *nomenklatura*. This new alliance between the presidential faction and the Agrarian Democrats in the parliament elected the former Communist Party first secretary Petru Luchinschi as the new parliamentary chair (Socor 1992, 1993). Yet, this alliance too was short-lived, as the new parliamentary leadership and president began to disagree over economic reform and cultural policy. The president turned once again to the popular front for support. In the 1994 parliamentary elections, the Agrarian Democrats won a solid majority of seats, and in the 1996 presidential elections Luchinschi defeated Snegur. Yet, this did not lead to a cohesive alliance between the new president and parliamentary majority because by 1996 the Agrarian Party had already begun to fragment and quickly lost its parliamentary majority (Crowther, 1997; U.S. CSCE 1998c).

In Russia the confrontation between legislature and executive and between central and regional governments created a balance that prevented any one faction from establishing its hegemony in this period. The constitutional history of this period is filled with crises in which a compelling conterfactual case can be made that had there been no "double-tripartite balance" among president, legislature, and regional authorities, and within the regions among the party of power, industrial managers, and farm managers, authoritarianism would have triumphed (e.g., McAuley 1992; Melvin 1998). Consider just four of the more important recurring critical issues in which the constitutional outcome could have been very different.

First is the failure of the Russian president to create a dominant presidential party in this period. At various times the president and his staff undertook preparations that would have made this possible, but they encountered resistance from other political actors who refused to subordinate themselves to the presidency and whose support the president needed. On one hand, Boris Yeltsin attempted to ban significant opposition parties. For example, on 6 November 1991 he banned the Communist Party, but this was overturned in December 1992 by the Constitutional Court. Had Yeltsin not been checked at that moment by his desire to gain allies on the design of a constitution, he might not have relented. On the other hand, the Russian president at various times began preparations for a "presidential party." Early in 1992 Gennadii Burbulis announced creation of a "presidential party" that would support economic reforms. In February Democratic Russia held a conference of Public Committees for Russian Reforms that were to become the foundations of this official partylike organization. Burbulis ordered state officials to set up local Public Committees for Russian Reforms in places of residence and workplaces and to provide information, offices, and special telephone communications facilities to these committees (Roeder 1994). In November 1992 Yeltsin called on all "democratic forces" to unite in a party that he would head. Yet, these plans in 1992 failed to galvanize a following. Two and a half years later, as preparations for the parliamentary elections got underway, Yeltsin tried again and announced formation of two electoral blocs, which would be headed by Viktor Chernomyrdin and Ivan Rybkin and would "be able to forcefully eject all extremists from the political arena" (see the discussion in *The Current Digest of the Post-Soviet Press* 47 (May 24, 1995): 1–6). While some prominent regional leaders announced they would join Chernomyrdin's bloc (Our Home is Russia), many did not; moreover, major agricultural and industrial leaders announced they would not join either (Tregubova 1995; Yuryev 1995). If successful, these plans would have been invaluable in the construction of an integrated electoral machine. The resistance from autonomous bureaucratic leaders blocked these attempts.

Second, the Russian president did not transform the legislature into a rubber stamp, because regional leaders blocked his attempts. The republic and provincial leaders were shrewd in trying to maintain balance between president and parliament in Moscow so as to maximize their own freedom of action. For example, in early 1993 the heads of the republics urged postponement of a referendum that might give the president the authority to prorogue the Congress of Peoples Deputies. The presidential coup of September–October 1993 presented Yeltsin with his best opportunity to turn the legislature into a rubber stamp, but the regional leaders resisted the president's attempt to subjugate the legislature. On 30 September 1993 heads of sixty-two of the eighty-nine regions in the Russian Federation assembled to demand that Yeltsin rescind his dissolution of the Congress of Peoples Deputies (Todres 1993). When given a relatively free hand to write the constitution, Yeltsin was, nonetheless, constrained by knowledge that he could not successfully make an end run around these regional leaders—even if he resorted to a public referendum to ratify it. In order to mobilize enough votes to cross the 50 percent threshold in turnout and in votes, Yeltsin had to rely on the regional leaders and their administrations (Lubarksii and Sobyanin 1995).

Third, the Russian president did not transform the regional governments into an integrated administrative machine. Yeltsin introduced presidential representatives in the provinces who would serve an intelligence and coordination function, reporting to the Control Department of the Presidential Administration, but these did not displace the governors or legislatures. In November 1991 the Congress of People's Deputies gave the president special powers to remove elected executives and appoint heads of administration in the provinces and cities. By presidential decree following the dissolution of the Congress of Peoples Deputies in 1993 the president confirmed his power to appoint the governors. Yet, the division at the national level between Russian president and Congress of People's Deputies, and then between the president and State Duma, meant the president needed the regional leaders as allies and needed the votes they could deliver in elections. These prevented Yeltsin from replacing leaders of regional mobilizational machines with toadies and creating an integrated electoral machine (or circular flow of power). In October 1992 the president set up a Council of Heads of the Republics as a consultative body, using it to rally regional support against the national parliament. In August 1993 he created the Federation Council to bring republic and regional representatives together in order to consult on constitutional and policy matters. In the elections of 1993, 1995, and 1996, Yeltsin struck deals with regional leaders to mobilize votes for his constitution, his parliamentary allies, and his own candidacy.

Fourth, to this list of counterfactual examples, one could add the decisions that most immediately would spell a shift toward authoritarianism—the decision to suspend elections. The Russian president did not call off the State Duma elections scheduled for December 1995, the presidential elections scheduled for June 1996, or regional elections beginning in the summer of 1996. Prior to each of these elections the president and his men had reason to fear that the outcomes would go against their interests. Prior to the Duma and presidential elections, members of the Presidential Administration actually floated a proposal to postpone the elections. What stayed the president's hand? Lilia Shevtsova and Scott Bruckner (1997, 24) make an argument that is very close to the larger argument made in this chapter. "Authoritarian tendencies in Russia are stymied by the inability of any single group to monopolize power for an extended period; intolerance among regional elites for the reestablishment of strong central authority; a widespread feeling that, to survive, Russia needs to be a responsible member of the world community; and the center's inability to count on effective armed-forces support."

Ironically, the very rough and tumble of politics that observers often lament as a sign of the failure of the postcommunist transition may, instead, be its virtue. Not only is this open and inclusive contestation a manifestation of democracy, it may be the greatest obstacle to authoritarianism as well.

Discussion

The emergence and survival of democracy in such inhospitable circumstances as the postcommunist societies and economies of the former Soviet Union is one of the twentieth century's more remarkable and enormously encouraging developments. Yet, it also poses something of a puzzle for social science, because prevailing theories of democratization seem unable to explain this pattern. Through such anomalies, the experience of the postcommunist democracies—and particularly, the post-Soviet democracies—speaks loudly to all theories and calls for rethinking conclusions drawn from other parts of the world. These anomalies should prompt a dialogue with students of democracy everywhere.

In order to begin to explain the pattern of outcomes in the Soviet successor states, I started with a puzzle: In only a few instances did the leaders of the union republics and successor states fail to defend the existing authoritarian constitution or find a nondemocratic alternative that made few changes to the status quo. Why did some leaders fail either to preserve the existing authoritarian constitutions or to find a proximate solution? Our theories must explain the choice of democracy over its alternatives— various forms of authoritarian regimes and authoritarian projects—and must explain the choice within the context of authoritarian regimes. In order to fill this lacuna in existing theories of democratization, I began with a simple model of constitutional politics within authoritarian regimes as an ongoing bargaining process. The model begins by identifying who is empowered to participate in the bargaining that can change the existing rules of politics. The most important constraint on the outcome of different bargaining processes is the institutionally defined balance of power within the state. Yet, the model also underscores that maintaining an existing authoritarian constitution and agreeing on a new authoritarian pact are not simple undertakings, because these regimes are caught between the horns of the twin dilemmas of authority and accountability that complicate the task of designing authoritarian constitutions and threaten to bring instability to authoritarian regimes. In the face of these dilemmas, the least hospitable circumstance for preserving authoritarianism or creating new authoritarianism is pluralism within the state. The conclusion is an insight that goes back in modern political thought at least to the Baron de Montesquieu, who argued persuasively that the defense of liberty from tyranny requires dividing the powers of the state and checking power by power.

Although I contend that the question addressed by this chapter is important, it is admittedly (and deliberately) narrow. First, I have limited the dependent variable to choice of constitutions by authoritarian leaders. Among the issues I have excluded from consideration is the introduction of violence into domestic conflicts. Contests for the control of the central government—excluding for the moment ethnic conflicts for secession— have escalated to protracted violence in Tajikistan and Georgia. This omission is deliberate—not only because it represents a different dependent variable, but also because it would require a different model to explain it. Suffice it to say that it was not in republics with the most dispersed power that these civil wars broke out. Second, I have used a definition of regime-type, following on that of Schumpeter, that is purposefully minimalist. Precision comes at the expense of richness. This does not address such issues as the quality of regimes in these states. As many commentators have recently argued, but perhaps none more eloquently and passionately than Anatol Lieven (1998), the democracy in the post-Soviet states that I laud suffers a level of venality and corruption that should cause outrage. I have not attempted to address these other dimensions, but to argue that these dimensions should be distinguished for purposes of analysis, since they do not always appear together, and to argue for the central importance of accountability of decision makers in distinguishing democracy from its alternatives.[10]

The specific institutional constraints found in the Soviet successor states are unique, but the principle of intrastate pluralism and the problem of credible commitments in authoritarian regimes are not; the model is applicable to a number of transformations and transplacements. Several authors cite bureaucratic conflicts within authoritarian regimes as critical to the initiation of a transition from authoritarianism. Alfred Stepan (1988), for example, notes that redemocratization in Brazil began in the 1980s when General Ernesto Geisel reached out for allies in civil society in order to stop the erosion of the position of the general-president and his staff and to counterbalance the rising power of the security-intelligence bureaucracies. Arturo Valenzuela (1991) explains how Air Force General Gustavo Leigh pressed for a return to democracy in order to counter Pinochet's growing power over the previously coequal heads of the armed services. In each of these instances, conflicts among autonomous bureaucrats—some of which saw looming threats to their own positions as a consequence of weak guarantees of the existing authoritarian constitution—were critical to the attempt to renegotiate the authoritarian pact. Although the occasion for the political choices in each of the Soviet union republics was an exogenous shock from Moscow, a shock is not a necessary element of the model of ongoing constitutional politics within authoritarian regimes. Exogenous shocks, like the death of an autocratic leader, are certainly common occasions for renegotiation of authoritarian pacts. The exogenous shock in the Soviet cases is fortuitous for analysis, because it permits us to compare several cases at exactly the same point in time. (The reasons for the exogenous shock, of course, must be explained—something I attempt in Roeder [1993].) Yet, exogenous shocks are not necessary to explain the beginning of a successful renegotiation of an authoritarian pact. As the examples of Brazil and Chile underscore, the slow accumulation of decisions reached to address other problems may shift the balance of power in a regime so that bureaucrats seek to protect themselves by new authoritarian institutions or even democratization.

The model presented in this chapter focuses on proximate institutional causes, in part because so many of the distant economic and cultural causes seem unable to explain the pattern of outcomes that we have observed in the Soviet successor states. My focus on proximate causes has received harsh criticism, because it purportedly borders on tautology. Yet, Herbert Kitschelt (1999, 19–20), who raises this charge, substitutes a distinction between the rational-legal and patrimonial cultures of different communist bureaucracies for my distinction between unified and divided control over union-republic bureaucracies; neither distinction is "deeper" or "shallower" than the other. The evidence for this charge of causal shallowness mistakes or misrepresents as ultimate, independent variables what is actually careful process-tracing of the bargaining within authoritarian regimes that followed upon different bureaucratic conditions created over decades of Soviet rule. My focus on political institutions at the heart of the old regime is part of the tradition of historical institutionalism that Valerie Bunce (1999b) and Pauline Jones Luong (2000) have used so artfully in the analysis of postcommunist politics in various countries. For example, Luong (2000, 663) explains the adoption of different electoral systems in Kazakhstan, Kyryzstan, and Uzbekistan by the bargaining among strategically minded politicians constrained by "the interaction between the preceding historical and institutional setting and the dynamic uncertainty that surrounds them." Yet, my institutionalism diverges from the sociological analysis of Bunce and Jones by stressing not socialization or identities, but constraints on the rational pursuit of interest.

The final outcome of the processes that I describe in this chapter is uncertain: The specific characterizations of regimes in the period 1990 to 2000 are initial choices and do not represent predictions about their future. The question answered in this chapter concerns the initiation of transitions from existing authoritarianism to specific alternatives—either alternative forms of authoritarianism or democracy. In this way this chapter is a complement to—and is, in turn, complemented by—the chapters of my coauthors. Steven Fish offers an account of the dynamics of failed democratization—backsliding toward authoritarianism—that may set in once a choice to begin democratization has been taken. Our analyses are similar—most obviously they both stress the role of political institutions in shaping subsequent outcomes. Yet, Fish sees a difference in our approaches that I am inclined to see as having only minor significance: Fish highlights the perils of hyperpresidentialism as an independent variable in the new democracies; in this chapter I treat as dependent variables institutions adopted as part of the process of responding to Gorbachev's pressures for democratization and to the breakup of the Soviet Union (compare Easter 1997; Frye 1997). Thus, in this chapter strategically minded autocratic coalitions have selected hyperpresidentialism in many successor states, such as Uzbekistan, because they saw this as essential to constructing an autocratic constitution. What may appear as a contradiction actually disappears if one discretely separates the institutional givens that preceded a specific choice from the institutional innovations that are part of that choice. Both Fish and I are careful to draw such distinctions in our chapters: We each focus on choices in different contexts, and so the institutions that are exogenous or predetermined in each context are similarly different.

Richard Anderson and Stephen Hanson explain changes in elite and citizen behaviors that complement the analysis in this chapter—these changes must take place in order to complete a transition to democracy. Yet, our epistemologies differ significantly. Anderson discusses the role of changing identities to answer a vital question—why do politicians and citizens suddenly begin to behave like members of a democracy when there are strong incentives of self-interest to free-ride? Hanson discusses the role of changing elite beliefs as the essential step in the consolidation of democracy—democracy will consolidate when the enforcers of a regime's institutions believe the formal rules of the institutions to be legitimate and value these as ends in themselves. My own model holds constant such cognitions as identities or beliefs, and I ask how variation in institutional constraints affects the pursuit of power interests. This distinction between our approaches captures the different epistemologies of political sociology and political realism. The approaches cannot be simply combined without doing violence to their respective assumptions. Indeed, each sets a research agenda for the other—can one's approach be extended to account (on its own terms and consistent with its own assumptions) for the phenomena highlighted by the other? For each of us, this is obviously a next step in our respective research programs.

THREE

THE DYNAMICS OF DEMOCRATIC EROSION

M. Steven Fish

SINCE THE demise of single-party regimes in 1989–91, the countries of the postcommunist world have followed virtually every conceivable path of regime change, ranging from smooth democratization to adoption of new forms of harsh dictatorship. Many countries did not follow a linear path. In some countries initial movement toward democracy was halted and even reversed. Arrested and reversed democratization is the subject of this chapter. I aim to explain why some countries that underwent democratization were able to build upon their early gains while others slid back toward authoritarianism.

At least nine of the twenty-eight postcommunist countries have experienced arrested or reversed democratization. Yet theories prevalent in the literature on democracy and regime change do not offer entirely satisfactory explanations for such a common, albeit unfortunate, end to antiauthoritarian transformations. I consider a wide variety of hypotheses for the reversal of democratization. Most conventional explanations prove not to hold great power. I find that a syndrome of factors, the most important of which is a political system that concentrates power in the chief executive, is the best predictor of backsliding. Superpresidentialism, or a constitution that invests formidable power in the presidency, turns out to be the greatest antagonist of the consolidation of democratic gains. The president's own preferences also matter, though the constraints the president faces are more important than the president's own traits. Even democracy's heroes dig its grave if unchecked by other forces. In addition to other branches of government, those other forces are opposition parties and foreign governments.

Postcommunist Regime Change: Variation in Trajectories

The criteria for classifying countries are the "freedom scores" that Freedom House issues for each of the world's countries. The scores represent averages of ratings on "political rights" and "civil liberties," which are measured separately. Freedom scores range from 1 (best) to 7 (worst).

"Political rights" captures electoral openness and fairness, while "civil liberties" encompasses rights of association and communication. The survey methodology essentially operationalizes Robert Dahl's celebrated definition of polyarchy and other more recent explications of Dahl's concept (Freedom House, various volumes; Dahl 1982; Schmitter and Karl 1996). I adopt Dahl's definition of *polyarchy*—a term he substituted for democracy, which he regarded as an ideal type. I also embrace the operationalization of it embodied in the Freedom House scores and the continuous measurement of democratization represented in the scores, which differs from a dichotomous notion that assesses whether a country is or is not a "democracy." Since Freedom House issues ratings each year as well as explanations for changes in countries' scores from the previous year, one may track change across time.

I place countries in four categories. (Table 3.1 shows the countries grouped in each category.) Category I consists of countries that received freedom scores of 1 or 1.5 in the most recent Freedom House survey (1999–2000). These are the best scores possible. The Czech Republic, Estonia, Hungary, Latvia, Lithuania, Poland, Slovakia, and Slovenia received such scores (all scored 1.5). Their scores are the same as those that Belgium, the United Kingdom, Italy, and Uruguay received and are one-half point better than those of Chile, Greece, South Korea, and Taiwan. Regime change in these polities, with the exception of Slovakia, has been unambiguous and unidirectional. By the end of the 1990s all had become, by any normal definition, democracies.

Category II consists of countries that received scores ranging between 2 and 4 in the 1999–2000 survey *and* that exhibited trends toward lower (better) scores during the first postcommunist decade. The countries in this category—Georgia, Macedonia, Moldova, Mongolia, and Romania—are not full-blown democracies. Yet all made substantial gains and sustained their progress during the 1990s. They are labeled "democratizers."

Category III encompasses countries that in at least one of the yearly surveys conducted since 1991–92 scored lower (better) than a 5 but received scores in the most recent survey that were higher (worse) than their best score during some previous year. Within the nine countries in this category, the scores of five deteriorated by one full point or more, which represents a severe degradation of democratic gains, while the scores of the four other countries depreciated by one-half point, which signifies milder erosion. Countries in this group are Albania, Armenia, Belarus, Bulgaria, Croatia, Kazakhstan, Kyrgyzstan, Russia, and Ukraine. I label them "backsliders."

Category IV is composed of countries that moved directly from Communist Party regimes to new forms of authoritarianism without ever undergoing substantial democratization. These countries never scored lower

TABLE 3.1
Democracies, Autocracies, Democratizers, and Backsliders

	Freedom Rating, 1999–2000	Lowest (Best) Freedom Rating (and latest year with that rating)
Category I: Democracies		
Czech Republic	1.5	
Estonia	1.5	
Hungary	1.5	
Latvia	1.5	
Lithuania	1.5	
Poland	1.5	
Slovakia	1.5	
Slovenia	1.5	
Category II: Democratizers		
Georgia	3.5	
Macedonia	3.0	
Moldova	3.0	
Mongolia	2.5	
Romania	2.0	
Category III: Backsliders		
Albania	4.5	3.0 (1993–94)
Armenia	4.0	3.5 (1994–95)
Belarus	6.0	3.5 (1992–93)
Bulgaria	2.5	2.0 (1995–96)
Croatia	4.0	3.5 (1991–92)
Kazakhstan	5.5	4.5 (1991–92)
Kyrgyzstan	5.0	3.0 (1992–93)
Russia	4.5	3.0 (1991–92)
Ukraine	3.5	3.0 (1992–93)
Category IV: Autocracies		
Azerbaijan	5.0	
Bosnia	5.0	
Tajikistan	6.0	
Turkmenistan	7.0	
Uzbekistan	6.5	
Yugoslavia	5.0	

(better) than a 5 in the yearly Freedom House ratings. They are Azerbaijan, Bosnia, Tajikistan, Turkmenistan, Uzbekistan, and Yugoslavia (Serbia and Montenegro). These countries are called "autocracies."[1]

The main purpose of this chapter is to explain reversion toward authoritarianism (or "de-democratization"). I therefore focus particularly on countries in Category III, the backsliders, though examining and testing hypothesized explanations for de-democratization requires systematic cross-national analysis of all the countries in the region and comparison across categories. Before investigating cases, I attempt to furnish a reasonably comprehensive overview of the causal arguments found in writings on democratic reversals.

Causes and Agents of Authoritarian Reversion: Hypotheses

I lump the causes of democratic reversal into two broad categories: *fixed conditions* and *proximate circumstances*. The former encompasses structural, sociocultural, and historical features that may vary across countries but that change slowly or not at all within countries. The latter refers to more mutable and immediate factors that may vary appreciably across time within a single country. Discussion begins with the former category.

The first fixed condition that may render a country structurally unfit to function as a democracy is gross inequality in the distribution of wealth and the concomitant presence of a mighty upper class. While large inequalities might not prevent a democratic breakthrough, they may subsequently inhibit the advancement of democratization. Inequalities may be particularly likely to shorten the life expectancy of a fledgling democracy or semidemocracy when the upper class is both economically powerful and numerically small, and therefore capable of disrupting democratization and fearful of mass empowerment via open elections. Scholars have used the economic-inequalities and class-power hypothesis to explain the demise of democracy in the 1960s and 1970s in Latin America and have adduced it as a basis for skepticism regarding the durability of democratic gains in the 1980s and 1990s in countries such as the Philippines, South Africa, and El Salvador (Rueschemeyer, Stephens, and Stephens 1992; Gibson 1996; O'Donnell 1973; Jowitt 1996b).

The second structural condition is overall level of economic development. Some analysts have held that democracies that reach a certain level of economic development rarely or never suffer authoritarian reversion. Conversely, democracy will be crisis-prone and tenuous in countries below some critical threshold of development. Analysts differ over whether there exists some intermediate stage of development in which democracy is particularly vulnerable, though most recent literature suggests that the richer the country, the more secure democratic gains (Przeworski et al. 1996; Przeworski and Limongi 1997; Huntington 1991; O'Donnell 1973).

A third possible structural influence is the size of the polity. Many theorists have held that small size facilitates the creation and sustenance of a republic. Some assume that a smaller population is more governable. The technical problems involved in maintaining democracy, from holding free elections to enforcing the law across the national territory, may be simpler in Costa Rica and Slovenia than in Brazil and Russia. But precisely the opposite hypothesis may also be advanced: If maintaining democracy is simpler in a smaller polity, so enforcing an authoritarian regime may be easier as well. The extent and subtlety of control that Singapore's rulers exercise provides a case in point (Montesquieu 1995; Dahl and Tufte 1973).

Sociocultural profile may also affect a country's "fitness" for democracy. Ethnically diverse societies are often seen as worse candidates for sustained democratization than are more homogeneous societies (Horowitz 1985, 1993; Rabushka and Shepsle 1972).

The fifth "fixed condition" is political culture. Predominant religious tradition is often viewed as the most politically relevant aspect of culture. Scholars view certain religious traditions as more conducive to democratic advancement than others. Predominantly Christian societies are often regarded as more receptive to democratization than are non-Christian societies. Many scholars see Islam as creating a particularly inhospitable environment for the endurance of popular rule. Even the one major democracy in the Muslim world, Turkey, is prone to bouts of authoritarian politics (Lipset 1996; Huntington 1984; Waterbury 1994).

The sixth condition is the legacy of democratic rule. Many analysts regard collective memories and experiences of democracy at earlier historical stages as important to sustaining democratization at a later time. A tradition of democracy lends a "feel" or "instinct" for open politics that may help sustain new democracies through hard times, and the longer the legacy, the better (Bunce 1995; Dahl 1989).

In addition to these six "fixed conditions," more immediate, proximate circumstances and developments may also influence possibilities for the advancement or degradation of democracy. A high degree of ideological polarization may threaten neodemocracies. It may pose a particularly potent peril where political parties representing diverse interests are locked into policy positions by strong ties to informed, politicized constituencies (Sartori 1976; Linz 1978; Di Palma 1977).

A second potentially important circumstance is electoral rules. In the wake of the spectacular demise of European democracies in the interwar period, some writers argued that proportional representation (PR) raises the risk of polarization, while majoritarian systems filter out extremists and thus diminish the dangers of democratic erosion or demise. Other scholars espouse the opposite view. They assert that PR enhances governmental representativeness and accountability and by so doing spurs popular contentment and institutional consolidation (Hermens 1941; Rae 1971; Lijphart 1996; Lardeyret 1996).

Constitutional arrangements, and in particular whether the regime takes a presidential or parliamentary form, may affect the life expectancy of new democracies. Some scholars strongly contend that parliamentarism enhances the prospects for avoiding authoritarian reversion (Linz and Valenzuela 1994; Stepan and Skach 1993). Others claim that presidentialism is superior or at least no less conducive to democratic sustainability than parliamentarism (Horowitz, 1985, 1996; Faundez 1997; Shugart and Mainwaring 1997; Bernhard 1999).

Economic performance may influence democratization. Strong performance may safeguard new democracies against erosion or early demise. Economic crisis, on the other hand, may provoke popular discontent. It may force governments to adopt policies that exacerbate popular dissatisfaction, alienate powerful social groups, and undermine the cross-class coalitions that may enhance democratic stability (Wallerstein 1980; Stepan 1978). On the other hand, the stability of closed regimes may also be vulnerable to changes in economic performance, so that, by subverting closed regimes, bad economic performance in some instances may actually create the conditions for democratization (Remmer, 1996).

According to many writers, economic policy doctrine, no less than economic performance, may affect the prospects for maintaining democratization. While the question of what types of economic doctrine best support democratization is a source of debate, the preponderance of opinion has pinned blame for democratic erosion on radical liberalization and stabilization programs. According to this argument, liberal programs require reducing popular consumption and rejecting popular demands for policies that would yield broad-based improvements in living standards. Liberal doctrines, especially in countries where the state has traditionally played a large role in the economy and the provision of public welfare, may necessitate coercive measures to grapple with popular discontent (Przeworski 1991; Callaghy 1994; Pion-Berlin 1983; Roberts 1995).

War may also spark democratic reversal. The human and material costs of war may reduce popular support for a new democratic government, and the requirements of prosecuting war may lessen state officials' tolerance for dissent. Wars may also enhance the popular appeal of antidemocratic forces, including chauvinists and nationalist extremists.

The seventh proximate circumstance is external intervention. The intervening power may impose a nondemocratic regime or create conditions that counter democratization.

In sum, ideological polarization, electoral rules, constitutional arrangements, economic performance, economic policy doctrines, war, and external interventions serve as the proximate circumstances that have been adduced to explain democratic reversals. These factors, together with the "fixed conditions" discussed above, cover the main causes of democratic reversals found in the social science literature.

Discussion of causes without agents, however, would be incomplete. By whose hands is democratization reversed? One of five agents is usually responsible. The first is a revolutionary party or movement. The capture of power by an antidemocratic party or movement is most likely under conditions of ideological polarization. The second possible agent of de-democratization is a separatist ethnonational movement. Democracy-degrading separatist movements are more likely in ethnically diverse societies than in homogenous ones. The third candidate agent is the military. Military activism in politics is especially likely where one finds extreme inequalities in wealth and powerful upper classes that have close ties to military institutions and lack confidence in their own ability to compete effectively in open politics. It is also common under circumstances of severe ideological polarization or deep economic crisis. Involvement in war may also empower and embolden the armed forces and lead to military coup. The fourth potential agent is the president. Some of the recent literature on regime change casts strong presidents as antagonists of democratization. Presidents are presumably more likely to possess the resources needed to engage in counterdemocratic behavior in constitutional systems that grant them wide scope for independent action. Finally, foreign armies may undo democratization. They do so following external military intervention.

The Standard Hypotheses and the Evidence

How well do the candidate causal factors outlined above explain democratic reversals in the postcommunist world? Additionally, in terms of agency, is one or are several of the "usual suspects" responsible for dedemocratization?

Many hypotheses cannot be tested rigorously. Where quantitative analysis is possible, I present the results of some simple bivariate regressions. For several reasons, I do not engage in multivariate regression here. First, many of the variables are not readily quantifiable. Second, the number of hypotheses under consideration is large relative to the number of cases (countries), and even for some quantifiable variables, reliable data are missing for many countries. Third, since this chapter deals with a dynamic phenomenon (changes in countries' democratic status, as reflected in Freedom House freedom ratings), standard regression cannot fully capture the relationships under consideration. Treating recent freedom ratings as the dependent variable, as I do here, facilitates examination of some hypotheses, but truly adequate quantitative analysis would have to grapple with incremental change and involve time series. Given the limited quality and quantity of available data, the fairly short period of time under examination, and the problems of establishing appropriate lags, such analysis would be premature, even though it is hypothetically feasible in strictly technical terms.

The first structural factor, economic inequalities and class power, cannot be tested satisfactorily due to insufficient data for many countries. What evidence is available, however, suggests that the countries that have undergone democratic erosion (Category III countries) did not suffer from inequalities sufficiently great at the time of regime change to render them structurally unfit for democracy. Nor is there compelling evidence that countries in this category suffered from greater inequalities than did Category II countries (World Bank 1996). Some countries in Category III, such as Russia and Albania, did experience explosions of income and asset inequalities during the 1990s. Yet others, such as Croatia and Belarus, did not undergo such dramatic transformations. And while inequalities in Russia and Albania may now impede further democratization, the initial erosion of democracy in these countries and others in the category cannot be attributed to inequalities. Soviet-type socialism, whatever its many pathologies, did leave behind a rudimentary economic equality as well as near universal literacy. Few if any countries in the postcommunist world manifested inequalities in income, wealth, and class power as severe as those found in, for example, Brazil, South Africa, and Central America (World Bank 1995, 1997). A structural-inequalities and class-power hypothesis holds little promise for explaining patterns of democratization and de-democratization in the postcommunist region.

Level of economic development at the outset of regime change may be linked to the risk of authoritarian reversion, but the relationship is not strong. A bivariate regression of Freedom House scores for 1999–2000 on GNP per capita as of 1990 shows a relationship that is statistically significant only at a rather undemanding level, and the goodness of fit is unimpressive (see table 3.2). Between-group variance is adequately large relative to within-group variance for the differences in mean scores across categories to be statistically significant. Yet Category II countries actually score substantially lower on GNP per capita than do Category III countries. Initial level of economic development does not predict which countries would subsequently experience counterdemocratic political development.

TABLE 3.2
Bivariate Regressions of Freedom House Scores on Structural Factors

Variable[a]	Significance (t-test)	Number of Cases
GNP per capita, 1990[b]	−2.43*	26†
Population, 1990	0.42	28
Largest ethnic group as percent of total	−1.89	28
Average GDP growth, 1990–94	−1.01	22††
Economic liberalization[c]	−6.71*	26†

* Significant at .05 level or better. All negative t-tests indicate a positive relationship with democratization, because Freedom House scores range from 7 (least democratization) to 1 (most democratization).

† Data missing for Bosnia and Yugoslavia.

†† Data missing for Bosnia, Croatia, Macedonia, Moldova, Slovenia, and Yugoslavia

[a]Sources of data: World Bank, 1995; Random House Geographical Dictionary 1992. Also see Fish 1998[b].

[b]Mean scores for GNP per capita are $4,010 for Category I, $1,604 for Category II, $2,498 for Category III; and $1,233 for Category IV.

[c]Mean economic liberalization scores are 8.79 for Category I, 6.84 for Category II, 6.57 for Category III, and 3.95 for Category IV. Scores range from 1 (least liberalization) to 10 (most liberalization). On these scores, see Fish 1998b.

The size of the polity is unrelated to democratization. A bivariate regression of Freedom House scores on population size yields no statistically significant link. Differences between categories are also not statistically significant.

Ethnic homogeneity/heterogeneity fails as a predictor as well. The percentage of the population accounted for by the largest ethnic group provides a rough but useful measure of the extent of ethnic homogeneity. A bivariate regression of Freedom House scores on this indicator for homogeneity fails to show a statistically significant relationship. Cross-category comparison also fails to reveal any consistent pattern.

Culture, as defined by predominant religious tradition, does appear to be related to overall democratic achievement. All Category I countries are overwhelmingly Catholic or Protestant; five of six countries in Category IV are predominantly Muslim. But Categories II and III both present mixed bags, and no consistent confessional difference appears to distinguish one category from another. In Category II, four countries are Eastern Christian/Orthodox and one is Buddhist. Category III consists of one Catholic country, five Eastern Christian/Orthodox countries, and three predominantly Muslim countries. Even if consistent differences in religious tradition are discernible between the democracies and the autocracies, such differences do not appear to account for divergence between the democratizers and the backsliders.

The historical legacies of democracy cannot explain a great deal of variation in the postcommunist region precisely because the "variable" does not vary very much. In this respect, this candidate explanation resembles the economic inequalities and class power hypothesis, but provides perhaps an even clearer case of low cross-national variation. As Bunce (1995, 89) has rightly noted in a comparison of the postcommunist region with others that have undergone democratization in recent decades, "Eastern Europe has no such democratic tradition. The so-called democratic experiments of the interwar period lasted less than a decade and are best understood, in any case, as authoritarian politics in democratic guise."

Thus, with the possible, partial exception of the cultural factor, none of the "fixed conditions" normally associated with democratic erosion carry great explanatory potential. Do the circumstantial variables fare any better?

For the most part they do not. Ideological polarization and an attendant ratcheting-up of conflict by parties closely tied to antagonistic classes or other social groups have rarely if ever characterized postcommunist politics. While intense conflict has often punctuated political life, sustained ideological polarization that includes mass mobilization has been conspicuous by its absence. The only countries in which political parties are tied to mass constituencies and consistently present coherent, conflicting programs are actually found in Categories I and II.[2] Nowhere in Categories III or IV were parties strong and representative enough during the 1990s to pose the threat of a Chilean- (early 1970s), Brazilian- (early 1960s), or German- (late 1920s–early 1930s) style polarization that could reverse democratization.

Nor are electoral rules, and PR in particular, linked to democratic erosion. All three categories that are occupied by countries in which some semblance of meaningful elections has been held (Categories I, II, and III) show considerable within-category variation in electoral rules. Many countries have altered their rules one or more times since 1989–91. The backsliders category includes countries with fully majoritarian rules for elections to the legislature (e.g., Belarus and Ukraine before 1998), predominantly majoritarian systems with a proportional component (e.g., Albania, Armenia, and Kazakhstan), mixed systems modeled roughly on the German system (e.g., Russia and Ukraine in 1998), and PR systems (e.g., Croatia and Bulgaria). Electoral systems are similarly diverse within Categories I and II. Democratic erosion cannot be attributed to PR; but nor does PR prevent erosion.

The constitutional framework, in contrast, may indeed be related to the trajectory of regime change. Among the eight democracies (Category

I), six (the Czech Republic, Estonia, Hungary, Latvia, Slovakia, and Slovenia) have parliamentary systems; Poland has semipresidentialism; and Lithuania may be characterized as a semipresidential or moderate presidential system. Four of the six autocracies (Category IV) have presidential systems. Thus, parliamentary constitutions are overrepresented among the democracies and presidential systems among the autocracies. Clear patterns become somewhat more difficult to discern when comparing Categories II and III. The democratizers (Category II) include one parliamentary system (Macedonia), two semipresidential ones (Mongolia and Romania), and two cases of presidentialism (Georgia and Moldova). The backsliders (Category III) include two parliamentary constitutions (Albania and Bulgaria); one semipresidential constitution (Croatia); and six presidential constitutions (Armenia, Belarus, Kazakhstan, Kyrgyzstan, Russia, and Ukraine). Presidentialism may be related to propensity for de-democratization; but some countries with presidential systems have neither experienced backsliding nor remained mired in dictatorship. The "presidential" hypothesis will be addressed at greater length below. As will be shown, presidentialism—or, more precisely, a particular type of presidentialism—may indeed powerfully affect patterns of regime change.

While data are missing for some cases, economic performance does not appear to be related to democratization. All countries in the region experienced severe economic crises during and after the fall of Soviet-type regimes, though the depth of crisis varied across countries. A bivariate regression of Freedom House scores on average GDP growth rates during 1990–94 shows no relationship. Within-group variance is too large relative to between-group variance for intergroup differences to show a statistically significant relationship.

Economic doctrine may affect the propensity for democratic degradation—but not in the way that most analysts have argued. Many students of postcommunist politics contend that policies of crash economic transformation have compromised democratization (Orenstein 1998; Nelson 1996; Bresser Pereira, Maravall, and Przeworski 1993). The evidence provides no support for this view. A bivariate regression of the 1999–2000 Freedom House scores on economic liberalization scores for the end of 1995 actually shows a positive and statistically and substantively significant relationship. Between-group differences are statistically significant. Not only does the evidence not sustain the notion that rapid economic reform undermines democratization; it contradicts it. But economic reform per se does not abolish the risk of de-democratization. Croatia, Russia, Albania, and Kyrgyzstan—backsliders all in democratization—each ranks in the top half of countries in economic liberalization.

War is certainly no friend of democratization. None of the democracies have been involved in wars since the onset of regime change, while four of the autocracies (all but Turkmenistan and Uzbekistan) have experienced war. Yet the presence or absence of war is not a particularly good predictor of backsliding. Two of the five Category II countries, Moldova and Georgia, suffered major armed conflict (in both cases civil wars aggravated by an external power). Five of the nine countries in Category III have not suffered war. Two (Croatia and Armenia) were involved in interstate wars; one (Albania) experienced a general breakdown in civil order, and one (Russia) suffered from a serious but geographically contained civil war. War obviously is not propitious for democratization. Yet some Category II countries have experienced it and managed to move forward with democratization, while most backsliders have not suffered from major armed conflict at all.

Finally, no country, with the partial exception of Bosnia, suffered invasion and replacement of its government by one appointed by a foreign power. Tajikistan's government became dependent for its survival on Russia's armed forces, but even Tajikistan was not invaded and its government has been made more by domestic actors than by a foreign army.

Just as most of the "usual" causes do not readily explain democratic erosion, neither are most of the "usual" agents responsible. Nowhere has an armed revolutionary party come to power and toppled an existing constitutional order. The postcommunist world in the 1990s did not know a disciplined, armed revolutionary party of any size and real political significance. Armed separatist ethnonational movements appeared in six countries, but these countries are spread across categories. Two of them (Georgia and Moldova) are in Category II; two (Croatia and Russia) are in Category III; and two (Bosnia and Yugoslavia) are in Category IV. Seven of the nine countries in Category III have suffered no separatist ethnonational movement. In the clear majority of cases, therefore, one cannot blame a separatist ethnonational movement for de-democratization.

Nor have politically assertive militaries been prominent agents of democratic degradation or demise. In remarkable contrast with Latin America and Africa, the postcommunist region has not known military coups. Azerbaijan experienced several attempts by poorly prepared fragments of the security services that were easily put down. In Armenia, President Levon Ter Petrosian was forced from office in late 1997 by pressure from the military and state security forces, though new elections were held in early 1998 for a new civilian president. The Armenian case is probably the closest that a country in the region has come to a military coup. Even there the military was not the main agent of democratic degradation. As the Freedom House scores reflect, Armenia shifted toward authoritarianism on Ter Petrosian's watch, well before he resigned the presidency under pressure (Freedom House 1996–97).

As will be discussed, presidents have served as agents of de-democratization. Still, the backsliders are not strictly limited to polities with *constitutionally* strong presidents. Albania's president was elected by the legislature. Like South Africa's president, in some respects he served as a de facto prime minister, even if he carried the title of president. Bulgaria has a parliamentary system with a weak president. Croatia's constitution is formally semipresidential in character, though the president was able to emasculate the parliament and push the de facto operation of government toward presidentialism. Two countries with presidential systems, Georgia and Moldova, are found in Category II. Presidentialism may be related to a propensity for backsliding, but investigating the quality or type of presidentialism, which will be done below, is important for grasping presidentialism's effects.

Foreign armies have not played a major role in democratic slippage. At most, one country (Bosnia) has suffered change of government or regime at the hands of a foreign power.

In sum, few of the normal causes or the usual suspects lie behind democratic erosion in the postcommunist world. The inadequacy of most conventional frameworks requires looking elsewhere for explanations and agents. The prima facie importance of chief executives as possible agents of democratic degradation suggests the importance of investigating executive leadership and the institutions within which executives wield power.

The Formula for Democratic Reversal

In all but one of the de-democratizers, the agent of degradation was a chief executive bent on aggrandizing his (all were male) own power. The only exception is Bulgaria, which is anomalous in several respects. In general, Bulgaria does not fit the pattern that holds in the other cases in Category III, and this country will be put aside in the following analysis.[3] In each of the other eight countries in Category III the chief executive was unambiguously the agent of degradation. It is crucial to note that Freedom House does not downgrade a country's rating merely for an expansion in the executive's power, so there is no risk of an endogeneity problem, wherein change in the dependent variable may drive change in the hypothesized causal variable. For example, Kyrgyzstan's rating improved in 1994–95 even as President Askar Akaev dissolved parliament and augmented his own powers via referendum. Kyrgyzstan's rating worsened only after Akaev moved against his critics in the media and journalists were imprisoned for "insulting the president's honor and dignity." Similarly, in 1994–95 Belarus's score improved from 4.5 to 4 from the previous year's survey because the country had a competitive presidential election, although the election was accompanied by the advent of a strong presidency and the end of parliamentarism. Only when President Aleksandr Lukashenko subsequently banned independent trade unions, reintroduced censorship, held dubious elections and referenda, and violated Supreme Court decisions did the country's score fall, plummeting to 6 in 1996–97 and staying there thereafter.

Not only is there no risk of an endogeneity problem in technical terms in assessing the effect of executive power on propensity for authoritarian reversion; there is similarly no hazard of an endogeneity problem, or of tautological reasoning, in conceptual terms. Only the view that strong executive power *is itself* the very definition of authoritarianism could produce the impression of endogeneity or tautology. Such a perspective would equate a *diagnostic feature* with a *hypothetically facilitating or sustaining condition*—a gross error, albeit one that is sometimes encountered in social science. What is more, strong executives are only one of several possible culprits. As discussed above, revolutionary parties, separatist ethnonational movements, politically assertive militaries, and foreign armies may also undo democratization. Indeed, in most reversals of democracy in the twentieth century outside the postcommunist world, one of these agents, rather than a sitting chief executive, bore responsibility. Furthermore, neither an assertive executive nor institutions that invest the executive with great power are necessary for authoritarian reversion. The substantial shifts (steady deterioration followed by steady improvement) in India's freedom scores during the 1990s did not result from large fluctuations in the prime minister's power, which did not occur, but rather from changes in the intensity of intercommunal and separatist violence and the ways that governments reacted to them. Many cases of de-democratization in the contemporary world occur under conditions of deteriorating central authority and disempowerment of presidents or other chief executives. Conversely, a rise in or solidification of presidential power does not always induce authoritarian reversion. Ghana's freedom ratings steadily improved in the 1990s as the government became more civilianized and as elections went forward, even as the president's powers in both formal and practical terms did not diminish (Freedom House, various volumes; Varshney 1998; Lyons 1997; Gyimah-Boadi 1997). Some polities with powerful executives have maintained a high degree of democracy. Great Britain and Canada, with their mighty prime ministers and unified executive authority, have long served as models of popular rule (Lipset 1996). Indeed, the uniformity in the postcommunist region of the chief executive's culpability for authoritarian reversion is striking in part since it is—or at least seems to be—peculiar. So too, as will be discussed, is it remarkable how consistently institutions that grant the executive freedom of action undermine democratization in the postcommunist region.

To return to the discussion of cases, the decline in Albania's rating resulted from the banning of some opposition politicians from running for parliament, electoral fraud, and crackdowns on antigovernment protesters—all of which were perpetrated by the then-president, Sali Berisha. Similar causes worsened Armenia's Freedom House score, and the agent of degradation in every instance was the then-president, Levon Ter Petrosian. The decline in Croatia's rating from 3.5 to 4 in 1992–93 was not necessarily induced only by actions taken by the president, Franjo Tudjman. Effects of the war, including displacement of citizens and occupation of parts of the country by Serbian (Yugoslav) forces played a role. But part of the blame for the decline in the rating and especially for the failure to improve after the termination of the war resulted from Tudjman's practices of intimidating rivals and throttling the media. The fall in Kazakhstan's rating followed President Nursultan Nazarbaev's moves to curb press freedoms, crack down on political opponents, and stack parliament with his own followers and then quickly dissolve the body when some fractions proved to be less than enthusiastically supportive of him. Russia's score fell three times during the 1990s, each time by a half-point, in large part due to President Boris Yeltsin's increasingly erratic and despotic behavior, including his attempts to meddle with the media and his brutish campaign in Chechnya. The Freedom House survey attributed Ukraine's decline between 1992–93 and 1993–94 to adoption of an "undemocratic electoral law." The country's failure thereafter again to attain its previous level appears to have been influenced by President Leonid Kravchuk's use of the media as his personal mouthpiece during his (nevertheless unsuccessful) bid for reelection against Leonid Kuchma. As president, Kuchma continued the tradition of highhandedness, deploying top aides to pressure media outlets to hire his own loyalists and running roughshod over laws on local self-government in order to assert personal control in many cities (Freedom House, various volumes; *Europa World Yearbook*, various volumes).

In most Category III countries, the chief executive enjoyed status as the father of his country. He was the hero of national independence, of democracy, or both. In most cases the executive did at some point in time enjoy a substantial measure of charisma in the strict Weberian sense, meaning that a large portion of the population viewed him as a doer of extraordinary deeds. Berisha, Tudjman, Ter Petrosian, Nazarbaev, Akaev, Yeltsin and, more ambiguously, Kravchuk were widely viewed at home as the fathers of both national independence and democracy. Most enjoyed personal prestige akin to that held by India's Jawaharlal Nehru, Kenya's Jomo Kenyatta, and Zambia's Kenneth Kaunda at the time of national independence. The prominent exception is Lukashenko, who did not play a preeminent role in Belarus's politics until shortly before he was elected president in 1994. Belarus did not have a founding father figure. In sum, the agent of de-democratization in countries that underwent such change was the chief executive; and in most cases he enjoyed hero status at the time of regime change.

The crucial common institutional condition that united the countries of Category III was a constitutional system that concentrated power in the president or that could readily be manipulated in a way that facilitated such concentration of power. Such a system may be referred to as a "superpresidency." There are many varieties of such a form of regime, but in broad outline it tends to have most or all of the following traits: a very large apparatus of presidential power that greatly exceeds other state agencies in size and in the resources it consumes; a president who enjoys power to legislate by decree; a president who de jure or de facto controls most of the powers of the purse; a relatively emasculated legislature that cannot readily repeal presidential decrees and that has little authority and/or meager resources for overseeing the executive branch; provisions that make impeachment of the president extremely difficult or even virtually impossible; and a judiciary that is controlled wholly or largely by the president and that cannot in practice check presidential prerogatives or even abuse of power.

Such a system, in one form or another, was conspicuous in the backsliders. Albania's parliamentary system provided for a president elected by the legislature who enjoyed all the powers of a powerful prime minister without having to suffer competition from a separate, directly elected executive. The constitution was readily malleable in the hands of the assertive Berisha. From the time of independence, Armenia's constitutional structure invested great authority in the presidency. Belarus began its post-Soviet life with the republic's Supreme Soviet in place as the highest governing body, but in 1994 it scrapped parliamentarism in favor of a strong presidency filled by direct election. Croatia's constitution was the only one among Category III countries that provided for a genuine division of powers between the president and the legislature. But Tudjman, taking advantage of the executive-enhancing pressures that the war created, manipulated several ambiguities in the constitution and marginalized the legislature. The Kazakh and Kyrgyz regimes from the onset of independence provided for exceedingly strong presidencies. Russia started its post-Soviet existence with an equivocal division of power. On paper the legislature held supreme authority, but in fact the president enjoyed wide-ranging decree powers. Russia subsequently resolved the ambiguities with the adoption of a superpresidential constitution. Ukraine did not adopt a new post-Soviet constitution until mid-1996, but both before and after ratification of the new fundamental law, the president enjoyed formidable power, although his command was not as unchecked as that of most of the other executives in Category III.

The choice of a constitution that concentrated power in the hands of the president occurred *independently* of the degradation of democracy. In fact, the transfer of great power to the president—in most instances the hero of regime change—was widely regarded by both important revolutionary elites and populations more broadly as a blow in favor of democratization and against entrenched forces of the old regime. Even in Belarus, citizens voted for a strong presidency hoping to fracture the corrupt, holdover *nomenklatura* elite. The manner in which the institutional concentration of power subsequently facilitated democracy's emasculation therefore has a paradoxical character (Huskey 1997; Olcott 1997[a, b]; Fish 1995; Mihalisko 1997; Bojcun 1995; Urban 1997; *Europa World Yearbook*, various volumes).

Most countries in Category III had a plebiscitary moment during which the executive achieved or at least appeared to achieve an overwhelming popular endorsement. Usually this moment came in a referendum held outside the framework of normal electoral politics; sometimes it took the form of an impressive victory in a national election. Where the executive attempted to engineer a plebiscitary victory and failed, he was subsequently thrown out of office, but not before he had reversed democratization. The latter case is illustrated by the experience of Albania's Berisha, who lost a national referendum that he fully expected to win in November 1994. The referendum proposed a new constitution that virtually would have codified dictatorship, giving the president even the right to preside over the Supreme Court. Undaunted, Berisha pressed ahead in the May 1996 parliamentary election, in which he engaged in fraud and deployed troops to crush protests by his opponents. Some regions subsequently fell into anarchy, and new elections were held in mid-1997, leading to Berisha's ouster. Armenia's Ter Petrosian experienced a similar end. He resigned the presidency under strong pressure a year after winning reelection in balloting that many observers regarded as fraudulent. Prior to the flawed election and his ouster, however, Ter Petrosian did enjoy a plebiscitary victory that may have encouraged his autocratic behavior. His triumph came in a referendum held in July 1995, in which nearly 70 percent of voters endorsed a new constitution that granted the president full control over all branches of government, thereby converting an already strong presidency into a virtual dictatorship (Freedom House, various volumes; *Europa World Yearbook*, various volumes; Fuller 1996).

Rulers in Belarus, Kazakhstan, Kyrgyzstan, and Russia each triumphed in his plebiscitary moment. In November 1996 Belarus's Lukashenko called a referendum to legitimate his "reformation" of parliament—which amounted to ousting deputies who opposed him—and to expand his already formidable powers. The government never published the full results, but it claimed that over 70 percent of voters supported Lukashenko's proposal. In the spring of 1995 Kazakhstan's Nazarbaev dissolved parliament and called a referendum on extending his term, which was to end in 1996, to 2000. According to official figures, 95 percent of voters supported the measure. In a second referendum held in August of the same year, voters supposedly overwhelmingly endorsed Nazarbaev's call to confirm a new constitution that established a puppet legislature and enshrined the president's right to rule by decree. Between 1994 and 1996, Kyrgyzstan's Akaev triumphed in multiple referenda he called to win fresh doses of popular approval and enhanced powers. Russia's Yeltsin also won several plebiscites. In a referendum of April 1993, in a result that surprised most observers, a majority endorsed Yeltsin's program and his call for new parliamentary elections. Yeltsin failed to act until September, when he attempted to dissolve parliament. After a bloody confrontation in which Yeltsin's forces beat back a challenge by recalcitrant deputies and their supporters, Yeltsin called for a referendum on his own draft of a new constitution, which provided for overwhelming presidential prerogatives and a relatively weak legislature. The new constitution was confirmed in a vote that some observers regarded as flawed.[4]

Chief executives in Croatia and Ukraine did not benefit from such crowning referenda, but rather enjoyed their plebiscitary moments during regular elections. Croatia's Tudjman won an overwhelming majority in his bid for reelection in June 1997. Ukraine's Kuchma wrested from the legislature the right to name the cabinet and to control appointments of officials sent from Kiev to help run local and provincial governments. Kuchma won such powers only after threatening to take the issue to a referendum, which most parliamentarians expected he would win. The Ukrainian constitution, adopted in mid-1996, provides for a very strong president, albeit not one who may ignore the legislature and overrule it at will. Kuchma won reelection handily in late 1999.

Plebiscitary moments and institutions that encode superpresidentialism were often closely related. The plebiscitary moment itself frequently took the form of a referendum on enhancing (often already expansive) executive powers. In four of the five countries in which executives sought to generate a dramatic plebiscitary moment through referenda, they won—at least according to official results—impressive popular endorsements. Only Albania's Berisha was rebuffed. Each executive strove assiduously to expand his own powers. Only Berisha and Ter Petrosian, as of the end of the 1990s, were ousted in the attempt. Lukashenko, Tudjman, Nazarbaev, Akaev, Yeltsin, and Kravchuk (and then Kuchma) all to some degree succeeded in aggrandizing their office. The plebiscitary triumph may well have goaded leaders who earlier demonstrated a personal commitment to pluralism and toleration—most notably, Yeltsin, Ter Petrosian, Akaev, and perhaps even Nazarbaev—toward greater haughtiness.

As such, the plebiscitary moment may be seen as a facilitating condition and sometimes an integral part of the dynamic of executive aggrandizement, though not an independent explanatory variable or a crucial condition for authoritarian backsliding.

The second factor that does, like the institutional concentration of power in the president, serve as a bona fide explanation for reversion, is the condition of political oppositions to chief executives. In Albania, the Socialist Party, Social Democratic Party, and the Democratic Alliance (a union of mostly liberal groups that split with Berisha's Democratic Party) enjoyed a reasonably strong presence in Albanian politics and were able to organize some opposition to Berisha's attempts at self-aggrandizement. Their strength helps explain why Berisha failed in his plebiscitary attempt, even as he did degrade the country's democratic status.

In all of the other backsliders, however, political-societal opposition to presidents was mostly poorly organized and inarticulate. The problem was precisely oppositional *weakness*—and specifically organizational and communicative weakness—and not merely "fragmentation," as is often claimed in writings on political parties. Any political parties or party systems in any polity may safely be labeled "fragmented." I have in mind oppositional *weakness*, meaning specifically a marked inability to communicate with citizens and to mobilize people and resources. Opponents of Ter Petrosian and his Armenian National Movement, most notably the Communist Party, the nationalist ARF-Dashnak, and the National Democratic Union, began to show some strength in 1995, but they did not form a powerful opposition (Dudwick 1997; Fuller 1996). In Belarus, Lukashenko's opposition comprised small groups of well-intentioned but politically inept liberal intellectuals and romantic nationalists who assigned higher priority to belarussifying words on street signs than to ensuring that food reached tables. Tudjman's Croatian Democratic Union (HDZ) did not face serious opposition until the time of Tudjman's passing at the end of the 1990s. Several of the main alternative parties, such as the Croatian Peasants Party, maintained structures and programs separate from that of the HDZ, but in practice did not strongly oppose it. The communist-successor Social Democratic Party of Croatia spent most of the first half of the 1990s on the defensive, establishing its "national" (pro-independence) credentials. Liberal forces proved unpragmatic and diminutive. Tudjman's physical decline and death, however, invigorated the opposition, and parliamentary and presidential elections held at the beginning of 2000 dealt the HDZ severe setbacks. Croatia now potentially serves as an intriguing case of redemocratization after de-democratization. How its politics evolve in the post-Tudjman era will raise important issues for comprehending regime change, though those matters lie beyond the scope of this chapter (Lukashuk 1998; Irvine 1997; Pusic 1998).

Nazarbaev's opponents in Kazakhstan enjoyed a window of opportunity in the short-lived unicameral legislature in 1994–95, before the president dissolved the body and pushed through a new constitution. But they squandered their chance, focusing largely on establishing perquisites for themselves. Akaev's opponents in Kyrgyzstan proved to be scarcely more imaginative or effective. Despite the persistence of a regime that even in the face of Akaev's increasingly expansive conception of his own role allowed for the formation of opposition groups, Akaev's opponents showed themselves incapable of organizing serious political parties. Nor did Russia's Yeltsin have to suffer a potent opposition. His liberal opponents were notoriously inept and poorly organized. The preeminent nationalist party was led by a bizarre eccentric, and he and his subordinates were so easy to buy off that Yeltsin could rely on their votes in parliament despite their professions of militant opposition. The Communist Party of the Russian Federation (KPRF) proved to be the strongest source of opposition to Yeltsin, but its leaders were uninspiring figures and its parliamentary deputies repeatedly yielded to the president's blandishments and threats. The Ukrainian presidents faced some opposition. Yet the virtual nonexistence of genuine political parties, save a clutch of highly corrupt and politically unambitious communist successor organizations and one nationalist party whose appeal is highly circumscribed in regional terms, gave the president wide scope for independent action (Huskey 1997; Collins 1997; Olcott 1997[b]; McFaul 1997; Fish 1997[b]; Prizel 1997).

Chief executives in Category III countries not only faced weak internal oppositions. They also encountered insubstantial opposition from outside their own countries and enjoyed a powerful external patron. This external patronage serves as the third variable explaining backsliding toward authoritarianism. Berisha's anticommunism and penchant for rapid economic reform made him a darling among Western governments and international lending institutions, who did not back away from supporting him until Albania sunk into anarchy in 1997. During the first half of the 1990s Albania obtained more capital from loans from World Bank Group countries as a percentage of GDP than did any other country in the post-communist region (Fish 1998[b]).

Armenia's Ter Petrosian enjoyed support from both Russia and the West. Ter Petrosian enjoyed long-standing ties with Yeltsin. He also was popular among the Armenian diaspora in the United States, many of whose members held him in high esteem for his central role in the movement for independence and in the largely successful war against Azerbaijan. Both the Russian and U.S. governments ignored Ter Petrosian's moves against his opponents in 1994 and 1995 and the strong evidence of serious irregularities in the September 1996 presidential elections (U.S. State Department official, 1997; Huttenbach 1995).

Belarus's Lukashenko benefited handsomely from unstinting Russian aid. Alone among leaders of former Soviet republics outside of Russia, Lukashenko called for reestablishing a post–Soviet Union and sometimes advocated a full union of his country and Russia. Lukashenko was wildly popular among Russia's nationalists and communists, and supporting Lukashenko served as an inexpensive way for the Yeltsin government to appease antiliberal forces at home. While hardly embracing Lukashenko, Western governments, through their silence and inaction, signaled that they regarded Belarus as located firmly within Russia's sphere of influence (Mihalisko 1997).

The United States and Germany steadfastly supported Tudjman in Croatia. Western support stemmed from Tudjman's role in resisting Serbian aggression and his pivotal part in implementing the Dayton Accords for ending the protracted war in Bosnia, a pact that the Clinton Administration cherished as one of its greatest foreign policy accomplishments. Actions that under other circumstances might provoke Western ire, such as Tudjman's maintenance of tight controls over the media and his promotion of officers charged with war crimes by an international tribunal, drew only the most perfunctory rebukes and did not compromise Western support (Cohen 1997).

Kazakhstan's Nazarbaev received strong backing from the Russian government due to his demonstrated ability to enforce political quiescence in a country that makes up a large portion of Russia's southern border and his commitment to resisting violence against the large ethnic Russian population in his country. Western governments did not protest Nazarbaev's increasingly autocratic behavior. Western oil corporations' interest in developing Kazakhstan's vast reserves powerfully intensified governments' distaste for offending the president (Olcott 1997[a]).

Like Ter Petrosian and Nazarbaev, Kyrgyzstan's Akaev maintained excellent relations with both the United States and Russia. Akaev enjoyed good personal relations with Yeltsin. The U.S. government, which targeted Kyrgyzstan for aid and democracy-promotion efforts, treated Akaev as the best hope for open politics in a region otherwise mired in sultanism. It was loath to abandon its commitment to the courtly, intellectual president even as he turned toward a style of rule more typical of his counterparts elsewhere in Central Asia (Huskey 1997, 1993; Collins 1997).

Yeltsin also enjoyed an extraordinarily clement external environment. Even the protracted war in Chechnya cost Yeltsin little support among Western governments or international lending agencies. Russia's large size and prominence in the international system mean that Western governments ultimately must accommodate whomever rules there. Western governments also viewed the main alternatives to Yeltsin as so distasteful that they stood by him unconditionally.

Ukraine's presidents likewise benefited from a profoundly benign international environment. The U.S. government, which looked upon Ukraine as the key to checking a possible revival of Russian imperialism, provided strong backing for both Kravchuk and Kuchma. By 1997 Ukraine had become the third largest recipient of U.S. aid, exceeded only by Israel and Egypt, and the size of the USAID office in Kiev dwarfed its counterparts in other postcommunist countries. While both Kravchuk and Kuchma enjoyed American support, so did both cultivate good relations with Russia. Kravchuk's policies of Ukrainianization of education and state service drew some criticism from Russia, but Russian leaders appreciated Kravchuk's attempt to build a nonethnic basis for citizenship that did not disenfranchise ethnic Russians. The Russian government also supported Kravchuk's successor, an eastern Ukrainian whose inner circle was made up largely of Russophones like himself. Like Ter Petrosian, Nazarbaev, and Akaev, Kuchma had the remarkable good fortune of backing from both the United States and Russia (Prizel 1997; Bojcun 1995).

The formula for democratic reversals is now complete. The agent of degradation was the president. He usually enjoyed the status of a national father figure, the hero of independence and democracy. He typically enjoyed success in a plebiscitary moment, which provided him with an endorsement of popular confidence and a signal that he could scarcely do wrong in the eyes of his people. The three main conditions that enabled the chief executive to operate in a manner that degraded democracy were: *superpresidentialism*—that is, an institutional environment that created few hard constraints on presidential highhandedness; a *weak domestic opposition;* and the presence of a powerful *external patron.*

The Backsliders in Regional Perspective

These generalizations, however fitting as a formula for democratic erosion, acquire full support as hypotheses only in a comparative framework. Even if they hold true for countries in Category III, they do not constitute a compelling explanation if they obtained with equal force and regularity in countries that did not experience degradation.

The generalizations do not hold among countries that did not undergo backsliding. The conditions that enabled executive usurpation and, in turn, counterdemocratic behavior, were not present. Demonstrating this point requires brief examination of the countries in Categories I and II in light of the analysis offered above.

The Czech Republic did have a father figure in the person of Václav Havel. But Havel occupied the presidency in a parliamentary system, while the more powerful prime ministership was taken over by the technically competent but less personally appealing Václav Klaus. Havel's office offered him precious little opportunity, even had he been so inclined, to act autocratically. But his enormous personal authority, along with his vaguely social-democratic views, enabled and inclined him periodically to intervene in politics in a manner that trimmed Klaus's potentially overweening ambitions. What is more, within two years of becoming prime minister, Klaus faced a sophisticated opposition, which demonstrated its strength clearly in the fall of 1997, when it performed strongly in elections and forced Klaus to resign (Wolchik 1997[a]).

The other country in Category I that had a genuine father figure was Poland. Lech Wałesa, the courageous organizer of the anticommunist Solidarity trade union movement, was that person. But from the outset of his tenure in office Wałesa was hemmed in by a semipresidential regime that granted him more power than the Czech president enjoyed but that nevertheless severely limited his capacity for independent action. Wałesa also faced an assertive and powerful opposition—both the liberal Democratic Union and the renovated former communists who formed the Democratic Left Alliance (SLD). Wałesa was unable to engineer a defining plebiscitary moment. Reelection in the November 1995 presidential race might have handed Wałesa the plebiscitary endorsement for which he yearned, but his SLD opponent, Aleksander Kwasniewski, defeated him. Wałesa was enraged by his defeat; indeed, he contested the election and threatened to attempt to retain office. Given Wałesa's pugnacious personality, his reaction surprised few Poles. But fewer still concerned themselves that Wałesa could have annulled the election and clung to office. The distribution of power in the political regime and the strength of Wałesa's opposition ruled out an Armenian outcome. It was also inconceivable that the major Western powers would have countenanced any such mischief. Wałesa was admired in the United States, but the U.S. government never placed Wałesa's fortunes above democratization in Poland or conflated the two—a situation that contrasted with policy toward Russia during the Yeltsin period. A combination of internal and external constraints ensured that Poland's president, whatever his personal inclinations, could not engage in the counterdemocratic actions undertaken by his counterparts in countries in Category III (Michta 1997; Barany 1995; Curry 1995).

None of the other countries in Category I had founding-father figures. Vytautas Landsbergis, Lithuania's first president, enjoyed substantial popularity at the time of independence, but he never held anything resembling the overwhelming authority possessed by Havel, Wałesa, or the leaders of Category III countries. In 1992 an electorate desiring more competent administration turned him and his party out of office. Estonia and Hungary had no figure who could be called the founding father. Slovenia's first president, Milan Kucan, who remains in office after multiple successful reelection bids, was a popular figure who in some senses may be regarded as enjoying father-figure status. Like Havel, however, he assumed the presidency in a parliamentary system. In Lithuania, Estonia, Hungary, and Slovenia, moreover, vigorous oppositions emerged within the first few years of independence (Mahr and Nagle 1995; O'Neil 1997; Clark 1995).

Given the presence of these internal constraints, external checks were not necessary to block the growth of executive absolutism. It nevertheless merits mention that none of the Category I countries or their leaders developed a relationship with Russia that could have enabled executives, in the style of Lukashenko, to rely on Russia for political protection. Most Category I countries, moreover, formed close ties with Western governments, and several of them, most notably the Czech Republic, Hungary, and Poland, lay at the center of Western efforts to promote a democratic and market-oriented postcommunist Europe (Parrott 1997).

The only country in Category I in which one finds some of the conditions that I argue cause backsliding is Slovakia. It is therefore unsurprising that Slovakia's democratization was also by far the most problematic among Category I countries. Slovakia's Vladimir Meciar, who as prime minister presided over the Velvet Divorce with the Czech Republic, suffered defeat, then returned to power as prime minister in 1994, only to be ousted again in 1998, pretended to a founding-father role, though his unbalanced personality circumscribed his popular appeal and authority. Slovakia's constitution provided for a puissant prime minister and a very weak president. It concentrated the lion's share of executive power—and, via his parliamentary majority, legislative power as well—in the prime minister. Meciar took advantage of the constitution and, between 1994 and 1998, single-handedly degraded his country's democracy with a stream of arbitrary actions. He attempted to muzzle the press, pushed through laws aimed at curtailing the rights of the Hungarian minority, and deployed thugs to attack his political opponents. Meciar did enjoy some Russian backing. He benefited from Russia's search for clients in East Europe whose antiliberal and anti-Western orientation hampered the development of close ties with the West. While the Russian government supplied Meciar with some energy supplies at cut-rate prices and endorsed his bid for reelection, however, it did not back Meciar nearly as staunchly as it did, say, Lukashenko. The defeat of Meciar's party in the fall 1998 elections ended his reign and brought a decidedly more pro-democratic coalition to power. Slovakia's Freedom House rating moved from 3 to

1.5 between the 1997–98 and 1999–2000 surveys, bringing the country into company with the democracies. The Meciar experience shows that baleful concentration of power in the executive is also possible in parliamentary systems, and that the counterdemocratic results may resemble those seen in regimes with overweening presidents. But Slovakia also shows that concentration of power in the prime minister, at least as long as the political system is not closed completely, is not likely to injure open politics as severely as superpresidentialism does, mainly since parliamentarism furnishes stronger incentives for party development than does superpresidentialism. Indeed, throughout his tenure in office, Meciar's autocratic ambitions constantly collided with spirited opposition parties, which managed to topple him before he could assert full personal control over the regime. Even more clearly than Croatia, Slovakia illustrates the possibility of redemocratization after de-democratization. Like in Croatia, however, in Slovakia the sustainability of recent gains remains an open question (Fish 1999).

Even more interesting and revealing as referents for comparison with the backsliders of Category III are the democratizers of Category II. Alone among countries in Category II, Georgia had a founding-father figure. He was Zviad Gamsakhurdia, the nationalist former dissident who was elected president with 86 percent of the vote in May 1991. But immediately after taking office, Gamsakhurdia launched violent attacks against his opponents, who responded by driving him out of office in an armed assault on the presidential palace in January 1992. Thus, Georgia's founding father had only one-half year to wreak havoc on his country's transition. His behavior undermined democratization, antagonized nonethnic Georgians, and precipitated civil war. Toward the middle of the decade, however, democratization resumed, as Georgia adopted a new constitution and Eduard Shevardnadze was elected president. Shevardnadze enjoyed wide fame as the Gorbachev-era Soviet foreign minister. He was, notably, a *Soviet* leader who had no major part in his country's independence. He lacked the qualities of the founding fathers found in most Category III countries. What is more, although the new Georgian constitution, adopted in August 1995, provided for a strong executive presidency, it did not create a superpresidency. Shevardnadze could not ignore parliament, which acquired substantial powers under the new constitution.

The other countries in Category II lacked a founding-father figure. Neither Macedonia nor Mongolia ever had a dominant politician who could pretend to such a role. The first presidents of postcommunist Moldova and Romania, Mircea Snegur and Ion Iliescu, respectively, had some such pretensions but never enjoyed anything resembling the personal authority and mass appeal of the leaders of Category III countries. Both Snegur and Iliescu were political chameleons and quickly came to be seen as such by their electorates. Snegur's alternatively warm and cold relations with the Moldovan Popular Front, as well as his limited oratorical and managerial skills, helped prevent him from emerging as a real father figure. Iliescu's personal career as a high party official, his close ties to Russia in a largely Russophobic country, his transparent opportunism, and his—to many Romanians—almost comical attempts to claim the mantle of the great revolutionary did not prevent him from winning reelection, but they kept him from acquiring vast personal authority (Fish 1998[c]; Davies and Ozolins 1994; Crowther 1997; Calinescu and Tismaneanu 1991; Tismaneanu 1997).

Differences between Category II and III countries were not limited to the personal status of leaders. The institutional configuration of power and the strength of oppositions also differed substantially across categories. Georgia's presidential system, as mentioned, invested meaningful power in parliament. Macedonia's parliamentary regime provided for a system with a relatively high concentration of power, but a diverse and relatively well-developed party system helped ensure that all executives faced strong, organized oppositions. Moldova adopted a form of moderate presidentialism that lodged considerable power in the legislature. Neither Snegur nor his successor, Petru Lucinschi, could possibly ignore the legislature in the formation of the government or in policy making in general. Neither enjoyed nearly the power over the government afforded, say, the Russian president. Furthermore, the division of powers in Moldova, as well as the strength of the organized opposition grouped in part around Lucinschi, ruled out any attempt by Snegur to block a normal transfer of power, even had he been inclined to make such an attempt (Carothers 1996; Crowther 1997; Plakans 1997).

Like Poland, Mongolia and Romania adopted semipresidential systems fashioned on the French model. Substantial institutional barriers to executive absolutism are present in both systems. Thus, any attempt by Iliescu to maintain himself in power after losing the 1996 presidential election to the liberal intellectual Emil Constantinescu, or to rig the elections in advance, would have proved exceedingly difficult. Romania's semipresidential system, the strength of opposition parties, and Iliescu's own less than overwhelming personal appeal circumscribed his room for maneuver. The power of Mongolia's president is even more limited. The president is nevertheless strong enough to provide a check on prime ministerial absolutism, as was shown during 1992–96, when the relatively liberal president, Punsalmaagiyn Ochirbat, regularly wielded his veto powers and personal authority in broader society to block the ambitions of the conservative prime minister, Puntsagiyn Jasray. Mongolia also developed a vigorous multiparty system that included several well-differentiated parties with deep roots in society and strong local organizations (Carey 1996; Tismaneanu 1997; Fish 1998[c]).

In Category II countries, like in Category I countries, strictly internal conditions were probably adequate to check the growth of executive absolutism. The external environment still merits mention. Executives in Category II countries did not enjoy the support of powerful external patrons who would have offered succor in a play for self-aggrandizement. Shevardnadze's relations with Moscow were deeply strained. Shevardnadze enjoyed good relations with Western leaders, but none ever treated him as an indispensable client or the leader of a supremely important country. No post-Soviet Macedonian leader has ever enjoyed particularly good relations with Russia; nor has any been regarded as an invaluable ally by Western governments. Snegur antagonized Russia with his attempts to recover Moldova's Trans-Dniestria region from separatists supported by Moscow. At the same time, he failed to secure patrons among Western governments, who for the most part treated him with indifference. Romania's Iliescu found himself in a situation that largely resembled that of Snegur. In order to boost his revolutionary credentials he held Russia at arm's length. Yet Western governments did not hold him in high esteem or regard him as an important ally. No postcommunist Mongolian leader ever enjoyed an intimate relationship with a powerful external patron. Despite Russia's traditional interest in Mongolia, the post-Soviet Russian government did not regard any Mongolian leader as a valuable client.

Observations, Discussion, and Prescriptions

This chapter has argued that the opportunities and constraints that chief executives face are crucial to whether or not a country continues to democratize after an initial antiauthoritarian breakthrough. When the institutional and political environments were permissive, the executive seized the chance to aggrandize his own power. Executive usurpation consistently was accompanied by reversal of previous democratic gains. The former is distinct from the latter. In practice, however, the latter followed the former with remarkable regularity.

This general scheme certainly may not hold universally. South Africa's Nelson Mandela may serve as a counterexample, as a chief executive who engaged in self-limiting behavior for the good of his country. George Washington and Charles de Gaulle may also exemplify such leaders. A leading student of Indian politics has argued that Nehru consistently placed adherence to the law and established norms above expanding his own power. According to this scholar, Nehru's "remarkably democratic temper" crucially abetted the survivability of Indian democracy (Varshney 1998, 46).

Such cases raise questions concerning the importance of leaders' own beliefs for democratization. It is tempting to argue that in the postcommunist experience, only actors' strategic calculations have mattered, and these calculations depended on constraints and opportunities. The yawning gap between leaders' reputations at the outset of regime change and their subsequent behavior in power would seem to reinforce such a conclusion. In most Category III countries, the very politicians who started their tenure during revolutions as heroes of democracy subsequently blocked further democratization. Personal political inclinations mattered less than the institutions that defined the domain within which leaders operated. There is precious little evidence that Romania's Iliescu had a more "democratic temper" than did Yeltsin, Akaev, or Ter Petrosian. Indeed, his democratic credentials were considerably weaker at the outset of transition than were those of the Russian, Kyrgyz, and Armenian leaders, and Iliescu did strive to enhance his own power during his six-year tenure in office. But unlike Yeltsin, Akaev, and Ter Petrosian, Iliescu was boxed in by a semipresidential system. So too was the heroic but personally authoritarian Wałesa, who also faced a formidable array of political opposition from the early stages of his presidency. Personalities and personal inclinations were not nearly as crucial as the three constraints on executive power whose importance has been highlighted in this chapter: constitutional dispersion of power, domestic oppositions, and external patrons.

And still, leaders' own ideological predispositions and specifically their commitments to open rule cannot be considered entirely irrelevant. The Czech Republic's Havel and Slovenia's Kucan accepted presidencies in parliamentary systems, thus bounding their own power from the outset. Both subsequently sought to empower their own office, but neither seriously challenged the law or jeopardized democratization to expand their own authority, and neither called into question the legitimacy of the parliamentary system. How either leader would have acted had he occupied an office of great power cannot be known. Among the rulers who presided over the degradation of democracy, beliefs and values might have affected at least the *degree* to which leaders damaged democratization. Yeltsin might have resisted the urge to scrap pluralism entirely due to a rudimentary personal revulsion against a full-blown retreat to tyranny—a feeling that manifestly never troubled Lukashenko (Breslauer 2000).

This chapter's negative findings—that is, the inadequacies of most of the usual explanations for democratic degradation—are as interesting as the positive findings. Only two of the many explanations found in the literature on authoritarian reversion—constitutional frameworks and economic policy doctrine—clearly are related to propensity for demo-cratic backsliding. Both are what were above dubbed "proximate circum-stances"; neither is a "fixed condition." The results suggest that polities undergoing regime change do not necessarily suffer under a tyranny of initial conditions. They make their own fates.

To the extent that these two variables are important, their effects are fully intelligible only within the constraints-and-opportunities framework put forward in this chapter. As discussed, economic reform is, in contra-distinction to much of the prevailing wisdom, closely and positively re-lated to democratization. The phenomenon is explicable in terms of the importance of the pluralization of economic power in a regime in which economic power was until recently both fused with political power and highly concentrated. Rapid liberalization helps to pluralize economic power, thereby creating a firmer financial basis for the emergence and development of nonstate organizations that can check the growth of exec-utive absolutism. Conversely, the nonpluralization of economic power re-stricts the growth potential of societal organizations, including opposition parties (Bunce 1998; Fish 1998[b]).

Constitutional frameworks greatly affect the chances of democratic backsliding, with presidentialism serving as the apparent culprit. But pres-identialism caused de-democratization mainly because it often facilitated executive arrogation. Potent presidencies did not always undermine de-mocracy, as the Georgian, Moldovan, Polish, Lithuanian, Mongolian, and Romanian cases show. These countries had presidential or semipresi-dential regimes and all fall within Categories I or II. In each of these six countries, reasonably powerful legislatures, most of which included a siz-able complement of opponents of the president, controlled the danger of presidential arrogation. From the standpoint of democratization, the problem is concentration of power. What is more, it is a specific type of concentration of power—namely, concentration in the executive at the national level. Other studies have noted the primacy of elites in the degra-dation or collapse of democracy even where mass actors appear to have played major roles (Bermeo 1997). In the postcommunist world, one elite actor in particular—the chief executive—bears the bulk of the blame for de-democratization.

How the chief executive's relations with other elite actors may shape political outcomes provides a vitally important topic for investigation. Philip Roeder emphasizes the demand for personalist authoritarianism—specifically among republican-level elites in the Soviet Union—in his treat-ment of the problem. Roeder's chapter goes much further than my own in its investigation of the matter, but I suggest the merits of also stressing the supply of antidemocratic personalism in intra-elite relations, and spe-cifically the supply of anti-institutional impulses and pressure that an uncontrolled chief executive brings to politics. In his chapter in this volume, Stephen Hanson speaks of democratic consolidation as a state in which the enforcers of democratic institutions can be counted on to behave in ways compatible with, and oriented toward, the perpetuation of formal institutional rules. Unchecked or weakly controlled executives, in the cases under examination, consistently undermine precisely what Hanson sees as the key to democratic consolidation—namely, the perpetuation of formal institutional rules.

The logic of the anti-institutional bias of superexecutivism is found in the incentives that the ruler has or does not have to build institutions. If a single politician enjoys supremacy, he or she will often continually impair the development of foci of organization and power that could potentially challenge him or her. In his study of postcolonial state-building, Joel Migdal, without making the point argued here, shows how rulers—even those who seek real social transformation, not mere self-aggrandizement—often encounter and indulge an anti-institutional urge. Rulers even disable institutions that they built themselves. Since institutions may become wellsprings of rival power centers, rulers often find themselves pursuing deinstitutionalization just as quickly as they succeed in institutionalization. Strange as it may seem, Migdal (1988, 207) writes, rulers "have themselves crippled the arms of the state, especially those organs that ultimately could have given the leaders not only mobilizational ability but also . . . enhanced security." With special reference to Egypt under Gamal Abdel Nasser, Migdal asserts that the ruler's efforts at transformation run up against "the vast, but fragmented social control embedded in the nonstate organizations of society," which in turn "has dictated a particular, pathological set of relationships within the state organization" (207). Migdal focuses on how society, with its multifaceted and weblike structures of authority and control, molds the state. Prior-existing centers of societal power, including local influentials and strongmen, gain control of the ruler's agents and agencies of transformation, perpetually forcing him to undermine his own agents and agencies and engage in counterinstitutional behavior in order to thwart any challenges to his supremacy.

Migdal furnishes a useful look at the deinstitutionalizing impulse, but he does not fully uncover its logic or show precisely under what conditions it—or a contrary urge—might govern the ruler's actions. There is no reason why "the vast, but fragmented social control embedded in the nonstate organizations of society" must necessarily serve as the main source of the ruler's fear that his agents will elude his control. Migdal studied countries where societies rich in long-standing clan or tribal ties, chiefdoms, rich peasants, and other sources of nonstate authority meshed with and co-opted state agents and thereby threatened the ruler's transformational goals and supremacy. Even without the societal challenges that figure prominently in Migdal's accounts, one can easily imagine the ruler fearing loss of control over his agents—especially if they are able to break out of vertical, dependent relations with the ruler and work within institutions that might escape the ruler's monitoring and command. In fact, post-communist societies did not enter the post-Soviet period with, nor did they subsequently give birth to, dense, weblike societies of the type that Migdal found in his postcolonial cases (Fish 1995; Howard 2000). Soviet-type regimes decimated societies and groups based on ascriptive ties, including clans and tribal structures. Yet some postcommunist rulers' anti-institutional behavior has been at least as conspicuous as Nasser's. Yeltsin, for example, like Nasser, feared institutions because they threatened to depersonalize power by enabling his agents and helping them to elude his control (Breslauer 2000).

The logic of politicians' stances toward institutions may differ when power is dispersed. Politicians may still shun institutionalization. But where power is divided among or between branches or camps, politicians are often guided by an institution-building—rather than institution-thwarting—imperative. In fact, the cradle of most institutions is conflict between or among contenders for power. If one does not enjoy and cannot hope to achieve total mastery, one's best strategy is often to outstrip competitors in building institutions that can serve as sources of support, even at the risk that they may escape full control. The origins of most institutional development and innovation are found in *competition for the right to rule, rather than in ruling itself.* Charles Tilly (1990) argues that in primitive state-building, the stimulus to construct institutions stems from competition from rival states or proto-states, not from the practice of despotism within a single, unchallenged polity. Dankwart Rustow's (1970) celebrated theory of the genesis of democracy is based on the notion that hot competition between roughly evenly matched forces leading to deadlock engenders the growth of democratic institutions. Each party to the conflict comes to see that it cannot impose its will and rule alone, and must engage in cooperation and institution-building in order to compete with its antagonist and to ensure that its antagonist accepts its right to exist and to compete in perpetuity.

Even Migdal's own account suggests the paramountcy of competition and the dispersion of power for institution-building. Though Migdal does not draw out the logical implications of his own analysis, his story of the single case of successful postcolonial state-building, Israel, brims with conflict, rivalry, and balancing among the creators of the new state. Indeed, the strife among the new state-builders and their organizations, the absence of a single dominant personage or organized force in the anticolonial movement, and the consequent necessity of resolving conflict by creating institutions, serve as the most conspicuous differences between

Israel and the cases of failed state-building. Migdal himself does not high-light these differences but instead focuses on the acumen of Israeli politi-cians and the structural features of society.

In sum, the concentration of power, particularly if it is invested in an office held by a single individual, exerts counterinstitutional effects, yield-ing tendencies that directly oppose those that Hanson identifies with dem-ocratic consolidation. Conditions in which power is dispersed, in con-trast, may spur institutional formation and development.

Yet why have superpresidential systems been so much more antithetical to sustaining democratization than have parliamentary systems, which may also concentrate power rather than dividing it up? The advantages of parliamentarism touted by its apologists—greater representativeness and flexibility, the absence of a chief executive with a fixed term who views himself as a popular tribune, and greater transparency of govern-mental operations—are indeed found in most postcommunist parliamen-tary systems. Still, as Slovakia under Meciar shows, pure parliamentarism with a powerful prime minister can imperil democratization. Pace the predictions of parliamentarism's advocates, no amount of prime-ministe-rial abuse of power sparked a movement against Meciar by his party or coalition partners, and he clung to office for a half-decade.

In most parliamentary regimes, however, Meciar-style prime-ministe-rial absolutism did not appear, and even in Slovakia, citizens eventually toppled the prime minister at the ballot box. This good fortune has been partially attributable to the presence of presidents who, despite the limit-edness of their formal powers, enjoyed great authority by virtue of their status as heroic opponents of the old communist regimes. President Václav Havel's ability and inclination to check Prime Minister Václav Klaus's potentially overweening ambitions helped keep democratization on course in Czech Republic. Similar situations obtained in President Arpad Goncz's relationship with Prime Minister Jozsef Antall in Hungary and President Zhelyu Zhelev's stand vis-à-vis a succession of Socialist-led gov-ernments in Bulgaria. Slovakia's first president, Michal Kovac, did not enjoy such extraordinary authority. His formal powers, moreover, were even more limited than those of most of his counterparts. He lacked any dissolution power, had no real veto power (the veto override threshold in Slovakia was 50 percent plus one deputies), and he himself was subject to removal from office by a three-fifths vote of parliament (Wolchik 1997a; O'Neil 1997; Szomolanyi and Gould 1997).

The postcommunist experience therefore shows that one of parlia-mentarism's greatest assets for facilitating democratization is also among the least commonly advanced or even recognized by parliamentarism's own propagandists. It is that parliamentarism may—though it does not always—provide for enough of a separation of power to help stay executive arrogation. Since parliamentarism is normally regarded—approvingly by its advocates—as ensuring mutual dependence of executive and legislative power, the possible merits of its tendency in practice to *divide* power are rarely recognized (Stepan and Skach 1993; Linz 1996). Where the parliamentary regime greatly concentrates power—as in Slovakia, with its feeble presidency and all-powerful unicameral legislature—democracy may languish.

But it is unlikely to suffer as badly as it does in superpresidential systems. While Slovakia's pure, hypermajoritarian parliamentarism opened opportunities for abuse of power, such opportunities were not as abundant as those that superpresidentialism furnishes. Meciar was never able to achieve full domination or to emasculate electoral institutions entirely, and he remained vulnerable to defeat. The same cannot be said of Belarus's Lukashenko or Kazakhstan's Nazarbaev, who did close their polities and establish authoritarian regimes. An important counterweight to Meciar's ambitions was the vigor and tenacity of opposition parties. Systems with powerful parliaments—be they fully parliamentary, semipresidential, or moderate presidential—have provided a far stronger stimulus to political party-building than have superpresidential systems. Even in the absence of voting based exclusively or mainly on party lists (that is, proportional representation, or PR), parties have developed and matured relatively rapidly in countries with authoritative parliaments. Roughly half of all seats in Hungary are allotted according to territorial districts; Mongolia adopted an American-style system of pure district voting, with no party-list component. Yet these two countries have among the best-developed party systems in the region. Thus, while PR may advance party development, it is not necessary for it. A regime that includes a large role for the legislature—that is, a regime other than a superpresidency—is normally sufficient. In a system such as Slovakia's, the incentives to build parties were strong. Reasonably vigorous multipartism, which included major organizations that opposed Meciar, guarded Slovakia's tenuous pluralism against Meciar's assaults (Fish 1997[a], 1998[c], 1999).

Superpresidency, in contrast, subdues the impetus for societal actors and ambitious politicians to invest in political party-building. A superpresidential system encourages the formation of small, compact societal organizations that are adept at applying pressure on and currying favor with individuals in ministries and other executive-branch agencies. Such groups, which often take the form of highly personalistic, well-endowed cliques representing business interests, constituted the growth area in the political-societal realm in Category III countries during the 1990s. Incentives to build political parties were far weaker than where parliaments had more power.

The causal arrow does not necessarily point in the other direction as well. The extent of concentration of power in the executive was not necessarily affected by the strength of parties. Moldova, Mongolia, and Romania did not start their postcommunist existence with anything resembling lively civil societies or parties, though they did to a greater or lesser degree develop them during their first postcommunist decade. They did not adopt constitutions that separated power in response to powerful pressure from below on behalf of such institutional design. In fact, there were no strong civil societies or opposition parties at all in these countries at the time when each adopted its constitution.

This chapter's findings may seem to be broadly consonant with a rationalist, choice-theoretic approach that assumes that the ruler acts in the interests of bolstering his own power within the boundaries that his environment imposes on him. But a caveat is in order. In many cases executives' self-aggrandizement did not benefit them personally. A level-headed assessment often would have shown that accumulating more and more power could compromise the ruler's chances to maintain himself in office, realize his goals, enjoy widespread popularity and esteem, and secure an honorable place in history. Ter Petrosian and Berisha pressed forward with wild self-aggrandizement in 1996–97 despite clear signals that doing so might encounter resistance and lead to personal ruin. Gamsakhurdia did the same in 1991. Similarly, in less dramatic but perhaps even more illuminating cases, one may question whether leaders such as Yeltsin and Nazarbaev really enjoyed as much genuine power, authority, and support as overweening superpresidents as they would in moderate presidential systems in which they shared some power—and responsibility and blame—with more puissant legislatures. Instead, all opprobrium for all problems fell on the president, a situation that brought Yeltsin to public disgrace by the time of his resignation at the end of 1999 and that sooner or later may bring Nazarbaev, Lukashenko, and others to ruin as well. Despite overwhelming evidence that more power can mean less, chief executives in Category III countries ceaselessly continued their efforts at self-aggrandizement. It is remarkable how little updating of beliefs goes on among the chief executives. The experience of Gamsakhurdia did not deter Berisha; that of Berisha did not deter Ter Petrosian; that of all three of these leaders did not influence Yeltsin; and the experience of all four of these presidents does not now subdue Akaev, Nazarbaev, or Lukashenko. Since the denouement of superpresidentialism is often the destruction or disgrace of the overweening president himself, and since this fact is, and for some time has been, so obvious, it would be difficult in all cases to characterize executives as rational utility maximizers or even as clear-headed optimizers or satisficers. "Arational gluttons for power" would be a more fitting characterization. Leaders may act instrumentally and selfishly, but their experience in office may cloud their judgment. The distorting effect of power-holding on personal judgment may be greater in systems that concentrate great power in the hands of the chief executive than in regimes in which power is dispersed. From Peru to Kyrgyzstan, the world of neodemocracies is littered with leaders who displayed little or no megalomania before assuming powerful presidencies but who acquired a host of megalomaniacal traits after spending some time in office.

This chapter's findings and analysis suggest several prescriptions for countries undergoing regime change. Given such inclinations on the part of even leaders who began their rule as champions of democracy and national liberation, and given that executive self-aggrandizement so often leads to policies that reverse democratization, the clearest prescription that emerges is the virtue of dispersing power. There is no substitute for institutions that circumscribe the power of the chief executive. A Madisonian approach to institutions, rather than simple avoidance of presidentialism, provides the firmest basis for avoiding democratic erosion. Overweening executives are much more common in presidential than in parliamentary regimes in the region. But presidentialism becomes an antagonist of democracy only in its "super" form; as long as the president must share power with the legislature, presidentialism per se does not necessarily lead to the debasement of democracy.

The second prescription would be *not* to start life as an autonomous, democratizing polity with a national hero at the helm of state. Heroism, like oil, is a curse that societies do not usually choose and that they rarely notice is a curse until it is too late to save democracy. Often the best that a country with a national hero can do is to mitigate the effects of the hero's presence, though the hero can actually facilitate democratization if he or she holds an office with highly restricted powers. To that end, installing the hero in an office whose formal powers are minimal (as in the Czech Republic) or substantial but highly circumscribed (as in Poland) serves as the wisest course. Lavishing the hero of freedom and self-rule with honor and glory and even office, provided that office is not invested with great power, is highly recommended. Placing the hero in an office with extensive prerogative ensures de-democratization.

Institutions that disperse power may not be sufficient to deter de-democratization. Albania's Berisha, Croatia's Tudjman, and Russia's Yeltsin started their rule under constitutions that formally limited their power, but all managed to break out of such constraints and reshape formal arrangements. Reasonably strong oppositions, both internal and external, may also be crucial to parrying executive arrogation. It makes little sense, of course, to "prescribe" a sturdy and capable domestic opposition, but the desirability of one for avoiding reversion is worthy of note.

External opposition may be more readily "prescribed," since great powers often have considerable room for choice in their policies toward fledgling democracies and semidemocracies. Westward location may help mitigate the dangers of authoritarian reversion. But as the Croatian case shows, it is not sufficient; and as the Georgian, Moldovan, Mongolian, and Romanian cases demonstrate, it is not necessary. The pull of Europe may countervail backsliding, but the formation or absence of a patron-client tie between the Russian or U.S. government and a particular executive is at least as important as a country's geographical location. Since strong U.S. or Russian support for a particular ruler raises the risk of democratic erosion, avoiding unconditional commitments to specific leaders is obviously the best policy for discouraging backsliding. In this regard, comparison of U.S. foreign policies under various circumstances is instructive. U.S. acceptance of Ter Petrosian's and Berisha's—and, for that matter, Yeltsin's—counterdemocratic actions in 1994–97 may be contrasted with U.S. resistance to the executive coup attempted by the then president of Guatemala, Jorge Serrano, in 1993. Strong American opposition, combined with formidable internal resistance, frustrated an *autogolpe* that would have aborted Guatemala's tentative democratization (Yashar 1997). In Guatemala, as elsewhere, external pressure was not as significant as domestic factors. But it may tip the balance, especially in small, weak, and dependent countries.

Reflections on the Argument and Its Limitations

The argument put forward here is predicated partially on the idea that the choice of institutions that define the distribution of power within the regime was not caused by the extent of democratization already accomplished in each of the countries in the region. That is to say, I regard choice of constitutions as an "exogenous" factor. My argument in this respect differs from that which Philip Roeder puts forward in his chapter. Roeder explains the choice of constitutional form, or of some of the institutions that helped define the type of regime, in terms of the structure of party organizations in the union republics at the time of the dissolution of the Soviet Union. Roeder treats institutional choice as a dependent variable or an outcome. Many other leading scholars have done the same (Frye 1997; Easter 1997; Bernhard 1999). I treat it as an independent variable. This approach is also found in the work of distinguished social scientists (Linz and Valenzuela 1994; Stepan and Skach 1993; Di Palma 1990).

I do not go nearly as far as Roeder in explicating the problem of constitutional origination; indeed, I have not heretofore explored this matter at all. But constitutional choice, in my own framework, could not have been predicted by the structure of republican party organizations and the interests of their leaders at the time of regime change. I hold that constitutional choice in many cases predated the backsliding away from (or advancement toward) democracy investigated here.

Romania adopted a French-style semipresidential constitution precisely because the French had such a constitution. As the Western country that paid Romania the closest attention and whose culture Romanians knew the best, France seemed the country to imitate. For Romanians, who suffered home-grown fascism in the interwar period, Stalinist rule in the 1970s and 1980s, and the region's only violent revolution in 1989, emulating a time-proven foreign model was more appealing than either inventing a new paradigm or returning to some earlier indigenous model. Romania's Constituent Assembly wrote the constitution in short order after the revolution, and the electorate approved it by referendum in 1991. The constitution and the structure of government it provides for do not express the interests of a particular politician or elite group. Nor, as mentioned, did the division of power result from demands from below; such demands, if they were present at all, were scarcely audible. Czechoslovakia, Slovenia, and Hungary immediately embraced parliamentarism after the old regimes' demise not because this system best served the interests of ascendant politicians, but because in the heat of revolution both citizens and emerging elites reached for the form of noncommunist regime they knew best from their countries' precommunist pasts.

In Russia, different influences and circumstances drove constitutional choice. Parliamentarism was never really even on the agenda, though not because no powerful politicians would have benefited from it. The superpresidentialism that Russia ended up with, moreover, grew out of a proximate political conflict that Yeltsin himself did not fully control. Yeltsin did, of course, seek a strong presidency for himself; but he neither created the office himself nor foreclosed a parliamentary alternative. Rather, the Russian superpresidency originated in the democratic movement's effort to demolish the communist system by withdrawing Russia from the Soviet Union, and to create an office for a politician who would bring such an event to pass. Public opinion itself, as expressed in the referendum on the question in the spring of 1991, created the presidency in Russia. What is more, voters founded the office for Yeltsin; everyone in Russia in the spring of 1991 knew who would capture the new office. The complete failure of Yeltsin's antagonists in the legislature to advance their plans for a parliamentary system between 1991 and 1993, moreover, was rooted in a public consensus, expressed in referenda in 1993, that Russia needed a strong president to guard its great power status—and, paradoxically, to battle conservatives in the holdover Supreme Soviet and to impel political reform (Urban 1997; Fish 1995).

A universal desire to guard the country against foreign pressure shaped constitutional choice in Mongolia. There, constitution makers were most concerned with fending off any future efforts by China or Russia to compromise Mongolia's autonomy. Rather than seeking concentration of power, however, Mongolia's leaders thought that dispersing power as widely as possible would provide the best protection against foreign manipulation. This belief is rooted in Mongolia's communist past. Unlike people in many other postcommunist countries, Mongolians view their previous communist regime less as a partyocracy than as a one-man dictatorship headed by a puppet. Such a view is justified by the way the country was ruled during most of the Soviet period. Thus, to Mongolian politicians, none of whom knew what kind of institutional configuration would benefit themselves anyway, patriotism and a concern for what was perceived as the national interest guided decision making and yielded a parliament-heavy form of semipresidentialism that reflected exquisite preoccupation with separating power (Fish 1998[c]).

In short, constitutional choice was not determined by some prior level of democratization. Nor were constitutional choice and the propensity for backsliding toward authoritarianism together determined by some common third factor. Thus, the extent of concentration of power is, in my own model, exogenous and nonpredetermined. If the *roots* of constitutional choice vary widely, however, the *consequences* of it are remarkably tractable to unqualified generalization. Throughout the region the concentration of power has been a recipe for stalled democratization and backsliding.

Although the analysis presented here does not suffer from an "endogeneity problem," it is vulnerable to a separate and more valid criticism—namely, that the analysis is potentially sensitive to modest changes in score on the dependent variable, and that small fluctuations in Freedom House scores, particularly within the first decade of transition, do not necessarily represent hard and fast trajectories of regime change. This is a legitimate concern. The core findings do not, however, hinge on blips or small undulations in freedom scores. Over the past four Freedom House surveys—that is, between the 1996–97 survey and the 1999–2000 survey, the latter of which provides measures for the dependent variable—only three of twenty-eight countries changed categories. Macedonia moved from Category III to II. Since Macedonia, along with Bulgaria, was an exception to the generalizations offered here regarding the backsliders, its change of category actually made the present argument less complicated and "cleaner." The change was entirely consonant with the thrust of this analysis. Slovakia moved from Category III to I, thus removing another parliamentary regime from Category III and strengthening the notion that mighty presidents pose a uniquely hazardous obstacle to the maintenance of democratization. Finally, Latvia moved from Category II to I, which had virtually no substantive effect on the analysis. Thus, while it would indeed be premature to conclude that countries are now forever stuck in the categories into which they are grouped in this chapter, some lasting patterns may be emerging. It is not too early to try to make sense of the forces underlying these patterns.

Even if the present analysis must be regarded as provisional, there are distinct advantages to positing a theory for a phenomenon before the empirical evidence is "all in." The advantages for scholarship are obvious from some writings on postcommunism that offered bold and logically coherent propositions long before the dust began to settle and patterns appeared to be firmly established (Jowitt 1992b; Tucker 1992). Such analyses not only help define clear scholarly agendas; they also offer propositions that truly lend themselves to post facto scrutiny in light of accumulated evidence and to assessment of where they were accurate and where—and why—they went wrong (Hanson 1995). Social scientists who eschew prediction may not agree with this view. Yet if a theory does not contain a predictive element—that is, if predictions cannot be logically inferred or explicitly expressed on the basis of the theory—then that theory *is not genuinely falsifiable.*

All of the propositions that the present chapter advances are falsifiable. They are falsifiable in the strong sense, meaning that future real-world developments, rather than mere scholarly criticism and reinterpretation of the past, could reveal them to be simply and obviously wrong. Such vulnerability to genuine falsification is possible only if generalizations are issued in time for them to be falsified—meaning only if they are put forward and developed at a relatively early stage in the unfolding of a historical phenomenon. If, over the next decade, countries in which great power is concentrated in the presidency make strides toward democratization that outstrip those made in countries in which power is dispersed, and if these differences become pronounced and lasting, then this chapter's central generalization and the logic underpinning it will be undone. To many observers and political actors who regard concentrated executive power as a weapon of reform, such a development would not be surprising. To me it would come as a shock—albeit a welcome one, given that over half of the population of the postcommunist region resides in the countries of Category III, with their "strong" executive presidencies. What is more, if vigorous opposition parties turn out to be more of a bane than a boon for democratization, then events will falsify another major proposition put forward in this chapter. Indeed, some observers have characterized muscular, assertive societies and especially opposition parties as potential hazards to open government, especially in countries laboring under great social stress and dislocation. The weakness of social mobilization and organization, in this view, may help stay authoritarian reversion (Bermeo 1997; Berman 1997; Hanson and Kopstein 1997). If such a perspective turns out to be right, the positive link I have made between the strength of opposition parties and progress in democratization will be proven wrong. The evidence, of course, might in time render a mixed verdict that does not make an "either-or" judgment possible. One scholar has recently argued that the character of the *relationship* between political parties and other forms of societal association powerfully affected the sustainability of democratization over the long run in the "first wave" democracies of Western Europe in the nineteenth century and first half of the twentieth century (Ertman 1998). A dynamic such as he found in the earliest democratizers might eventually obtain in postcommunist countries as well.

Examining the propositions put forward here across time and across polities in the postcommunist world represents the best way to test them and to use them to advance knowledge. Another important component of evaluation and analysis involves cross-regional comparison, a matter taken up briefly in the following and closing section.

Cross-Regional Comparison

Why—and indeed *if*—postcommunist reversals of democratization differ from those in other regions remains to be explained and cannot be fully investigated here. Several possible sources of cross-regional difference are worthy of note. First, the actors that often challenge democracy in other regions differ substantially from their counterparts in the postcommunist area. Due to the legacy of Soviet-type regimes, militaries in the postcommunist world are accustomed to subordination to civilian authority and do not normally conceive of themselves as political actors. Officer corps are not thoroughly inbred and segregated from broader society. In these respects militaries differ from those in places such as Argentina, Chile, Brazil, and Turkey.

Would-be revolutionary movements and parties are as rare in the postcommunist region as are politically assertive armed forces. The region contains extremist and militant organizations of every conceivable stripe. But almost everywhere their appeal is strictly limited. The manifest lack of support for messianic organizations may be found in the public skepticism and exhaustion left by long decades of ideocratic rule by avowedly millenarian parties. Public disillusionment and fatigue may also help explain why levels of politicization and mass mobilization, not to speak of genuine polarization, also are scarcely evident and therefore have not been at the root of democratic erosion. Political fatigue and skepticism, however, may also help account for why strong, well-organized oppositions to overweening executives have failed to materialize in so many countries, leaving would-be usurpers with much room for maneuver.

The weakness, absence, or dissimilarity of the usual suspects helps furnish insight into why militaries, highly politicized mass publics, and other possible agents have not played a major role in democratic erosion in the postcommunist world. But the mere absence from the stage of such actors does not provide a positive explanation for why chief executives *have* occupied center stage in democratic degradation. Here the extraordinary weakness and disrepair of political institutions, and state institutions in particular, may play a considerable role. Decrepit institutions are normally more vulnerable to takeover by a single strong figure than are firmly established, well-functioning structures. The dissolution of the communist-party system induced deep crises of state power. State structures did not collapse completely; Category III countries do not include any close analogues to Zaire/Congo in the late 1990s. Still, they were less robust and coherent and more vulnerable to plebiscitary takeover than state structures in most Latin American, Southern European, and East Asian countries during their transitions since the 1970s.

What is more, statehood itself—that is, the very identity of the country as a distinct, sovereign national unit—has been far more problematic in the postcommunist world than in most other regions (Bunce 1999b). All the countries of the former Soviet Union and the former Yugoslavia, as well as the Czech Republic and Slovakia, emerged from larger multinational entities. Strong individual leaders may not only act as readily identifiable substitutes for strong institutions; they may also embody the new state itself. For a leader to play such a part, he or she normally must enjoy hero status at the time of regime change, and a large section of the citizenry must be prepared to invest in him or her a great deal of national-symbolic significance. As shown in this chapter, the region—and especially Category III countries—has not lacked such hero figures. The ability of a leader successfully to portray himself or herself as the central agent and personification of statehood is naturally much more difficult in countries where statehood is not problematic.

The postcommunist political condition in some respects resembles that of early postcolonial Africa. There, state apparatuses were also fully formed but exceedingly weak. Organized oppositions to the new indigenous rulers were also underdeveloped. Statehood itself was similarly unsettled. Many new rulers also enjoyed clientelist ties to powerful external supporters, as Cold War competition virtually guaranteed every African ruler the patronage of one or another of the superpowers. In the years following independence, strongmen who enjoyed status as national liberators and founding fathers engaged in self-aggrandizement and ran roughshod over embryonic institutions of self-government. In many respects

African countries during and after decolonization differed starkly from many postcommunist countries, including in terms of levels of economic development and cultural and historical traditions. But the causes of authoritarian reversion emphasized in this chapter were also present in early postcolonial Africa. Patterns of de-democratization in the two regions, moreover, bear a striking resemblance.

As in Africa, in the postcommunist world superexecutivism and personalization of power will not have the "stabilizing" or "developmental" effects that many executives and their apologists claim for them. In fact, the situation that Kohli (1997) notes has prevailed in many "follower democracies" in the Third World is already evident, and will certainly obtain in the future, in the former Second World as well. According to Kohli (p. 76), "the typical resort to personalistic, concentrated executive power as a post-transition, stabilizing measure only postpones the deeper need to work out a society's power conflicts." In both the Third and postcommunist worlds, executive usurpation "postpones" conflicts precisely because it is so often accompanied by measures that stifle free competition and check the development of the organizations and habits of behavior necessary for managing and resolving conflict. Personalism and executive usurpation also have another pernicious effect, one that is already tragically manifest in Africa and that will soon be in evidence in the postcommunist world: the distortion of statebuilding and the diminution of state sovereignty in the context of the larger polity. The massing of power in the executive, which is so often carried out in the name of "strengthening the state" and "promoting state effectiveness," in practice yields precisely the opposite result. By concentrating and personalizing power, it arrests the development of the institutions, including public bureaucracies, legislatures, courts, and legal systems, that are crucial to the emergence of an autonomous and effective state apparatus.

FOUR

THE DISCURSIVE ORIGINS OF RUSSIAN
DEMOCRATIC POLITICS

Richard D. Anderson, Jr.

TWO PROFOUND CHANGES have occurred in Russia: The political authorities have started competing for votes that all adults are eligible to cast, and the people have begun casting votes that decide who wins the contest for power. Until 1989 the votes for which the Soviet Union's ultimate rulers competed were cast only by Central Committee members who never numbered more than about three hundred persons (others voted, but they did not choose between rival candidates, and no one competed for popular votes). Until the late 1980s Soviet citizens were banned from taking sides in the contest for political power and incurred penalties, often extraordinarily harsh, if they tried. Since 1991 they have been free to take sides, and both the incumbents and their opponents actively solicit them to do so. It is certainly true that Russian democracy is grossly imperfect. Russia's observance of civil liberties leaves much to be desired, and there is reason to believe that its record has been worsening of late, particularly in connection with the warfare in Chechnya. It is also true that Russian democracy is unconsolidated and may prove impermanent. But the very appearance of democracy in Russia is nevertheless worth analyzing, because Russian politics since 1991 presents features entirely absent from Soviet politics before 1985. How did these features appear, and how did they appear so suddenly?

The suddenness with which *nomenklatura* and subjects turned into politicians and citizens poses a challenging puzzle for theories of democratization. In the brief period from 1985 to 1991 Russians began to act as members of a democracy—to use Joseph Schumpeter's definition—in which elites compete with one another for citizen support and citizens take sides. Even before Russia's first competitive elections in 1989, thousands of Russians began influencing the selection of their leaders by taking to the streets. The first demonstrations that forced a provincial party first secretary into resignation evidently occurred in Iuzhnosakhalinsk, capital of Sakhalin province, where first an estimated 1,000 and then an estimated 4,800 demonstrators turned out in May 1988 (Berezovskii and

Krotov 1990, 221–22). When Russians learned that instead of the demonstrators suffering repression, the first secretary had resigned, new demonstrations spread to one city after another across the territory of Russia. Ultimately some fifteen million Russians participated in the wave of demonstrations (Bahry and Way 1994, 335). The suddenness with which the transformation took place in Russia—and has occurred in many other new democracies—raises the two questions that I will address here: Why do politicians begin competing for a popular vote? Why do citizens take sides in this competition?

Most theories of democratization simply take these defining elements of democracy for granted and fail to explain why they appear. Many focus on causes, such as economic or cultural constraints, that are much slower to change and cannot account for the suddenness that characterizes the shift in the behaviors of politician and citizen. Even those theories that focus on conditions susceptible to rapid change, such as elite coalitions or political institutions, do not provide an explanation for why some nomenklatura and a few subjects become politicians and other subjects become citizens. Moreover, social science theory that emphasizes the strategic pursuit of interest suggests that such a change *cannot* take place: When individual Russians consider taking sides in politics, they run head-on into the well-known paradox of voting that presents a compelling disincentive to participation. In the form of a collective action dilemma, the same considerations make it rational for both nomenklatura and subjects to free ride on the political activity of others. Incentives for competition among politicians and participation by citizens can exist only if one postulates that some individuals *enjoy* competing and participating, yet such an explanation provides no independent causality at all and is unable to explain why those same individuals were previously passive.

A new kind of theory is needed. In this chapter I propose a discursive theory of democratization that explains the two central changes that must take place to produce competition among elites and partisanship among publics. First, an authoritarian elite becomes unable to remain unified when its identity—as a coherent unit distinct from the population—begins to fade. Identity fades if and because political leaders change their discourse. Loss of identity in turn erodes the elite's determination to repress political activity by persons formerly excluded from politics. Second, a new elite political discourse converges on the ordinary language of the people formerly excluded from political activity and cues members of the public to affiliate themselves with political contenders. Dictatorship crumbles and democracy emerges when political discourse changes from linguistic cues that isolate the elite from the people to linguistic cues that merge the elite into the people. Political identities no longer divide society horizontally between rulers above and ruled below; they begin to divide it vertically among parallel coalitions of citizens who side with politicians competing for occupancy of "top" offices.

A discursive theory of democracy complements the principal ideas advanced by my colleagues in this volume. The observance of civil liberties may seriously deteriorate, as Steven Fish argues, when a leader—even an elected leader—concentrates excessive power in the executive, but even so, discursive identification of governors with governed may be sufficient to sustain electoral politics stripped of many of the ordinarily accompanying liberties. If, as Philip Roeder shows, diversified institutional settings create variegated sub-elite identities, then individuals promoted to positions of political leadership after careers in separate institutions may be less likely to converge on the unified discourse that would enable them to sustain authoritarian rule. And as Stephen Hanson argues, if such a democracy remains unconsolidated—by my definition, vulnerable to new discourses restoring isolation of the elite from the people—it may be because there is no cadre of officials who derive their own identity from enforcing procedures that enable the people to express their identification with political contenders by voting.

A Discursive Theory of Democratization

A discursive theory of democratization begins from a conception of social identities—"rulers," "subjects," "politicians," "citizens"—that form as responses to linguistic cues. It is a shift in discourse that causes the bifurcated social identities of an undemocratic regime to break down and the unified democratic identity of citizen to emerge in their place.

Transition to democracy means the extension to all or nearly all adults who live under the power of a given state the opportunity to take sides in the contest for power.[1] The alternative to a transition to democracy, maintenance of nondemocracy, requires that the rulers prevent subjects from taking sides in their contest for power. The rulers accomplish this by inflicting penalties on any subject who tries to take sides. Infliction of penalties requires solidarity among the rulers, who include not only the immediate contestants for supreme power but also the enforcers of their power. Although these enforcers are often overlooked, their role is essential because of the numerical disproportion between the ultimate rulers and the ruled. In any state, democratic or not, the number of contestants for national political power is tiny—two, three, four, ten, at most perhaps a few hundred. The number of persons, whom those who win the contest for power in an undemocratic state exclude from politics by threatening to inflict penalties for taking sides in the political contest, is enormous. This number can run into the hundreds of millions. In an undemocratic state the numerical disproportion between ultimate rulers and ruled precludes any possibility that the ultimate rulers might inflict the penalties themselves. They are compelled to depend on persons beside themselves to enforce the exclusion from politics of the millions who live under their rule. In undemocratic states of different kinds, those who enforce exclusion from politics on behalf of the ultimate rulers bear different names—barons in a monarchy, soldiers in a military dictatorship, literati under the Son of Heaven, officials in bureaucratic authoritarianism, nomenklatura appointees in a communist dictatorship. Despite the difference in names, however, all these kinds of enforcers have in common that they possess some collective name—that is, they bear a *distinctive social identity*, set apart from and considered superior to that of the population as a whole, symbolized by the name they bear as a category.

Nondemocracy requires this distinct social identity. In the absence of a social distinction between those who inflict penalties and those who suffer them, even undemocratic rulers who want to preserve their rule become incapable of achieving this goal. The task of explaining democratization consists in part in discovering how the social identity of enforcers of rule can suddenly disappear. When people who have borne the social identity of enforcers lose it, they cease to inflict penalties on subjects who try to take sides in the political contest among the leaders. The other part of the task is explaining why the subjects begin taking sides. If they do, they lose the identity of "subject" and turn into citizens. And the social identity of "citizen," I will argue, is the result of the formation of the social identity of "politician."

Discursive Sources of Social Identities

In order to explain how the social identity of enforcer disappears, it is useful to start by explaining how it can exist. This question is of course a specific version of the general question: How do social identities exist at all? The explanation of social identities turns on the concepts of "text" and "discourse." A "text" may be defined as a single communicative event. A "discourse" may be defined as a set of procedures for composing and interpreting texts (Beaugrande 1985, 47). A discourse arises as speakers or writers, in the process of communicating among themselves and with others, produce texts that bear common traits from which both those who emit and those who encounter the texts compile procedures for composition and interpretation. They then use this discourse to guide the composition and interpretation of future texts.

As individuals encounter texts, among the consequences are inferences by the individuals about their own and others' identities (Gumperz and Cook-Gumperz 1982, 1). Because people use texts to infer identities, lin-

guists have found that people impute two kinds of meaning to texts—
"informational" and "relational" (Schiffrin 1987, 12, Brown and Yule
1983, 1–3). Informational meanings communicate what the speaker and
the audience infer about objects in the world around them (including their
own presence), while relational meanings communicate what selves the
speaker and the audience infer.[2] In the process of communication, people
continuously define and redefine their identities, both by the narratives
they tell and retell about themselves and by their inferences about themselves drawn from narratives told by others (Schiffrin 1996). That is, identity is a variable over time, not a constant across time. Of course, over
time a person's identity may not vary much, but if it does not, its relative
stability may be attributable to the person's repeatedly encountering texts
with stable characteristics, generated by a stable discourse, from which
the person repeatedly draws similar inferences about his or her identity.

Relational meanings can cue someone to recognize either a personal
or a social identity. Decades of experimental research have distinguished
behaviors that occur when texts cue a personal self from behaviors that
occur when texts cue a social self. Three findings are pertinent here. First,
when a text draws someone's attention to a social identity, that person
will voluntarily accept costs to the self (and impose costs on others sharing
the same social identity), if these sacrifices widen the perceptual gap separating bearers of the person's own social identity from bearers of some
contrasted identity. Second, when a text draws a person's attention to
social rather than personal identity, the person becomes more aware of
differences between groups bearing opposed social identities and less
aware of interpersonal differences among bearers of a given social identity. Alternatively, when attention is drawn to personal identity, the person
is equally aware of interpersonal differences regardless of the social identity borne by the persons being compared. To the extent that the social
self is cued, the personal self recedes, and so does awareness of other
personal selves. Third, the most arbitrary cues, such as dressing one group
of laboratory assistants in red coats and another in white coats, or labeling one group "kappa" and another "delta," are sufficient to make bearers of one identity pay costs in order to penalize bearers of the opposed
identity and to shift awareness from interpersonal to intergroup differences. Most important, the bearers of the two social identities do not even
need to exist. Merely telling a subject that there is another group, and
asking the subject to allocate among individuals in the own group and the
other group, is enough to produce both the behavioral and the perceptual
changes. In short, discursive cues to personal or to social identity change
both perception and action. (These conclusions are drawn from an enormous literature synthesized in Turner et al. 1987, 22–66).

These findings bear direct implications for politics. In a striking exception to the problems of external validity that often arise when one scales up findings originally made in laboratory or small-group studies, the findings of social identity theorists point directly to macropolitical empirical relationships that are well established in the study of democracy. Voting is well known to be an instance of a collective action game analytically isomorphic with those studied in the laboratory by social identity theorists. Experiment has shown that people are more likely to pay costs of contributing to collective action when presented with discursive cues indicating that their contribution will spread the difference between the rewards to members of their group and to members of the opposing groups. Voting is costly in time and attention. In an exact parallel to the experimental findings, survey research has established that partisan identification is the most important reason why people pay the cost of voting (Rosenstone and Hansen 1993). When partisan identification causes people to vote, of course, their votes do spread the perceived difference between candidates by designating one as a "winner" and the other as a "loser."[3]

Political Identity in Nondemocracy and Democracy

Political texts cue people to make decisions whether they share identity with contestants for political power—with rulers in a nondemocracy, with politicians in a democracy. The issue is whether political discourse bifurcates society along a horizontal cleavage, with rulers and their enforcers of rule above and ruled below, or divides society along one or more vertical cleavages separating a politician and his or her voters from rivals and their voters. In the former case, nondemocracy, political discourse must cue recognition of *two separate identities*—that of rulers (with their enforcers) and that of ruled. In the latter case, democracy, political discourse cues *one shared identity*—that of citizen—linking politicians to voters.

Of course, within each separate identity characteristic of a nondemocracy, and within the shared identity characteristic of a democracy, there are plural personal and social identities.[4] In any nondemocracy, the rulers recognize differences between each other and among their enforcers, for example, in the Soviet case, between party officials and economic managers. In democracy the politicians use discourse to cue recognition of plural partisan identities. But these identities within the basic categorization are far more fluid and diffuse than the rigid division between rulers and ruled characteristic of nondemocracy. This rigid division forms the horizontal barrier, which is crossed only by entry into or expulsion from the ruling group, and normally no more than once by any person. (By contrast, Soviet party officials and economic managers could and did switch occupational identities with some frequency). The discourse of democratic politicians, on the other hand, not only assumes that individuals can, but positively invites them to, change sides across the vertical divide separating political parties—a divide whose very existence is obscured by the many "independents" and "leaners" whose political identities straddle or border it.

Besides being more fluid, the multiple partisan identities within the unified identity of citizenship differ in principle from the dual identities of a nondemocracy. In democracy, political discourse assigns positive definitions to all the opposing partisan identities. In nondemocracy, discourse defines the cleavage between rulers and ruled by a "privative opposition"—a paired opposition in which one member of the pair is defined by some positive quality and the other member is undefined except by the absence of the quality defining the first member (Forsyth 1970, 6). *In nondemocracy, discourse cues a positive identity only for the rulers and the enforcers of their rule.* Despotic discourse deprives the ruled of any positive political identity at all. Privative opposition, juxtaposing a positive identity for the rulers and the agents of their rule to a negative identity assigned to the population at large, is observable in the use of "not" or its variants to introduce reference to the population living under despotic rule. This reference by negation appears in the Soviet distinction between "communists" and "nonparty persons" (*bespartiinye*), the two political categories into which Soviet citizens were divided.[5] In non-democracy, the identity of the populace is the residual of the identity of the rulers. In democracy, the various political identities are not each other's residuals. Empirically Democrats may include nearly everyone who is not a Republican, but "Democrat" is not defined as the residual that remains once "Republican" has been defined, and neither party name contains any variant of the word "not."

Despotic Discourse

Definition of political identity as a privative opposition is the cause of both prerequisites for the existence of any form of undemocratic rule—the willingness of its enforcers to engage in repression and the political passivity among populations living under despotic rule. Experimental research on social identity finds that when a person is assigned a *positive* identity, he or she discriminates against members of opposing groups. Someone informed of membership in an in-group will attempt to widen the perceptual difference between bearers of his or her social identity and bearers of an opposed identity *by imposing penalties on the latter.* Someone not informed of membership in a group will not make this attempt. Informed by Soviet texts that they were different from the population at large, nomenklatura officials did actively penalize members of the broader population who engaged in activities reserved to the nomenklatura. While political repression may have been the particular specialty of the security police, a very wide range of nomenklatura officials performed some repressive duties. Educators and industrial officials, for example, penalized persons under their supervision for reading *samizdat*—literature whose authors had transgressed upon the prerogative of nomenklatura appointees to authorize publication. The officials removed such persons from universities or fired them from jobs. On the other hand, when people read in the Soviet press that they were *bespartiinye*, they necessarily also found out that there was no party to which they did belong. Thus people should have been expected *not* to discriminate against Communists. Indeed, as long as Soviet political discourse remained stable, the Soviet people largely remained politically inactive. It was necessary to induce people to vote by promising private rewards (what would be called "case work" in a democratic legislature) and to falsify voting records in order to make it appear that everyone had voted.

It may seem strange to attribute both repression and passivity to discourse, rather than to the incentives used by the rulers to reward enforcers of their rule for performing repression and to the disincentive to act presented to the population by repression. Yet, the attribution to discourse is coherent, while the argument from incentives is incoherent. First, discursive theory offers a simple and coherent explanation for the motivations of both the enforcers and the population. These motivations are consequences of a discourse that cues a bifurcated social identity. Cued to recognize opposing social identities, a person becomes motivated to increase the perceived difference between groups. Rulers therefore allocate benefits to bearers of their own identity (e.g., privileges to the nomenklatura) and penalties to bearers of the opposed identity (e.g., the population's inferior incomes). Not cued to recognize the sharing of any positive identity with each other, members of the population remain inactive and, in return for individual rewards, may even cooperate with the rulers in imposing penalties on other persons outside the ruling group.

Second, attribution of repression and passivity to incentives is incoherent, because in any argument attributing them to incentives, a collective action problem arises that would cause enforcers to shirk in administering repression. Collective action problems necessarily arise whenever costs in time and effort to repress exceed whatever intrinsic benefits are conferred by the activity of repressing. Distribution by rulers of particularistic, material incentives to reward enforcers for repression cannot explain the existence of repression: The rulers possess incentives that they *can* distribute to the enforcers only as a result of revenue gathered through collective action by the enforcers. Yet, if enforcers can shirk, it is always an equilibrium for each of them to shirk by free riding on the others' effort. If the enforcers are too numerous for each to monitor all the others (as they must be to maintain any authoritarian order with a population sufficient to qualify it as a state), the equilibrium where all shirk is the only equilibrium that can exist. Thus all shirk, no revenue is gathered, and no incentives exist for the rulers to distribute. Discursive theory argues that the social identity separating enforcers from the ruled is necessary to provide enforcers the motive not to shirk—that is, the motive to gather the rulers' revenues that enable the rulers to provide private incentives to each enforcer.

Third, discursive theory also offers a more coherent account of why undemocratic rulers must engage in repression. Repression is not necessary to prevent collective popular action against the despotic regime. After all, even if every member of the broader populace wants to overthrow the state (a very doubtful proposition), each person is, nonetheless, likely to free ride on the revolutionary action of others. Again in populations too large for each person to monitor all others, this is the only demonstrable equilibrium—everyone shirks and no collective action against the regime occurs.[6] In short, the disincentives already suffice to prevent people from demonstrating, *if incentives are all that motivates people*. If the material disincentives to collective action against the despotic regime already suffice, then why must despotic regimes engage in repression? Discursive theory argues that repression is necessary to authoritarian regimes, because it disrupts the cueing of political identity by persons outside the regime. Human beings are characterized by a generalized propensity to construct positive identity.[7] They try to define these positive identities through various discursive pursuits, such as talking about politics. Like any nondemocracy, the communist regime sought to co-opt some of the individuals most active in political discussions while repressing the others, for fear that their political self-identification would communicate itself to the *bespartiinye*. This would have been dangerous to the regime, because those relegated to a negative political identity could be expected to identify against the regime with anyone who offered them a compelling positive identity. It is this possibility that necessitates repression.

By blocking the development of a positive identity among their subjects, undemocratic rulers make it possible to maintain their rule with the scarce resources available to them. In the Soviet case, the relative infrequency of self-definition taking political forms was in fact the enabling condition for the success of repression. Even at the height of repression under Stalin, those Soviet citizens who experienced political violence to their own persons were a minority. Later, as violence receded, it became even more selective, targeting precisely those individuals whose efforts to communicate a positive political identity to the population at large threatened to undermine the rulers' strategy for keeping the people passive. Had it been otherwise—had the Soviet state signaled a positive political identity to the general public or failed to block dissidents from doing so—the small minority of enforcers could not have repressed the massive majority of the population.

Democratic Discourse

If nondemocracy requires a privative opposition that assigns a positive identity to the rulers and their agents but a negative identity to everyone else, the emergence of democracy depends on eliminating that privative opposition. That is, if nondemocracy is sustained by a political discourse that assigns negative identity to everyone but the rulers and the enforcers of rule, democratization begins when political discourse assigns a positive identity to other members of a population. This transition is clearly expressed in the slogan of post–Nazi German democrats: *"Wir sind wieder wer!"* ("We are someone again!") Given a shared positive identity universal to the population, members of the population may assign positive and negative values to various identities within the population. Partisans of various political organizations within democracies may mildly or even intensely dislike each other, but they do not deny that their partisan opponents share with them the trait of bearing a political identity. Undemocratic rulers do deny this trait to the ruled.

People acquire increasing opportunities to take sides in politics if and when discourse begins to change. If the privative opposition erodes, an authoritarian regime loses its *capacity* (not necessarily the will of its rulers) to repress, not because the institutions that formerly conducted repression disappear but because their personnel become uncertain whether they still want to repress. By 1991 the discourse of the Gorbachev Politburo had greatly diminished the former separateness of politics (a statement for which I shall give evidence below). As a result, at the demonstration in Moscow on 28 March, as *Moscow News* reported, "the 100,000 marchers and 50,000 troops in Moscow 'did not regard each other as enemies'" (quoted in Russell 2000, 5). Indeed, videotapes taken of demonstrations in Moscow during 1990 and 1991 show demonstrators laughing and talking with police, who in the authoritarian era would have been beating and arresting them instead. It is not the case that no policemen or soldiers retained the former distinctive identity. Instead the Politburo was now able to find only some, and relatively few, reliable enforcers of its authority. "Control and repression in the workplace," as Fish (1995) showed, continued throughout the Gorbachev period, but it began to vary substantially from place to place as the discursive distinction between nomenklatura and workforce collapsed.

Once political discourse stops cueing a population to distinguish its rulers from itself, then discourse begins to build partisan identification. This partisan identification in turn motivates people to take sides and to vote.[8] In order to vote, citizens first must perceive some kind of difference between the candidates—either a partisan difference or a performance difference—and they must share an identity with at least one. The act of taking sides by voting strengthens partisan identification with some candidates. When a voter approves, over and over again, of the candidates nominated by his or her party and repeatedly disapproves of candidates nominated by other parties, the voter builds partisan identification. If so, the stable partisan identities characteristic of a democracy emerge simply as recurrent, repetitive inferences from perceptions of difference between candidates.[9] For the differences necessary to the formation of partisanship to be perceived at all, the voter must encounter a discourse that avoids cueing him or her to attend to the differences between himself or herself and the candidates as a group. The emergence of partisan identities in turn overcomes the collective action problem in voting; cued with a partisan identity, the voter becomes motivated to spread the perceived difference between his or her preferred candidate and candidates belonging to opposed partisan identities. The voter does this by casting a ballot by which the voter designates his or her candidate the "winner" and the other candidates "losers."

In summary, what distinguishes democracy from nondemocracy? The distinction rests on the political identities that people infer from the textual cues that they encounter. Both undemocratic and democratic elites emit texts, composed and interpreted by a given discourse. Texts communicate both informational and relational meanings. When people encounter texts from political elites, they learn not only what the elite is telling them about the physical and social world (the informational meaning) but also whether they share an identity with the elite (the relational meaning). What they learn about identity has action consequences. Political discourses that bifurcate society along a horizontal cleavage into the opposing identities of rulers above and ruled below motivate the enforcers of rule to engage in the repression that maintains undemocratic rule. This repression aims not at intimidation of the majority (which remains passive when cued with a negative identity) but at preventing anyone among the populace from communicating a positive political identity that would motivate people to begin taking sides in politics. If the distinctive discourse of a nondemocracy erodes, the enforcers lose interest in repressing, while the population begins to see that there are sides to take in politics. (There always were sides to take, but they were invisible to the population because discourse cued perception of a distinctive social identity that distracted attention from differences between individuals competing for power.) Contestants for power, whether insiders or external challengers, begin to perceive the population as a political resource and move discourse further toward ordinary language. A democratic political discourse unifies society into a common citizenship of governors and governed and cues people to make the distinctions among individuals that provide perceptual anchors for partisan identities. Accumulating over time into vertical cleavages that affiliate some citizens with one set of contestants for political office in opposition to rivals affiliated to their own citizen supporters, partisan identities motivate people to pay the costs of voting. Elections are a ubiquitous democratic institution—*not* a quintessential democratic institution—because voting makes it easier to take sides and the relatively diffuse partisan identities that form within a shared social identity of citizenship can motivate people only to put forth a limited effort for the sake of penalizing candidates of the opposing party.

Initiating Transitions to Democracy

According to discursive theory, at the root of the transition to democracy lies the finding of research on social identity that each person requires some cue from outside in order to infer his or her own identity. Transitions to democracy begin when the populace receives cues less suitable for stimulating recognition of the bifurcated identity characteristic of nondemocracy and more suitable for stimulating recognition of the unitary identity characteristic of democracy. These cues may be supplied by individuals within the populace, a Lech Walesa, or by individuals among the rulers, a Boris Yeltsin. The question is why these individuals start offering these new cues.

Every nondemocracy is actually an oligarchy, regardless of whether only one oligarch exercises supreme power in law or fact. Any outward semblance of unity in submission to a despotic ruler invariably conceals an intense internal contest for power among oligarchs. This contest for power in any undemocratic polity may be represented by a modified version of the game that Roeder (1993) calls "Oligarch's Dilemma." In modeling the contest as a game, I make no imputation of rationality to the contestants, who may understand the game but do not need to. Instead the game predicts who will stay alive in the contest by observing their strategies; such a game is as useful for analyzing the behavior of bacteria as for that of human agents. All such games oversimplify. The simplification is worthwhile to the extent that the game makes it possible to visualize the workings of otherwise obscure and complex political interactions.

In Roeder's original version of Oligarch's Dilemma, each oligarch faces a choice between two moves, which I may call "close" and "open" for the kind of politics that they entail. "Close" corresponds to emission of discursive cues that stimulate the bifurcated identity characteristic of non-democracy, while "open" corresponds to discursively cueing the unitary identity characteristic of democracy. All oligarchs are assumed to minimize the constraints on their power. The constraints are, in decreasing order of magnitude, the power of other oligarchs, the preferences of voters in a democracy, and the preferences of enforcers in a dictatorship. The assumption is interpreted as meaning that each oligarch's chances to remain active in the game improve if the oligarch's behavior displays the following priorities, listed in decreasing order of importance: (1) to eliminate other oligarchs, even if he or she must accept a new constraint imposed by voters; (2) to share power with other oligarchs at the cost of accepting the constraint posed by motivating enforcers of rule; (3) to share power with other oligarchs at the cost of accepting the constraints posed by motivating voters; and (4) to be eliminated. If all oligarchs play "close," all share power with enforcers but no one eliminates any other oligarch. If any oligarch plays "open" while others play "close," any oligarch who plays "open" gains the overwhelming support of the populace and uses it to eliminate the oligarchs who have played "close." But if all play "open," then they divide the support of the populace and no one eliminates other oligarchs.

Such a game is formally a prisoner's dilemma (open-close > close-close > open-open > close-open for every oligarch), and consequently its equilibria depend on whether it has a definite endpoint or is indefinitely iterated. When this game has a known endpoint, the observer can use backward induction to identify behaviors that keep oligarchs in the contest. While the notion that political contests can have a fixed endpoint is peculiar, the analysis is nevertheless instructive because of the rule that any oligarch who is caught playing "close" when another plays "open" is eliminated. All oligarchs must play "open" on the last round in order to prevent their own elimination on that round. Knowing that every oligarch will play "open" on the last round, each must play "open" on the next-to-last round, and therefore every oligarch observed to survive must have played "open" on every round. In this case, "close-close" will never be an equilibrium.

If "all open" is the only equilibrium, then the original version of Oligarch's Dilemma is not a very satisfactory model of transitions to democracy, for it implies that nondemocracy can never occur unless something outside the model bars every oligarch from ever playing "open." Nevertheless the model may be worth fixing, because it does portray the fundamental choice with which discursive theory is concerned—that is, political contestants choosing whether to preserve or transcend the bifurcated political identity that makes nondemocracy possible. The model can be fixed by introducing two modifications. First, postulate a lag of at least one round between one oligarch's decision to play "open" on a given round and the elimination of other oligarchs. Second, postulate a third choice: On any round, rather than playing "close" or "open," any oligarch can propose to expel another oligarch. This proposal eliminates the targeted oligarch if all others play "expel"; it fails otherwise.[10] The cost of playing "expel," however, is that the oligarch cannot simultaneously play "close," does not cue the enforcers to repress on that round, and therefore cannot play "expel" all the time without the polity reverting to democracy. It was this option, of course, that was successfully used against Yeltsin in October 1987.

While an unmodified Oligarch's Dilemma makes nondemocracy implausible, the possibility of retaliation by playing "expel" makes transitions to democracy unlikely. It eliminates the foreseeable endpoint for each individual oligarch, since any oligarch who plays "open" will ordinarily encounter a play of "expel" from every other oligarch on the next round, as they are otherwise eliminated in the following round when the populace enters on the side of the oligarch who first invites them into politics. Thus nondemocracy will ordinarily be a stable equilibrium, since by assumption all oligarchs survive longer under "all close" than under "all open" and the opportunity for any oligarch to end the game by playing "open" is foreclosed by the possibility of expulsion. Yet in this modified version, transitions to democracy are possible. The equilibrium can suddenly shift to "all-open" if it ever occurs that after a play of "open" the other oligarchs cannot agree on "expel." This case might arise because authoritarian oligarchies are dependent on masking their internal divisions by a show of submission to a supreme arbiter who reconciles their internal conflicts. If for some reason they are unable to agree on whom to appoint to that position, the incumbent may be safe from plays of "expel." In the Soviet case, it was Gorbachev rather than Yeltsin who initiated the transformation of discourse represented by the strategy of "open." Gorbachev was safe from expulsion by a majority of the Politburo, if such a majority against him existed, as long as the leading contenders to replace him, Egor Ligachev and Nikolai Ryzhkov, were mutually unacceptable to one another and each commanded enough support in the Central Committee to block each other's election.[11]

In short, competition within the elite engenders the shift from despotic to democratic cues by offering a reward, the elimination of rivals, to any contestant for power who shifts from the discourse of nondemocracy to the discourse of democracy. Because despotic contestants retaliate by expelling from the contest any contestant who tries to take advantage of this option, nondemocracy is normally stable. But in any contest there is at least a small probability that the various contestants' probability of winning will be nearly equal, and when that circumstance arises, one or more contestants may be able to exploit disagreement among rivals to safely take advantage of the option of inviting the general population to take sides in the political contest. Then to protect themselves, the rest of the erstwhile oligarchs must also seek support within the population, and the discourse of all contestants suddenly shifts from despotic toward democratic. If they all shift, the one who ultimately receives popular support may be the oligarch who has moved first, has taken the greatest risks, or has moved most fully. Thus Yeltsin rather than Gorbachev ended up as the ultimate winner, even though the strategy of opening politics to the public, under the name of glasnost, did succeed for Gorbachev in eliminating his Politburo rivals by 1990.[12]

Applicability Outside Russia

If discursive theory explained political developments only in Russia, it would have no merit as a theory. For any theory to hold, it must be capable of generating hypotheses that hold uniformly under specifiable conditions. Such a hypothesis from discursive theory concerns the relationship between discourse and democracy. Every undemocratic discourse should produce texts that signal the difference between the identities of rulers and ruled, excluding the ruled from a positive political identity, while every transition to democracy should follow a rapprochement with the vernacular—that is, adoption for political use of one or more of the languages most widely spoken among the population living under authoritarian rule. The evidence available to test this hypothesis is, unfortunately, seriously incomplete. For very many cases there is no evidence at all. For others, the evidence is often merely anecdotal. Here I can show only that very many cases correspond to the hypothesis. I know of no exceptions.

Undemocratic discourses fall into four categories. First, by far the most common language of rule in undemocratic regimes is a language foreign to the population. Ordinarily this is the native language of conquerors, as in the cases of European colonialism in Asia, Africa, and America, Amharic in the former Ethiopia, or Arabic across much of the Islamic world. But quite often rulers whose own native language is the vernacular consciously adopt some prestigious foreign language to set themselves apart from the local population. A striking example is the Magyar magnates' decision to exclude any language but Latin from their Diet, courts, and administration (Kann 1950, 116–23).

Second, a variant on the theme of adopting a foreign language wholesale has been the introduction of foreign usages to elaborate a distinctive "register" of a native language. After English was introduced in 1362 as the political language of England, replacing Norman French despite the persistence of Latin in the law courts, English rulers found it necessary to maintain distinctiveness by increased borrowing of learned Latin and Greek terms (normally through French), which continued until the eighteenth century to be used according to Latin and Greek syntax (Nist 1966, 158–59). Because instruction in Latin and Greek was confined to the public schools at which the sons of the elite were educated, only the rulers and their enforcers obtained the education necessary to speak and write what was known as proper English. Until 1815 Parliament observed a rule of rejecting all petitions not written in this register of English (Smith 1984, 30–34). Other examples of this kind include the *usul i-kalem*—the "bureaucratic style," in which the Ottoman empire was administered, that featured a heavy admixture of Persian and Arabic terms, each declined according to the syntax of origin (Lewis 1968, 426–31)—and, of course, the Russian of both czarist and imperial officialdom, which was marked by calques of Greek terms borrowed into Russian from Church Slavonic (Chernov 1984, 86, 102).

Where rulers eschew the device of adopting foreign languages or borrowing foreign elements, they rely instead on what linguists call "diglossia"—the division of language between "high" and "low" variants. Either may provide a language of rule, although it may be more common for rulers to seize the high version. The most famous case of rulers using "high" is, of course, Javanese, spoken in a society whose nobles confined themselves to an elaborate form known as *krama* that was not even taught to peasants speaking the "low" variant *ngoko* (Errington 1985). Greek offers a parallel case. When the Greek rebellion against Ottoman rule succeeded, a debate arose as to whether to adopt as the language of politics either the contemporary demotic, spoken by the population, or the ancient classical Greek, spoken by no one. A compromise was reached on a variant known as *Katharevousa*, an invented standard that mixed contemporary Greek with classical elements declined according to classical grammar and limited willingness to take sides in politics by signaling the elevated status and educational attainment of those who spoke about politics (Frangoudaki 1992).

Democratic political discourse invariably identifies politicians with the population—in almost every case by conforming to the vernaculars spoken by the population. Again far from every case has been studied, but various independent commentaries on the speech of politicians in democracy do note the ordinariness of their language. The linguist Michael Geis (1987, 8) writes that "the politically most efficacious language will be not exceptional language of the sort that attracts the attention of those interested in double-talk, for instance, but rather it will be quite ordinary language." The political scientist Murray Edelman (1988, 111) describes electoral language as "banal." As the text linguist Teun Van Dijk told a July 1997 conference, the main obstacle to analyzing the discourse of electoral politics has been its linguistic "non-uniqueness." Students of French campaigning have noted the confinement of candidate vocabularies to the most common French words (Cotteret et. al. 1976, 50–51), while analysts of Swedish political discourse describe its "ordinariness" (Svensson 1997) and the prevalence of "everyday communicative formats" (Economou 1997, 4). Where democracy exists in multilingual societies, politicians either interchangeably use all the widely spoken vernaculars (as in Switzerland, Belgium, or Canada) or communicate with each other in some neutral "link" language not among the vernaculars (such as English in India) while using their respective vernaculars to communicate to constituents (Laitin 1992, 38–45).

Not only do existing democracies practice politics in ordinary language. Multiple cases can be cited in which democratic transitions introduce sweeping linguistic reforms, founder where the rapprochement with the vernacular remains insufficient, and reintroduce linguistic distinctiveness with a reversion to nondemocracy. In France, Richelieu having established the Academie Française for the express purpose of devising an official French that would be identifiably separate from the various patois spoken by the king's subjects, the French revolutionaries disestablished it in favor of the common parlance. But the collision between the revolutionaries' desire to impose a uniform French and many citizens' desire to conduct politics in the variety of regional dialects and foreign languages (Basque, Italian, Spanish, German, Dutch, Breton) led the revolutionaries into the fatal error of reestablishing an elevated French that was then adopted by Napoléon's court as a new language of rule (Grillo 1989). In Turkey, Kemal Atatürk established a language commission to expunge the Persian and Arabic elements marking the Ottoman "bureaucratic style." Since the democratic element in his reforms gave way to military rule, the subsequent adoption of a democratic constitution in 1945 necessitated a second language reform in order to purge the recent bureaucratic encroachments on the Turkish vernacular (Lewis 1968).

In the North American colonies the revolutionary orator Patrick Henry challenged the King's English with "syntax and pronunciation often falling below the line separating the educated from the uneducated," while Tom Paine wrote *Common Sense* in a "billingsgate" that stimulated widespread protest against refinement in speech (Cmiel 1990, 50–52). But seeking to reestablish social order after the revolution, the framers of the Constitution deliberately limited occupants of the powerful new presidency to a "constitutional" rhetoric requiring tutelage of the citizenry in constitutional principle and prohibiting identification with citizens (Tulis 1987). In England the campaign for extension of the franchise was led by the linguist Horne Tooke, who challenged the claim, by which the rulers justified their right to rule, that because each word corresponded to some reality, those with the greatest knowledge of words were also those best able to know the state of things. Pointing out simply that prepositions correspond to no things, Horne Tooke devised a new grammar for men excluded from politics who found in the grammar the linguistic resources for formulation of their claims to voting rights (Smith 1984). Their initial triumph, the Reform Act of 1832, led directly to composition of a New English Dictionary that overthrew the previous Latin and Greek standards.

In Greece the overthrow of the colonels led the new democratic government to introduce a language law in 1976 requiring all public documents to be written in demotic, not in the *Katharevousa* required by the colonels even though they were themselves insufficiently educated to speak it correctly (Frangoudaki 1992). In Haiti a democratic movement shifted from the metropolitan French, used even under Papa Doc, to the Creole speech of the population (Valdman 1988). Postwar German writers described their language as "dirty," "sick," or "raped," and they self-consciously sought to devise alternatives to Nazi locutions (Widmer 1966). The first presidential candidate in Mexico to defeat a candidate of the ruling PRI, Vicente Fox, used a vernacular that supporters of the incumbent party dismissed as "vulgar" language.

Completing these illustrations, we should note that these examples of nondemocracy's association with linguistic distinctiveness and democracy's association with the vernacular raise an otherwise puzzling question that discursive theory resolves. The question is this: Why should rulers pay the cost of learning, let alone devising, a distinctive language of rule? Of course where rulers establish themselves by conquering a population speaking a foreign language, it is cheaper for them to govern in their native language than to learn that of their subjects. But why do Greeks devise and study *Katharevousa* when the demotic is available to them for free? Why does Louis XIV spend money employing intellectuals to construct an artificial French distinguished solely by "purity" from the French vernacular of his time? If a discourse that cues a distinctive political identity bifurcates society into agents and victims of repression, then this otherwise puzzling question has an answer. Undemocratic rule is maintainable only by repression, which can occur only if some persons identify themselves as its agents and other persons as its victims. This provides the incentive for authoritarians to learn and even to devise distinctive discourses of rule.

Some Russian Tests

Discursive theory hypothesizes that the political discourse of a nondemocracy cues recognition of a social identity bifurcated between rulers and ruled, while the discourse of democracy cues recognition of a shared social identity linking governors to governed. This general hypothesis should be testable by various methods currently used by social science—including both statistical and experimental tests. As an exploration of the plausibility of this hypothesis, I will report the results of two tests—one statistical analysis and one experiment. The first examines whether authoritarian Russian texts of the Soviet period create social distance between the elite "speaker" and popular "listeners." The second examines whether texts in the post-Soviet period lead "listeners" to take sides with one or the other "speaker."

From Communist to Democratic Russian

Discursive theory predicts that authoritarian communist Russian (not the Russian of contemporary communists competing in elections) not only should be distinguishable from the Russian vernacular (*literaturnyi russkii iazyk*) but also should be so configured as to communicate the separateness of its speakers. The propensity to communicate separateness can be measured by examining the *iconicity* of authoritarian, transitional, and electoral Russian. In linguistics, "iconicity" refers to any feature of language that replicates in linguistic form the meaning that the utterance is designed to convey. One example of iconicity is correspondence of the temporal or linear order of clauses to the chronological sequence of the events described by those clauses. Another is the striking cross-linguistic regularity with which speakers and hearers use the length of utterances as an index of the social distance between them, with longer utterances signifying less sharing of identity (Haiman 1985). The iconicity of social distance offered communist rulers an opportunity to speak a kind of Russian that would communicate the separation between rulers and ruled. If they used this opportunity, one should find that the transition to democracy began with a reduction of iconic distance in the speech of the Gorbachev leadership and that it has been virtually eliminated in the speech of post-Soviet electoral politicians.

One among many means of introducing iconic distance into texts is to increase the number of nouns in each clause. Sentence (1), pronounced by former first secretary of the Ukrainian Party Vladimir Shcherbitskii (and presented here only in translation), offers an example of the noun-rich style favored by authoritarian communist speakers:

TABLE 4.1
Decrease in Nouns Relative to Verbs

Type of Text	Nouns per Verb	F-Test of Difference Among Types of Texts (and Significance)	
		Transitional	Electoral
Authoritarian	3.4	14.92 (p = 0.0001)	35.92 (p = 0.00003)
Transitional	2.7	—	13.70 (p = 0.0002)
Electoral	2.0	—	—
Vernacular (Zasorina)	1.6	—	—

(1) The CC [a contraction of "Central Committee"] of our party and the government are engaged daily with issues of fuller satisfaction of growing demands and requirements of the population.

Sentence (1) achieves noun-richness by various techniques. It displays doubling (also common in Nazi German), or use of two synonymous nouns where one would suffice: "demands and requirements." It also displays nominalization, or use of noun forms where verb forms are possible, such as "with issues of fuller satisfaction" instead of "with issues that promise to satisfy more fully." A clause is minimally defined by the presence of a single verb phrase (consisting of one or several verb forms, most often one) specifying an action or condition and linking one or two nouns (or noun substitutes, such as pronouns) specifying the participants in the action or condition. Because hearers and readers expect to encounter, on average, fewer than two nouns in association with every verb phrase, adding nouns to clauses confronts audiences with longer than expected utterances. The ratio of nouns to verbs in a text is therefore one index of iconic distance. Although texts can be iconically distancing in the absence of an increase of nouns relative to verbs, use of this device is necessarily a sign of the presence of iconic distancing.

Table 4.1 shows the ratio of nouns to verbs in fifty texts by Politburo members from the extended Brezhnev era (1964–84), fifty texts by members of the Gorbachev Politburo from the transitional year 1989, and fifty texts by post-Soviet electoral politicians across the political spectrum. The table also presents a ratio calculated from a count of nouns and verbs conducted by a team of Soviet linguists examining other Russian texts. In order to test differences between periods, the table also shows the result of F-tests of the difference of means. As the theory predicts, as democratization proceeded in the Soviet Union and Russia, political leaders decreased iconic distancing, until in post-Soviet democratic Russia, iconic distancing in political language converged toward the distance customary in texts of all kinds. The difference among periods is highly significant, with at most a .0002 probability that the responses are drawn from the same distribution.

A second indicator of iconic distance is avoidance of the so-called deictic center, the pronominal point of reference at which a given language locates the self. Russian like English places the self at the first-person singular, "I," *ia*. The more a speaker avoids the first-person singular in favor of other pronouns, the more distancing the speaker becomes. As the "I-thou" of a conversation between familiars is replaced by a dialogue between a collectivity ("we") and the individual hearer, or as statements are attributed to a person or collectivity not even present (i.e., in the third-person singular or plural) or to an impersonal agent (third-person impersonal) (Diez 1986, 229–30), iconic distancing increases. Sentence (2), taken from a speech by former general secretary Brezhnev demanding more effective research from the Academy of Sciences, exemplifies how expectations that could have been expressed as personal wants were transposed onto an impersonal agent, in this case the Communist Party (again I give only the translation).

(2) The party summons you to this, comrades, it expects this of you.

As general secretary, Brezhnev certainly wielded the authority to have said: "I demand this of you, I expect it of you" had an impersonal discourse not served the necessity of distancing. The audience for his speech, of course, was not limited to the members of the Academy and high party officials who directly witnessed it. It was also the enforcers and the larger population who did or could encounter it in *Pravda*. To this larger audience his usage communicated distancing of the rulers from the ruled and a separate identity available for enforcers to adopt.

Table 4.2 shows how Soviet authoritarian speakers strenuously avoided the first-person singular, how the frequency of the first-person singular increased during the transition to democracy, and how the frequency became comparable to ordinary Russian usage in the electoral era. Once again, according to the F-tests the difference among periods is highly significant.

In short, these (and other) iconic indicators of linguistic distancing were strongly marked in Soviet authoritarian Russian, began to lose their predominance in the Russian of the Gorbachev Politburo, and disappeared from post-Soviet electoral Russian. In any language, iconic distancing communicates to the audience that speakers choose to represent themselves as bearing a distinctive social identity purposefully dissociated from that of the audience. The decision to avoid iconic distancing (whether

TABLE 4.2

Decrease in Ratio of Third-Person Singular and Plural to First-Person Singular

Type of Text	Ratio	F-Test of Difference Among Types of Texts (and Significance)	
		Transitional	Electoral
Authoritarian	9.8	10.26 (p = 0.0009)	44.96 (p = 0.00003)
Transitional	4.5	—	15.00 (p = 0.0001)
Electoral	2.0	—	—
Vernacular (Zasorina)	1.8	—	—

conscious or not) communicates to the audience that it shares a common identity with the speaker. If audiences who share an identity with the speaker will sacrifice in order to spread the perceived distance between the speaker and the rivals of the speaker, while audiences cued to recognize dissociation from the speaker will avoid taking sides in politics, both the distancing speech of Soviet authoritarians and the closure with the audience by Russian electoral politicians serve their respective purposes of discouraging or encouraging people to take sides. For the Gorbachev Politburo, on the other hand, a speech that neither preserved the former distance nor closed the gap with the Russian-speaking population both demoralized the agents of repression, by removing the cues that had formerly enabled them to recognize the separate identity of the rulers, and simultaneously left the leadership vulnerable to challenges mounted by those who positioned themselves closer to the vernacular. A vital finding here, of course, is that authoritarian discourse began to dissolve under Gorbachev, even before Russia became a democracy.

In short, communist Russian represented a discourse distinct from vernacular Russian. Transitional Russian began a rapprochement with the vernacular—a rapprochement that preceded the elimination of penalties for taking sides in politics. In the post-Soviet era, electoral Russian became nearly indistinguishable from ordinary language.

Taking Sides in Russian Politics

Discursive theory claims that changes in discourse move people from passivity to activity. Since empirical evidence measuring popular reactions to texts during the previous periods cannot be collected after the fact, and the critical changes in Russia took place a decade ago, I have turned to experimental techniques that engage Russian respondents in order to test this claim. Specifically, my Russian colleagues Valery Chervyakov and Pavel Parshin and I conducted an experiment designed to test whether exposure to authoritarian speeches would decrease respondents' political affiliation with the "speaker," while exposure to electoral speeches would increase it. In the experiment, each respondent read political speeches and commented on their meaning. We measured the respondents' perceptions of difference in social identity between the speaker and themselves by (1) whether the respondents distinguished between the texts used as cues in the experiment or saw them as indistinguishable and (2) whether respondents took sides by volunteering affiliative responses. We expected that when texts cue people to recognize an opposing social identity that divided rulers from ruled, awareness of differences between texts should diminish. We also assumed that a person taking sides with a speaker would respond to the texts with affiliative statements, while a person refusing to take the speaker's side would respond with disaffiliative statements. We also expected that texts from one segment of the contemporary spectrum—either the "democrats" and "centrists" controlling the government, or their "patriotic" opponents—would draw affiliative responses, while the other side might draw disaffiliative responses, depending on the popularity of the respective sides in the population from which the respondents were drawn.

The experiment was conducted by teams of Russian interviewers in Moscow and Voronezh in fall 1993. Voronezh was selected as a city where the patriots were likely to be popular, in contrast to prodemocratic or centrist Moscow (in 1993). Respondents were randomly selected.[13] Respondents were then randomly assigned to read either (1) one of six authoritarian communist texts from the Brezhnev era; (2) one of six texts from the first full year of the Gorbachev leadership, 1986; (3) one of six texts, four communist and two democratic, from 1989; (4) one of six texts, three "democratic," one "centrist," and two "patriotic," from the post-Soviet electoral era. They were then asked to respond to deliberately vague questions intended to elicit, without suggesting, comments about the text. Their responses were written down by the interviewers, and pairs of blind coders were instructed how to code the resulting interview texts.[14]

The experiment produced two results. One result confirmed the prediction that cues to a distinctive identity that separates the "speaker" from the respondent would shift the respondent's perceptions from the differences between individual contestants for power to the differences between the respondent and the "speakers." The other confirmed the prediction that cues seeking to build identification between the "speaker" and re-

TABLE 4.3
Proportion of Respondents Saying Speeches of a Given Era Were "All Alike"
(or equivalent) (Means, Standard Deviations, and Number of Respondents)

	Location of Experiment		
Era of Speech	Moscow	Voronezh	Total
Brezhnev Period	.8	.43	.62
	(.40)	(.50)	(.49)
	N=60	N=60	N=120
Early Gorbachev Period	.72	.47	.59
	(.45)	(.50)	(.49)
	N=60	N=60	N=120
Transitional Period	.43	.18	.31
	(.50)	(.39)	(.46)
	N=60	N=60	N=120
Electoral Period	.35	.09	.19
	(.48)	(.29)	(.40)
	N=60	N=90	N=150
Total	.58	.27	.41
	(.49)	(.44)	(.49)
	N=240	N=270	N=510

spondent would lead the respondents to take sides—contingent on the
political preferences of speaker and respondent.

First, with regard to shifting perceptions of social identities, table 4.3
records evidence, spontaneously volunteered by the respondents and not
requested by the interviewers, that the authoritarian texts from the Brezhnev years and the early Gorbachev period cued recognition by the respondents of a distinctive social identity separating the "speaker" and the respondent and that neither the transitional texts (communist or
democratic) nor the electoral texts cued the same recognition. Social identity theory predicts that when individuals encounter cues to a distinctive
social identity, they respond by becoming less aware of individual differences among speakers and more aware of group stereotypes. When these
cues are absent, respondents become more aware of individual differences
among "speakers." Table 4.3 reports the proportion of respondents in
Moscow and Voronezh who spontaneously described the speeches of a
given era as "all alike" (or some equivalent). As table 4.3 shows, such
statements remain stable in response to the texts from the Brezhnev and
early Gorbachev eras in both cities and decrease sharply in response to

TABLE 4.4

Analysis of Variance: Proportion Volunteering That Speeches Are "All Alike," by Era and by City

	F	Significance
Variance by Era of Speech	26.92	0.00005
Variance by City of Experiment	51.99	0.00005
Interaction	0.51	0.677

the transitional and post-Soviet eras. Evidently respondents perceived the Soviet texts as conforming to a stereotype and the post-Soviet texts as individuated. Even if these perceptions were, on average, accurate (and "all alike" is surely an exaggeration of the manifest similarities among texts of the Soviet period), it nevertheless is significant for a discursive theory that speakers of the Soviet period spoke so as to encourage, and speakers of the transitional and post-Soviet eras spoke so as to discourage, a response so strongly associated with perception of an opposing social identity. As the analysis of variance reported in table 4.4 shows, neither the differences between the earlier and later periods, nor Moscow's greater tendency to produce these responses, are conceivably attributable to random variation. (The difference between cities, however, may be attributable to interviewer effects, as local teams performed the study in each location.) This division of social identities and failure to distinguish differences among rulers also has implications for the second experiment—on taking sides.

Second, with regard to taking sides, experimental technique cannot directly monitor the impact of all textual cues that a person would encounter in a social setting, or the full range of behaviors that these might elicit.[15] What can be tested, however—and with controls for the effect of other influences—is the influence that varying linguistic cues have on the attitudinal correlates of taking sides. The second experiment examines whether exposure to a given text then cues the production of attitudes that—if rehearsed often enough over time—would turn into a predisposition to take sides with one or another contestant for political power. Table 4.5 reports a test of the effect of linguistic cues on attitudinal correlates of taking sides—that is, whether exposure to a political text generates affiliative or disaffiliative responses.[16] Such responses would either encourage or discourage a citizen from joining a party or an organization with a political agenda. We classified responses as affiliative if the respondent expressed trust, found the text meaningful, believed it dealt with issues

TABLE 4.5

Mean Number of Affiliative and Disaffiliative Comments per Respondent
(Maximum = 5) (Means, Standard Deviations, and Number of Respondents)

Era of Speeches	Affiliative Comments Location of Experiment			Disaffiliative Comments Location of Experiment		
	Moscow	Voronezh	Total	Moscow	Voronezh	Total
Brezhnev Period	1.18	2.00	1.59	2.82	2.08	2.45
	(1.76)	(1.90)	(1.90)	(1.90)	(1.85)	(1.90)
	N = 60	N = 60	N = 120	N = 60	N = 60	N = 120
Early Gorbachev	.92	1.77	1.84	3.13	2.15	2.64
Period	(1.57)	(1.84)	(1.75)	(1.78)	(1.83)	(1.86)
	N = 60	N = 60	N = 120	N = 60	N = 60	N = 120
Transitional	1.88	1.62	1.75	2.02	2.12	2.07
Period	(2.08)	(1.53)	(1.83)	(1.85)	(1.52)	(1.69)
	N = 60	N = 60	N = 120	N = 60	N = 60	N = 120
Electoral Period	2.45	1.34	1.83	1.28	2.2	1.79
(Democratic or	(1.87)	(1.67)	(1.84)	(1.28)	(1.65)	(1.56)
Centrist)	N = 40	N = 50	N = 90	N = 40	N = 50	N = 90
Electoral Period	1.35	3.53	2.8	2.65	.83	1.43
(Patriotic)	(1.79)	(1.91)	(2.12)	(1.66)	(1.43)	(1.73)
	N = 20	N = 40	N = 60	N = 20	N = 40	N = 60
Total	1.51	1.97	1.75	2.43	1.94	2.17
	(1.89)	(1.88)	(1.90)	(1.86)	(1.73)	(1.81)
	N = 240	N = 270	N = 510	N = 240	N = 270	N = 510

relevant to its time, thought it interesting, or voiced approval or agreement. Responses were disaffiliative if the opposite opinion was expressed on any of these scores.

The first three columns in table 4.5 report the proportion of affiliative responses for Moscow and Voronezh to various kinds of texts, while the last three columns report the disaffiliative responses in each city. These show the same pattern. In Moscow the democrats and centrists from the electoral era receive the most affiliative and fewest disaffiliative comments, while in Voronezh the nationalists from the electoral era receive the most affiliative and fewest disaffiliative comments. Table 4.6, reporting the analysis of variance for the experimental results shown in table 4.5, again leaves no doubt that none of this can be dismissed as simple random variation, although again experimenter effects cannot be excluded from having affected the difference between cities.

TABLE 4.6

Analysis of Variance: Affiliative and Disaffiliative Comments, by Era and by City
(Means and Standard Deviations Shown in Table 4.5)

	Affiliative		Disaffiliative	
	F	Signif	F	Signif
Variance by Era of Speech	3.84	0.0044	5.40	0.0003
Variance by City of Experiment	8.59	0.0035	9.79	0.0001
Interaction	9.11	0.00005	7.41	0.00005

The persuasiveness of these findings may of course be susceptible to the objection that Russians in 1993 were being asked to respond to political cues from four, seven, and as many as thirty years earlier. Perhaps much changed in the way Russians read old texts in 1993 from the way they had read the same texts in the past. There is no way of knowing, since we cannot go back. But the coders successfully complied with an explicit instruction not to code as disaffiliative any comments by respondents that the text was old or out of date. As the Voronezh results show, it was perfectly possible for groups of Russians to express more affiliation with, and less disaffiliation from, Brezhnev-era texts than they did in response to texts by contemporary democrats or centrists. In a country where politics during its first eight years after secession from the Soviet Union turned on the choice between an authoritarian Soviet past and a democratic present and future, comparison of texts from the present with those of the past may not be a political irrelevancy. Moreover, the emotional intensity of responses to Brezhnev-era texts—words such as "repulsive" or "nauseating," or conversely, "it brings me joy"—does not suggest that these texts had lost their relevance for Russian readers as of 1993. Even if one does accept that the difference in response to the textual cues is affected by the obsolescence of the authoritarian texts, still discursive theory would have been refuted had some form of electoral text not drawn more affiliative and fewer disaffiliative responses than the authoritarian texts.[17]

Experimental procedure is a causal test. Random selection and random assignment of respondents guarantees, at least in the abstract, that other differences among respondents will not systematically bias the results of the experiment. The respondents in this experiment were representative of the populations of their respective cities, with the exception of oversampling of educated respondents, which proved unrelated to the test variable. The groups of Russians do not vary across test conditions, and the structural conditions in which they exist do not vary either. The *only* difference in the experiment between the groups of respondents in each city was that each group read texts of a different kind. The group reading authoritarian communist texts disaffiliated in Moscow and was neutral in Voronezh, while each group reading electoral text found some kind of texts with which to affiliate. The only cause of the shift from disaffiliation to affiliation in the experiment was change in discursive cues.

Implications

The theory of democracy is in crisis. Analysts of democracy continue to direct their attention to structural variables that are already known not to correspond to outcomes across cases. Russia is prominent among the cases that have induced the crisis. The failure of social science to predict the fall of the Soviet regime is evidence of the crisis. Contrary to the stereotype of area specialists divorced from theory, Soviet specialists knew and applied the existing theory of democracy. They validly concluded that the Soviet economic slowdown did not presage democracy, that Soviet political culture was antithetical to democracy, that the Soviet Union lacked a bourgeoisie, that the Communist regime had prevented society from organizing autonomously, that factions in Politburo struggles would not attract support from an indifferent population. These valid conclusions led to the theoretically warranted prediction that the Soviet Union was headed for increased repression. This prediction was wrong. It is the theory that is to blame, not the knowledge of the case or the application of the theory.

Discourse analysis offers an alternative to all the theories of democracy that have been discredited by the Russian case and by other cases in the so-called third wave, as well as by earlier cases that have always been anomalous, particularly India. The variables of discourse and identity are new to the empirical analysis of democracy. A discursive theory holds that nondemocracy changes to democracy when political discourse ceases to cue recognition of social identity bifurcated into rulers (including their enforcers) and ruled and begins to cue recognition of social identity shared between governors and governed. The privative opposition, cued by undemocratic discourse between a positive identity assigned to the rulers (and their enforcers) and a negative identity assigned to the ruled, motivates the enforcers to engage in repression as a means of differentiating themselves from the ruled. The latter are deprived of any motivation to take political action, for there is no perceptible side in the contest for the population to join and no contestant emitting cues to identification that would motivate people to side with that contestant. Challenged by the human propensity to develop positive identity, including that arrived at through political action, this privative opposition sustains nondemocracy only as long as the enforcers of rule selectively repress those individuals who do or might communicate a positive identity to the population. Should political discourse change from maintaining the bifurcation of social identity to transcending it in favor of the assignment of positive political identity throughout a population, the enforcers lose motivation to repress at the same time as the population gains motivation to take sides. The result is a collapse of the horizontal social cleavage formerly separating rulers above from ruled below and its replacement by one or more vertical cleavages. The people, their attention no longer drawn by discourse to group differences between themselves and their rulers, become more aware of individual differences among contestants for political power. The contestants for power, themselves aware that popular appreciation of the differences among them can be a resource in their contest, establish the electoral institutions definitive of democracy. This theory attributes a lot of explanatory power to discourse, but the structural variables to which democracy is commonly ascribed are known not to be powerful at all.

Because discourse, as a set of procedures for composing and interpreting texts, must change whenever people compose and interpret texts sufficiently discrepant with an existing discourse, and because a wide variety of texts can be composed and interpreted in any given social, cultural, or economic conditions, the emergence of democracy does not depend directly on such structural conditions. Of course, there may be indirect links from structural conditions through discourse to democracy. Whether democracy emerges, and particularly whether it survives, depends on how political contestants respond to linguistic or discursive diversity. To the extent that social, cultural, and economic conditions motivate people to reduce linguistic or discursive fragmentation or to learn languages suitable for communication between discursively defined groups, structural conditions may indirectly make the linguistic or discursive situation more propitious to democracy. This is the reason for the one really compelling observation in favor of modernization theory—that all the democracies are found very late in history, after economic advance has made it both possible and desirable to pay for schooling that greatly reduces linguistic fragmentation.

Discursive theory has the merit of explaining a wide range of observations whose causes are not obvious from the point of view of the material sociology that undergirds many existing theories. In numerous cases undemocratic rulers have paid costs to establish artificial languages of rule, the existence of which is unnecessary if social differentiation or institutional incentives are sufficient to maintain their rule. These artificial languages of rule do not seem to exist in democracies. In the Soviet case, authoritarian communist rulers practiced a quantitatively distinctive discourse whose iconic features distanced the speaker from the population by elongating utterances and by removing the speaker from the deictic center. Both characteristics diminished as democratization began and have virtually disappeared from post-Soviet electoral texts. Structural conditions provide no grounds at all for making any predictions about length of utterances or frequency of use of the word *ia*. In Russia, of course, political texts have become shorter as the cost of newsprint has become more constraining, but in other democracies political texts have become shorter as the cost of newsprint has become *less* constraining. Russians respond to the distancing communist texts by stereotyping them and by disaffiliation or neutrality, while they respond to the electoral texts by distinguishing between types of political discourse and finding one that they are more willing to affiliate with and less likely to disaffiliate from.

Discursive theory offers an opportunity to overcome the crisis of democratic theory by revising Marx's dictum, which for more than century has guided social scientists. "Men make their own history," Marx (1869, 15) wrote, "but they do not make it just as they please; they do not make it under circumstances chosen by themselves, but under circumstances directly encountered, given and transmitted from the past." It is his concept of "circumstances," now known as "structure," that has led theorists of democracy into the trap in which they currently futilely writhe. A discursive theory emancipates the study of democracy from the dead hand of "structure." Democracy's emergence in Russia attests that persons do make their own identities, not of course just as each person pleases, but as they collectively choose by exchanging texts among themselves and jointly compiling a political discourse that defines whether they will bifurcate between rulers and ruled or share the social identity of citizenship. The identity that results in turn shapes the history of persons.

FIVE

DEFINING DEMOCRATIC CONSOLIDATION

Stephen E. Hanson

THE POLITICAL DYNAMICS of the postcommunist Russian Federation pose challenging theoretical problems for comparativists interested in democratization. On the one hand, during the first decade after the collapse of communism, reasonably competitive elections and referenda on issues of major social importance became a standard feature of Russian political life. Nationwide voting took place in nearly every year from 1990 through 2000; the president, parliamentary deputies, and almost all regional governors were forced to pass the test of electoral competition. The Russian constitution adopted in December 1993, despite its well-publicized flaws and frequent proposals for its reform, endured into the new century. In addition, basic democratic freedoms such as freedom of speech, freedom of religion, and freedom of assembly—although there were certainly serious problems in these areas as well—were more secure than at almost any time in Russia's previous history. Considering the intense skepticism about the prospects for Russian democracy expressed by analysts emphasizing the substantial institutional obstacles to democratic institution-building in the post-Soviet setting (Jowitt 1992b) and Russia's supposed cultural bias toward authoritarianism (Steele 1994; McDaniel 1997), this outcome must be acknowledged and explained.

On the other hand, post–Soviet Russian democracy clearly continued to be characterized by a high degree of uncertainty and instability. The violent outcome of the initial struggle between Yeltsin and the Congress of People's Deputies in October 1993 left an enduring legacy of cynicism toward and distrust of the executive. Party building in general was very limited, and civil society remained weak (Hanson and Kopstein 1997). The wide scope for presidentialism allowed by the constitution encouraged Boris Yeltsin to ignore the will of parliament on key political and economic issues and push unpopular measures into law by decree. Continuing controversies about central constitutional issues, such as the nature of Russian federalism, the role of the Constitutional Court, and the relative powers of the president and the two houses of parliament, undermined public confidence in the basic legal framework of the regime. A wide range of prominent Russian politicians, such as Lebed, Luzhkov, Zyuganov, and Zhirinovsky, have questioned the legitimacy of the current international boundaries of the Russian state. An economic crisis lasting almost the entire decade became identified in the public mind with "Westernization," significantly eroding public support for democratic values (Fleron and Ahn 1998). Finally, public revelations about political corruption at the highest levels of Russian politics—including instances of electoral fraud that may have saved Vladimir Putin from a second round of voting in the 2000 presidential elections—have called into question the legitimacy of the existing electoral regime (*Moscow Times*, 9 September 2000).

How should comparativists make sense of this mixed picture in order to classify the post–Soviet Russian regime in theoretical terms? Early optimistic theorizing about postcommunist democratization tended to assume that successful "transitions" to electoral rule would be followed by relatively smooth, rapid, and comprehensive democratic legitimation (Di Palma 1990). More recently, given the obvious deficiencies of Russia's government when judged according to modern democratic ideals, pessimistic scholars have concluded that the Russian Federation is no more than a "facade democracy" based on "institutional mimicry" of the West (Jowitt 1996a, 4; Brovkin 1996). Neither optimists nor pessimists, however, explain why electoral contestation continued to be so important in Russia while democratic institutions remained so weak.

The mixed performance of Russia's electoral regime has inspired a growing scholarly consensus that the Russian Federation during the 1990s was indeed a democracy—but one that remained very much "unconsolidated" (Shevtsova 1996; Fleron and Ahn 1998). Such a formulation is certainly intuitively appealing: It allows analysts to take Russian elections, parties, and campaigns seriously while bearing in mind the flaws and fragility of the electoral regime itself. Upon closer examination, however, simply to label Russia an "unconsolidated democracy" raises as many theoretical questions as it resolves. As Schedler (1998) has shown, the term "democratic consolidation" is used in several incompatible senses in the scholarly literature, reflecting diverse understandings of the nature of democracy itself. As the author puts it:

> [T]he study of democratic consolidation, at its current state of conceptual confusion, is condemned to stagnation. The aspiring subdiscipline of "consolidology" is anchored in an unclear, inconsistent, and unbounded concept, and thus is not anchored at all, but drifting in murky waters. The use of one and the same term for vastly different things only simulates a shared common language; in fact, the reigning conceptual disorder is acting as a powerful barrier to scholarly communication, theory building, and the accumulation of knowledge. (Schedler 1998, 92)

But Schedler's own proposed solution to this problem, to use the term "consolidation" solely to "refer to expectations of regime continuity—and to nothing else" (p. 103), begs the most important question we would expect a theory of democratic consolidation to answer: Just how is it possible to judge whether a particular democracy is likely to endure or break down?

In this essay I will argue that it is indeed analytically useful for comparativists to categorize the contemporary Russian regime as an "unconsolidated democracy"—once the concepts of "democracy" and "consolidation" are defined precisely and given a proper theoretical foundation. However, most of the existing literature fails to recognize that an adequate theory of democratic consolidation must logically be part of a more general theory of *regime* consolidation. Addressing this larger topic, in turn, requires an understanding of how new political institutions are originally generated in environments of widespread social turbulence—but strangely enough, this is a problem most democratic theorists tend to assume away. Instead, taking the strongly institutionalized liberal capitalist regimes of Western Europe and North America as their point of comparison, analysts of democracy working within such diverse paradigms as modernization theory and rational choice theory end up setting impossibly high standards for the consolidation of new democracies. Given such standards, the finding of so many scholars that Russia's democracy is still "unconsolidated" as the twenty-first century dawns is both unsurprising and theoretically uninteresting.

In the following section of the essay, therefore, I sketch a proposal for how we might rethink the concept of democratic consolidation from an alternative, institutionalist point of view. I argue that regime consolidation should be defined as a situation in which the enforcers of state institutions can be counted upon with high probability to act in ways consistent with, and supportive of, formal institutional goals. Democratic consolidation, more specifically, can be said to occur when the staff of governing political parties, state bureaucracies, coercive apparatuses, and the judiciary consistently act to maintain or expand the functioning of electoral competition and legally defined citizenship rights. Such an alternative definition, I argue, helps to pinpoint the reasons for the divergent outcomes of democratization processes in Eastern and Central Europe as compared to most states of the former Soviet Union. In the Russian case, defining democratic consolidation as the dependable enforcement of democratic institutions would shift the analytic focus of democratic theorists from the problem of state-society relations in general to the more specific question of how dependable relationships between democratic elites and staffs might be forged under post-Soviet conditions.

Democratic Consolidation As a Change in Political Culture

Perhaps the most common way of thinking about the problem of democratic consolidation in the field of political science is to emphasize the need for a "political culture" and/or "civil society" supportive of democratic institutions. Larry Diamond, for example, defines consolidation as

> the process by which democracy becomes so broadly and profoundly legitimate among its citizens that it is very unlikely to break down. It involves behavioral and institutional changes that normalize democratic politics and narrow its uncertainty. This normalization requires the expansion of citizen access, development of democratic citizenship and culture, broadening of leadership recruitment and training, and other functions that civil society performs. (Diamond 1996, 238)

To be sure, Diamond cautions that the most important first step in building a strong democracy is the construction of strong institutions such as political parties and an unbiased judiciary; the presence of a civil society is "not decisive" in the early stages of democratization. Still, Diamond's vision of democratic consolidation implies a citizenry almost entirely oriented toward impersonal procedural rule. In this light, his gloomy prediction that given current social trends "many new democracies in Latin America, Eastern Europe, Asia, and Africa will probably break down in the medium to long run" suggests a judgment that only in the West does one find truly consolidated democracies (Ibid., 239).

Such an approach to defining democratic consolidation is rooted in the classic works of modernization theory, especially those of Parsons (1951), Almond and Verba (1963), and Eckstein (1966). Representative democracy, from this perspective, is basically a product of the general transformation of human societies from "tradition," based on communal identity, ascriptive status, particularism, and personal ties, to "modernity," based on individualism, achieved status, universalism, and impersonal procedures (Parsons 1951). The periodic selection of leaders by individual citizens voting under impersonal constitutional rules and the implementation of policies by these leaders in a manner consistent with the rule of law—both vital to the modern understanding of democratic politics—are held to be impossible within the context of agrarian societies based on solidary corporate groups. Thus, democratic institutions are thought to be viable only where such "modernizing" influences as industrialization, urbanization, Protestantism, and education have transformed traditional cultures sufficiently.

To be sure, there is by now a rather substantial literature demonstrating an undeniable empirical link between all the factors listed above and the existence of stable democratic regimes. A plethora of studies has replicated the original finding of Lipset (1960) that economic development and democracy are highly correlated. By itself, of course, this finding is compatible with alternative theoretical paradigms such as neo-Marxism, rational choice theory, and structuralism. However, Bollen (1979) also found a positive and significant correlation between the number of Protestants living in a country and the likelihood of democracy there, while Inglehart (1988) showed that popular satisfaction with government performance was significantly higher in Protestant European democracies than in non-Protestant ones. In addition, Rowen (1995) has shown that education levels and democracy are even more positively correlated than income and democracy. These empirical results have convinced a number of scholars that Parsons was correct in postulating the creation of a "modern" political culture as the key mechanism generating democratic stability.

Recently, adopting this reasoning, an increasing number of modernization theorists have been forced to conclude that democratic consolidation can only be achieved when a society's culture has been largely or even completely transformed in a "modern" direction. This idea, too, has its roots in Parsonian sociology, in which "system equilibrium" takes place only when the "cultural system" and "personality system" are largely in sync with the social system (Parsons 1951). Without a broader democratic culture, the reasoning goes, formal democratic institutions are likely to be undermined by particularism, corruption, and inconsistency in the application of laws. And since democratic institutions arose first in the West, the seemingly unavoidable implication is that global democratic consolidation requires universal cultural "Westernization."

Sometimes, this position is argued explicitly. Russell Bova, emphasizing that Freedom House analysts give Western democracies significantly higher average ratings on "liberty" than non-Western democracies, goes so far as to suggest that

> the relationship between democracy and Western culture at least raises the possibility that the correlation between democracy and liberty is spurious. Perhaps democracy and liberty are both products of Western culture, or, more to the point, perhaps democracy leads to liberty only in the specific cultural context of the West. The notion of cultural contingency is not far-fetched given that the emergence of the "democratic idea" in its modern form in the Europe of the Enlightenment was closely intertwined with—and, in fact, preceded by—the development of the doctrine of natural rights. (Bova 1997, 115)

Samuel Huntington's own standard for judging democratic consolidation—the famous "two-turnover test"—is not itself culturally defined; however, he clearly remains highly skeptical that "third wave democracies" will endure for long in non-Western "civilizations" (Huntington 1991, 1996):

> Modern democracy is a product of Western civilization. Its roots lie in the social pluralism, the class system, the civil society, the belief in the rule of law, the experience with representative bodies, the separation of spiritual and temporal authority, and the commitment to individualism that began to develop in Western Europe a millennium ago. In the seventeenth and eighteenth centuries, these legacies generated the struggles for political participation by the aristocrats and rising middle classes that produced nineteenth-century democratic development. These characteristics may individually be found in other civilizations, but together they have existed only in the West, and they explain why modern democracy is a child of Western civilization. (Huntington 1997, 6)

Francis Fukuyama (1995), too, claims that democratization in the non-Western world has largely taken place on the levels of "ideology" and "institutions"; democracy remains unstable there, he argues, due to insufficient modernization on the levels of "civil society" and "culture."

The idea that the development of a modern, essentially Western "culture" is the prerequisite to true democratic consolidation provides, it would appear, a rather simple explanation for Russian democracy's bumpy ride so far: namely, that the attempt to institutionalize democratic proceduralism in the postcommunist context was bound to encounter cultural resistance, given Russia's insufficient level of modernization. Thus, Huntington counsels supporters of global democracy to focus their attention on Latin America, whose culture "closely resembles Western culture"; Orthodox Christian countries should be given only secondary priority (Huntington 1997, 11). Similarly, Bova emphasizes that "Russia . . . has always been torn between East and West and between Slavophiles and Westernizers, giving rise to a culture that is less unambiguously Western than that of the Czechs, for example" (Bova 1997, 117). For this reason he cautions Westerners not to overemphasize pure democratic proceduralism in the Russian context. Russian democracy's best hope, he argues, is to reform the constitution to allow for stronger executive power; this might better fit a "political culture where the preference for order and 'governability' has always been and continues to be a central political and social value" (Bova 1998, 197). Even then, however, Bova expects the process of democratic cultural transformation to be at best a slow and arduous process. Harry Eckstein largely concurs with Bova's analysis, emphasizing that "short of extremely underdeveloped societies, it is hard to think of a less likely case for successful democratization than Russia" (Eckstein 1998, 376).

Given the continuing turbulence in the Russian Federation and the very real chance that its fledgling electoral democracy may fail, the cultural definition of democratic consolidation and accompanying Parsonian hypotheses concerning its absence in Russia have become increasingly widespread. Upon closer examination, however, modernization theory contains no compelling causal mechanism that might satisfactorily explain the cultural correlations it emphasizes. Indeed, the key forces of cultural modernization postulated by Parsons—industrialization, education, and urbanization—were all highly developed under the Soviet regime. Thus, only a decade ago modernization theorists were generally very enthusiastic about Russia's democratic prospects. During Gorbachev's perestroika, a number of scholars argued that these modernizing forces had generated a "civil society" that was forcing the Communist Party leadership to allow for democracy and liberty (Lewin 1988; Starr 1988; Hosking 1991). The collapse of the Soviet Union, too, was hailed as a "vindication of modernization theory" (Pye 1990; Fukuyama 1993). Early poll data showing widespread public approval of democratic values in post-Soviet states, especially among urbanized and educated sectors of the population, were seen as further empirical proof of the validity of modernization theory's claims (Reisinger, et. al. 1994). It is somewhat odd, then, to see so many modernization theorists claiming, just a few years later, that Russia's cultural "authoritarianism" is the chief obstacle to democratic consolidation.

In fact, none of the literature cited above makes more than a cursory attempt to explain why Russia, which from a Parsonian point of view is "certainly . . . a 'modern' country" (Eckstein 1998b, 375), should nonetheless now be considered culturally antimodern and antidemocratic. Having dispensed with the idea that economic development, education, and urbanization necessarily generate the civic individualism and proceduralism necessary for democratic consolidation, analysts utilizing the political culture approach end up embracing a reified and static understanding of both "Western" and "traditional" culture. Apparently, new democracies in countries that "missed out" on the Reformation, the Enlightenment, and Lockean liberalism—Russia among them—are doomed to remain perpetually unconsolidated.

Yet cultures evidently do change. We should recall that modernization theorists—in some cases, the same ones dubious about democracy in postcommunist Russia—were once equally skeptical about the prospects for the development of a "civic culture" and stable democracy in Catholic Southern Europe and post–Nazi Germany (Eckstein 1961; Almond and Verba 1963). Several countries whose intellectual traditions were central to the philosophical debates of the Enlightenment, including France and Germany, were ruled by monarchs, emperors, and dictators for many generations afterward. Protestantism, for that matter, hardly promoted procedural democracy for the first two centuries of its existence. If it now turns out that Stalinist industrialization and urbanization have also produced or reinforced an "antidemocratic" postcommunist culture in Russia, then evidently we need a new, non-Parsonian theory of the central mechanisms of cultural change in order to explain the empirical correlations between Protestantism, education, and development elsewhere. Until such mechanisms are specified and validated through scientific inquiry, it is premature, and perhaps even tautological, to ascribe the difficulties of democratic consolidation in the Russian Federation to deficiencies in Russian culture.

Democratic Consolidation As Acceptance of the "Rules of the Game"

As compared to cultural versions of modernization theory, rational choice theory appears at first glance to be far more flexible in allowing for the possibility of democratic consolidation in diverse social environments. Rational choice analysts take as their foundational assumption the view that every individual, regardless of his or her "cultural" setting, can be understood as a fundamentally self-interested rational actor. Wherever institutions—understood as the formal and informal "rules of the game" in a given society (North 1991)—tend to reward democratic behavior such as building parties, contesting elections, and obeying laws, and to punish antidemocratic behavior such as fomenting coups or insurrections, democracy as a system should remain stable. The primary problem for would-be democratizers, then, is to get the initial constitutional rules right. Democracy can be considered "consolidated" when political competition under these rules becomes "the only game in town" (Przeworski 1991).

The literature on democratic institutions analyzed from a rational choice point of view, starting with the seminal works of Downs (1957) and Riker (1962), is far too vast to summarize here. The idea that people are at least in some basic sense rational power seekers informs much of the contemporary analysis of the relative merits of parliamentarianism versus presidentialism, of proportional representation versus single-member districts, of federalism versus unitary states, and so on (Shugart and Carey 1992). In polities with long-established democratic institutions, rational choice institutionalism can lead to valuable insights and interesting empirical findings.

Attempts to explain how "rational actors" build new institutions in the first place, however, have been markedly less successful. In the context of the highly uncertain environment of postcommunist Russia, in particular, proposals for "constitutional engineering" (Ordeshook 1995; Ordeshook and Shvetsova 1997) run into an immediate theoretical difficulty: Why should any rational actor in the Russian Federation today remain bound by formal rules that others ignore and that may not exist at all in a few months' time? Indeed, sophisticated rational choice theorists have shown that institutions that enforce rules guaranteeing public order of any sort—democratic or otherwise—are themselves a "public good" that rational actors in situations of high uncertainty can never provide (Olson 1965; Taylor 1976; Elster 1989). No single individual by himself or herself can create stable political institutions, yet every individual benefits from the increased predictability and security provided by such institutions once they are established. Thus, rational actors should "free ride" on the efforts of others to enforce public order. Only those with sufficiently long time horizons can overcome the resulting collective action problem (Taylor 1987). Unfortunately, adopting a low rate of "time discounting" in an environment of rapid and turbulent change is itself ostensibly irrational (Hanson 1998). Rational choice theory, it seems, predicts that as long as high levels of social uncertainty persist, every political actor should choose to pursue short-run opportunistic goals rather than enforce procedures with integrity.

Of course, political uncertainty in some sense exists in established democracies as well. Indeed, Adam Przeworski, who has provided what is undoubtedly the most sophisticated theoretical explanation of how rational actors might choose to abide by democratic rules after a transition from authoritarian rule, has argued that democracy is tantamount to the "institutionalizing [of] uncertainty"—an agreement by powerful actors to abide by rules that may or may not bring them to power in any given time period (Przeworski 1991, 14). Such an agreement depends upon a perception on the part of key social interests that they are not permanently shut out of the power structure. If actors think that efforts to gain power that violate the democratic order face a real risk of punishment, even after electoral defeat they may well be willing to wait for future opportunities for electoral contestation. For these reasons, social policies in new democracies should be attentive to the concerns of those particularly badly affected by the predictable economic and social dislocations of democratic transition.

But even Przeworski's model of institutionalized uncertainty requires a greater degree of predictability than exists in a chaotic environment such as postcommunist Russia. This becomes clear once we examine Przeworski's definition of democratic consolidation in more detail:

Democracy is consolidated when under given political and economic conditions a particular system of institutions becomes the only game in town, when
no one can imagine acting outside the democratic institutions, when all the
loser wants to do is to try again within the same institutions under which
they have just lost. Democracy is consolidated when it becomes self-enforcing, that is, when all the relevant political forces find it best to continue to
submit their interests and values to the uncertain interplay of the institutions.
(Ibid., 26)

How do new democracies reach this point? Przeworski claims that the
institutions of democracy can become self-enforcing when they are understood not only as "rules of competition," but also as "codes of punishment" that mandate the sanctioning of those who violate democratic procedures:

To administer sanctions, actors must be able to undertake actions the effect of which is to lower the payoffs to others. Institutions enable such punishments and make them predictable; they have a priori rules according to which
punishments are meted out, the physical means of administering punishments, and the incentives for specialized agents to administer them.
(Ibid., 27)

Thus, it turns out that the institutionalization of democratic "uncertainty" nonetheless requires a very high level of certainty about the enforcement of laws against subversion. Yet the sorts of predictable institutional sanctioning bodies that enforce democratic laws in established
democracies are precisely what are lacking in most post-Soviet countries
today. Nor is it at all clear from Przeworski's theory how rational individual Russians might provide them.

Przeworski, to be sure, is aware of these dilemmas of institution building in new democracies. Indeed, he concludes his book on a pessimistic
note:

To be consolidated, democratic institutions must at the same time protect all
major interests and generate economic results. Yet the institutions that have
emerged from recent transitions to democracy seem to be to a large extent
haphazard, adopted under the understandable pressure to terminate fundamental conflicts as quickly as possible. Hence, the new democracies are likely
to experience continual conflict over basic institutions. The political forces
that suffer defeat as a result of the interplay of these institutions will repeatedly question the political framework. (Ibid., 188)

Arguably this prediction has largely been borne out by events in Russia,
where proposals to change the basic nature of the regime have been ad-

vanced continually by both government and opposition forces. Yet at the same time, other postcommunist democracies—including Poland, which initially adopted the policies of "shock therapy" so vehemently opposed by Przeworski—seem far more institutionally stable by comparison. What explains this pattern of mixed results? Apparently, key political actors in East-Central Europe were able to adopt long time horizons when evaluating their chances under democratic institutions, while those in Russia were not. But nothing in rational choice theory per se, or Przeworski's argument in particular, really explains why this difference should have emerged. If anything, Przeworski's (1991, 92–93) emphasis on the inconsistency between Catholicism and democracy would lead us to expect conflicts over fundamental principles to be at least as high in Poland and the Czech Republic as in Russia. It is telling, in any case, that such a careful analysis of rational commitments to democratic procedures in times of high uncertainty ends up arguing for the importance of ostensibly irrational belief systems in determining the prospects for democratic consolidation.

Ironically, then, rational choice theory appears to lead us in the same direction as modernization theory in the search for sources of democratic consolidation: toward the investigation of the sorts of "civil society" and "political culture" within which universal, unquestioning compliance with democratic procedures might indeed be rational. Instead of modernization theory's emphasis on social norms of individualism, proceduralism, and universalism, rational choice investigations of culture examine patterns of cooperation among individuals with high levels of "trust," "community," and "patriotism" (Ostrom 1990; Taylor and Singleton 1993; Levi 1997). Still, in every case, such analyses conclude that cooperative individual behavior depends upon past experiences of successful cooperation with one's fellows and/or with the state. Like modernization theory, rational choice never specifies the precise conditions under which consolidation might nevertheless occur in turbulent new democracies where civic participation is weak. Ironically, despite its rejection of reified assumptions about antidemocratic "cultures" in the non-Western world, consistent rational choice analysis seems to generate a similar despair about the prospects for democratization outside the existing Western liberal capitalist core.

This unexpected convergence of modernization theory and rational choice theory is most vividly demonstrated by Robert Putnam's *Making Democracy Work*, which skillfully blends theories of "civic culture" with a search for adequate rational choice microfoundations. Putnam argues that the higher levels of satisfaction with democratic institutions in Northern Italy compared to Southern Italy can be explained with reference to the "social capital" that has been built up over time in the former region.

Rational actors with long-term time horizons are likely to cooperate to provide public goods; repeated experiences of successful cooperation, in turn, generate high levels of confidence about the future gains of cooperative action in the present. Thus a society with many trusting and trustworthy individuals develops "virtuous circles" of cooperative action. By contrast, a society with many distrustful people oriented toward short-run payoffs—like that which, according to Putnam, exists in Southern Italy—generates "vicious circles" of perpetual defection. Such an environment leads to a high level of corruption, favoritism, and (justifiable) cynicism about formal democratic laws and procedures (Putnam, Leonardi, and Nanetti 1993; cf. Banfield and Fasano Banfield 1958).

Like the theorists examined above, Putnam is better at explaining the macropolitical results generated by cultures of trust and distrust than accounting for the emergence of such cultures in the first place. In this respect, Putnam's contention that Southern Italy is marked by high levels of distrust because of the exploitative policies of the Norman rulers who controlled the region centuries ago is undoubtedly the weakest part of his argument. Not every country invaded by the Normans, obviously, ended up with a weak "civic culture" in the twentieth century! Meanwhile, the highly "civic" Northern Italians seemed remarkably willing to support Mussolini as he smashed democratic institutions. Why didn't England end up like Sicily? Why did Milan become fascist? Putnam's theory provides no theoretical answers to these crucial questions. Without a satisfying theory as to how "civil societies" with high levels of trust get generated within some institutional contexts but not others, we are left with a rather static and reified categorization of democratic and antidemocratic cultures. In the case of Russia, too, to say that democratic consolidation has been impeded by the absence of large-scale social networks of trust and cooperation is surely accurate, but this gives us little insight into what forces might turn vicious circles into virtuous ones over time.

Toward a Dynamic Theory of Democratic Consolidation

Ultimately, contemporary theories of democratization derived from modernization theory and rational choice theory tend to generate static rather than dynamic definitions of democratic "consolidation." For modernization theorists, consolidation can only be reached when the vast majority of citizens accept democratic procedures as legitimate and when there is a high level of "congruence" between authority patterns in culture and authority patterns in politics (Diamond 1996; Eckstein 1998a). For rational choice theorists, consolidation can be attained only when all significant social actors discount the possibility of pursuing payoffs outside the legal "rules of the game" and interact with democratic institutions with high levels of civic trust (Przeworski 1991; Levi 1997). How such happy scenarios can ever emerge in societies with empirically high levels of social uncertainty, distrust, and turbulence, such as postcommunist Russia, is never directly analyzed. One is thus left with the impression that outside a small core of "civic" nations, the democracies of the "third wave" are likely to remain perpetually unconsolidated. Yet the historical record makes it clear that new democracies can emerge and solidify in diverse global settings, despite the obstacles posed by the wreckage and turbulence of authoritarian breakdown. Thus our current definitions of democratic consolidation seem to be of limited utility for orienting research that might explain "unlikely" democratic successes.

Perhaps the reason for this convergence of theoretical opinion lies in the common acceptance by Parsonians and rational choice theorists of "equilibrium" models of social order (Murphy 1996). If the consolidation of democracy means the attainment of a stable social (or n-person) equilibrium, then consolidation would seem to require that nearly everyone must actively support the procedural and legal framework. Anything short of full acceptance of the "rules of the game" by all significant social forces would seem to indicate a state of disequilibrium, and therefore of instability. Both paradigms thus end up with standards for democratic consolidation reflecting the ideals (and, one might add, not always the practices) of the most enduring democratic regimes of the West, and which are therefore largely inapplicable to emerging new democracies in the postcommunist world and elsewhere.

A concern that the concept of "democratic consolidation" may be inherently ethnocentric has led Guillermo O'Donnell to call upon scholars to drop the term altogether (O'Donnell 1996). Instead, O'Donnell argues, we should accept the possibility that the contemporary authority patterns in Russia and other non-Western countries may endure in their present form for the foreseeable future—a possibility that he thinks current theories of democratic consolidation tend to obscure. Yet this solution, too, leads to a static rather than dynamic approach to analyzing democratic development. Fully developed democracies, from this point of view, exist only in the "core" capitalist countries, while elsewhere we find "delegative democracies" with weak horizontal accountability and high levels of corruption (O'Donnell 1994; see also Zakaria 1997). Whether and how one type of democracy might be transformed into the other type, however, is left theoretically unclear. O'Donnell is surely correct to emphasize that new democracies should not simply be judged by the standards of the United States, Great Britain, or other core liberal powers. Yet in throwing out the idea of democratic consolidation altogether, he runs the risk of dichotomizing "liberal" and "delegative" democracies in a way that may inadvertently perpetuate the sort of Eurocentric analysis he is trying to attack.

If the concept "democratic consolidation" is to become theoretically useful, I would argue, it must be redefined as a stage in a larger dynamic process, rather than as a static endpoint (Rustow 1970). In addition, we need to see the problem of democratic consolidation as a special topic within a larger theory of regime consolidation. The first step toward both of these goals is to define democracy itself in institutional terms. In this respect, the recent work of Linz and Stepan represents a major theoretical advance. "Democracy is a form of governance of a modern state," they argue; "[t]hus, without a state, no modern democracy is possible" (Linz and Stepan 1996a, 17). From this point of view, the key problem for Russian democracy today is precisely that the Russian Federation lacks effective state institutions altogether. Its boundaries are constantly called into question by nationalist ideologues; its laws are poorly and inconsistently enforced; its officials are notoriously corrupt; and its executive behaves erratically and frequently autocratically. The implementation of a hastily designed program of economic "shock therapy," before any attempt to build effective political institutions, has led to the further fragmentation of authority in the country (Ibid., 386–400).

Yet Linz and Stepan combine this perceptive analysis of the importance of state building as a prerequisite for democracy—and the consequences of low "stateness" in Russia—with a standard for "democratic consolidation" quite similar to those criticized above. Thus they too argue that democracy is consolidated only when it becomes "the only game in town":

> Behaviorally, democracy becomes the only game in town when no significant political groups seriously attempt to overthrow the democratic regime or secede from the state. . . . Attitudinally, democracy becomes the only game in town when, even in the face of severe economic and political crises, the overwhelming majority of the people believe that any further political change must emerge from within the parameters of democratic formulas. Constitutionally, democracy becomes the only game in town when all the actors in the polity become habituated to the fact that political conflict will be resolved according to the established norms and that violations of these norms are likely to be both ineffective and costly. In short, with consolidation, democracy becomes routinized and deeply internalized in social, institutional, and even psychological life, as well as in calculations for achieving success. (Ibid., 1996a, 5)

Again, the definition of consolidation employed here requires a degree of social unanimity that is quite unrealistic even in the context of highly established democracies like the United States (as Timothy McVeigh, the

Montana Freemen, Louis Farrakhan, and other "significant" or potentially significant political actors would surely agree), let alone fragile new democracies like that in Russia. The finding by Linz and Stepan that Russia's democracy is still unconsolidated thus sheds little light on the dynamics by which democratic (or antidemocratic) forms of "stateness" in Russia might be established in the future.

Another extremely important contribution to building a dynamic theory of democratic consolidation comes from the work of John Higley, Richard Gunther, and their collaborators, who focus on the importance of "elite consensus" concerning the framework for political contestation in generating stable democracy (Burton, Gunther, and Higley 1992a, b; Gunther, Diamandouros, and Puhle 1995; Higley, Pakulsi, and Wesolowski 1998). Examining a wide range of new democracies in Latin America and Southern Europe as well as Eastern Europe, these scholars conclude that explicit agreements among elites concerning democratic rules are highly correlated with consolidated democratic outcomes. Where "antisystem" elites are excluded or politically marginalized, they find, an institutional environment is created in which the long-run allegiance of broader masses to democracy can be mobilized much more successfully. Yet they, too, ultimately see democratic consolidation as requiring that "all politically significant groups accept established political institutions and adhere to democratic rules of the game" (Burton, Gunther, and Higley 1992a, 3). While the authors acknowledge that this is an ideal type that no society ever fully achieves, such a demanding standard still tends to call into question the "consolidation" of almost every non-European democracy (see, for example, the classifications given in Ibid. 1992b, 325).

In the case of democratization in post–Soviet Russia, the elite consensus approach to defining democratic consolidation leads to particular analytic difficulties. Thus Higley, Pakulski, and Wesolowski (1998) argue that in postcommunist Europe, the presence of consensual elites is favorable for democratic consolidation, the fragmentation of elites is likely to lead to unconsolidated democracy, and divided elites are likely to give rise to authoritarianism. However, they admit that Russian democratic elites are hard to classify in terms of this scheme: They can be reasonably described as "consensual" in their rejection of the mass political terror of the Stalinist past, as "divided" in their attitudes toward Westernization and market reform, and as "fragmented" in terms of their dispersion among competing regional and clientelist networks. Higley, Pakulski, and Wesolowski tentatively suggest that Russia's elite is currently fragmented but could be an "incipient consensual elite" in the making. However, the authors provide no clearly specified dynamic theory of the process by which incipient elite consensus generates (or fails to generate) stable democratic institutions—let alone a broader societal consensus about the political "rules of the game." Indeed, they argue that the tendency toward democratic consolidation in Russia has been furthered by such dubious moves toward "consensual" politics as Yeltsin's destruction of the Russian Supreme Soviet in 1993, his sponsorship of the pro-regime "Our Home Is Russia" Party in 1995, and his co-optation of General Alexander Lebed before the second round of the 1996 presidential elections (Ibid., 24–25)—all of which arguably worsened Russian elite fragmentation in the longer term by eliminating the political space for formal democratic opposition, thus forcing political struggles into informal, extralegal channels.

However, Linz and Stepan's emphasis on democratic state building as the prerequisite for stable democracy, and Higley and Gunther's stress on elite accommodation can be utilized as the foundation for a quite different approach to defining democratic consolidation—one that sees consolidation, too, in institutional rather than social terms. Following the classic work of Dahl (1971) on "polyarchy," we can define democracy as a type of state in which formal institutional guarantees of electoral contestation and free citizen participation are in place. Democracy is then consolidated, from this point of view, when the enforcement of the key institutions of a democratic regime—in particular, legally defined state boundaries, free, fair, and genuinely competitive elections, and formal rights of citizenship—has become dependable and regularized. But dependable and regularized enforcement does not necessarily require, contrary to modernization theory and rational choice theory, any social "equilibrium" based on near-universal assent to democratic values and procedures. The reality is that almost every democracy must cope with a large number of important actors who can imagine acting, and sometimes do act, outside of the formal democratic "rules of the game." Indeed, an even larger part of every citizenry, even in advanced democracies, remains wholly alienated from the political process (Mann 1970). Yet, I would argue, it is still meaningful to speak of democracy as "consolidated" *wherever the enforcers of democratic institutions themselves can be counted on with very high probability to behave in ways compatible with, and oriented toward, the perpetuation of formal institutional rules.*

Such an institutional definition of democratic consolidation focuses analytic attention on the relationship between elites and their administrative "staffs," rather than on relationships among elites or between state and society. It singles out as the key problem for unconsolidated democracies not the absence of preexisting democratic or civic "cultures," but rather the ability to recruit a critical mass of dependable officials to administer formally democratic institutions (Weber 1968). As Cirtautas and Mokrzycki (1993) have argued, the initial "articulation" of democracy will only generate "institutionalization" to the extent that supporters of democratic values within key state bureaucracies find themselves promoted relative to antidemocratic and/or corrupt individuals—creating a sort of "feedback loop" between the pursuit of democratic values and the pursuit of material interests. Where—despite the existence of formal procedures for defending state boundaries, organizing electoral competition, and protecting civic rights—open supporters of democratic ideals find themselves marginalized while antidemocratic and/or corrupt elites gain increasing power and influence, it is appropriate to speak of democracy as "unconsolidated."

This dynamic definition of consolidation can be employed for the analysis of processes of institutional consolidation in nondemocratic regimes as well. Indeed, every form of political order requires enforcement by a staff that can be counted on with some degree of confidence to uphold the directives of the central authorities. To the extent that such a staff is lacking, formal "rules of the game" may mask highly particularistic informal practices that subvert the cohesion of the regime. One can in this respect speak just as coherently about unconsolidated Leninism or fascism as about unconsolidated democracy; indeed, the work of Huntington (1970) and Jowitt (1992b) on the "consolidation" of one-party regimes is quite consistent with the general definition of democratic consolidation proposed here. Thus the term "consolidation" can be used in a wholly value-neutral sense, although most scholars will undoubtedly prefer the consolidation of democratic institutions to nondemocratic forms of institutional consolidation.

The definition of consolidation offered here draws on some of the insights of the "old institutionalism" that have been largely deemphasized or ignored in much of the "new institutionalism" in political science. As Stinchcombe has argued, many contemporary institutionalists tend to forget that institutions that endure for long periods and, more important, that generate enough power to reorient their surrounding social environments in accordance with institutional norms, tend everywhere to be organized and run by elites who genuinely believe in the practices they enforce (Stinchcombe 1997). Institutions, as Selznick pointed out many decades ago, are in this sense organizational patterns of action that have become "infused with value"—that is, have acquired meaning as a way of life, and not only as a means to an end, for their members (Selznick 1957, 17). By contrast, if institutions are defined simply as the "rules of the game," both formal and informal (North 1991), it becomes exceedingly difficult to distinguish institutional consolidation from simple long-term arrangements that happen to be convenient for two or more parties. Indeed, by North's definition, every social environment contains a practically infinite set of local "institutions," ranging from formal constitutional systems to agreements to meet at a local pub after the conclusion of a sports contest.

Applying the term "institution" to each of these kinds of "rules" governing collective behavior tends to desensitize us to the central political significance of institutional practices that really do become standardized over time and space and valued as ends in themselves, both by those who organize them and by those who are recruited to maintain them into the future.

It cannot be denied that the analysis of institutions contained in the classic works of organizational theory such as those of Barnard (1938) and Selznick (1949), which emphasized the functional, almost organic unity of the formal and informal dimensions of successful institutions, was insufficiently attentive to the problem of explaining the microfoundations of macroinstitutional outcomes. However, an understanding of institutions as built around regularized leader-staff relationships that promote a sense of identification with institutionally promoted values need not depart from a careful methodological individualism. Recently, Jowitt (1998) has proposed a definition of institutions as "bounded, persistent, authoritative, partisan patterns of leadership and membership." From this perspective, the central problem for analysis of new democracies—and new regimes in general—is to investigate the theoretical reasons why individuals in environments of social uncertainty and turbulence sometimes and in some places make choices to build and reinforce such authoritative, standardized patterns of leadership and membership, but at other times and in other places pursue short-run individual interests instead. In the former case, we can speak of institutional consolidation; in the latter, we can expect institutional boundaries to be challenged, claims to authority to be undermined or ignored, and patterns of leadership and membership to fragment. While unconsolidated institutions may nonetheless persist for some time, they can be expected to remain perpetually vulnerable to both external challenges and internal corruption. If democratic institution builders are to win out over their various authoritarian competitors, then, their ability to generate compelling political visions may be as important as their ability to reach temporary political compromises.

Patterns of Postcommunist Democratization

The utility of the definition of democratic consolidation given above can only be demonstrated through its use in empirical, comparative research on the dynamics of new democracies in postcommunist Europe and elsewhere. Obviously, it is beyond the scope of this theoretical essay to investigate the levels of predictability in elite-staff relationships in several or all postcommunist democracies and nondemocracies, although this is precisely the long-term research agenda suggested by the Weberian approach to institutionalization outlined here. However, we can at least utilize this approach to generate alternative testable hypotheses concerning some of the main trends in Eastern European and post-Soviet political development since the collapse of communism in 1989–91.

Perhaps the most striking initial result of the first decade of postcommunist politics is the remarkable diversity of regime types now emerging in the territory formerly dominated by Leninist parties, ranging from the seemingly strong and stable democracies of Central Europe to the emergence of personalistic dictatorships in every Central Asian former Soviet republic (Rupnik 1999). This result appears particularly surprising in light of the presumed uniformity of the totalitarian political and economic institutions imposed by the Soviet Union on territories it controlled. Thus one of the key puzzles for students of postcommunist democratization is to explain how powerful one-party dictatorships in some parts of the region were seemingly quickly transformed into full-fledged Western democracies, while in other regions new forms of autocracy reemerged (see Fish's and Roeder's essays in this volume).

As we have seen above, the modernization and rational choice paradigms, and the definitions of democratic consolidation they generate, do not help us account for the distribution of these outcomes very well. Highly "modernized" countries like Russia, Ukraine, and Belarus—judging by widely utilized indicators of education, industrialization, and urbanization—remained either "unconsolidated" democracies or even repressive autocracies, while countries with large rural populations such as Poland and Lithuania progressed much more rapidly toward Western norms of democracy. Levels of uncertainty about key democratic institutions, including basic electoral rules, constitutions, and party systems, were arguably just as high in Poland during most of the 1990s as in, say, Ukraine or Russia; yet politicians and bureaucrats have over time become more firmly committed to norms of democratic proceduralism only in the former case (Wasilewski 1998). Defining democratic consolidation as a state of near total consensus concerning the "rules of the game" predisposes analysts in both schools to assume that the regional variance in democratic outcomes observed thus far must ultimately be rooted in widespread social orientations toward these rules—but as we have seen, existing theory does a poor job of demonstrating, let alone accounting for, these hypothesized stark cultural differences among countries.

Analysts focusing on the impact of regime types on political outcomes in the region—and thus operating at a somewhat lower level of theoretical abstraction than characteristic of modernization theory and rational choice theory—have had rather greater success in identifying specific factors influencing the strength or weakness of new postcommunist democracies. Thus, parliamentary regimes have performed better than presidential or semipresidential systems; countries with national "founding elections" have done better than those where regional elections preceded national ones; and countries where the communist party lost the first free postcommunist elections have reformed Stalinist institutions more thoroughly than those where former communist parties remained in power (Linz and Stepan 1996a, Fish 1998b). However, purely institutionalist approaches often overestimate the extent to which "good" constitutional and electoral rules can be implemented effectively in countries with very different kinds of Leninist legacies and in very different geographical contexts. Indeed, recent research has demonstrated that much of the variance in postcommunist development appears to be traceable to various types of institutional diffusion from neighboring countries, suggesting that the geopolitical location of postcommunist states may play a decisive role in determining their later political and economic trajectories (Kopstein and Reilly 2000).

In this context, accepting a definition of democratic—and authoritarian—consolidation as a situation in which staffs can be counted on with high certainty to act in ways consistent with and oriented toward the formal institutional order suggests alternative reasons for the variation in levels of democracy in postcommunist Eurasia. To begin with, this definition implies that the relatively consolidated democracies in Central Europe have emerged not because of more advantageous "civilizational" influences—indeed, recent analyses suggest widespread public disillusionment with many of the outcomes of post-1989 "transitions to democracy" even in comparatively successful countries like Hungary and the Czech Republic (Howard 2000)—but because of the increasingly reliable enforcement of formal legal norms governing state boundaries, political contestation, and citizenship rights by party and state officials in these countries. The behavior of democratic "staffs" in the successful postcommunist democracies, in turn, can be explained by examining how those officials who originally embraced "Westernization" as a value commitment attained material benefits greater than those who rejected this orientation, thus producing the sort of synthesis between "value-rationality" and "instrumental rationality" among enforcers typical of legitimate political orders (Weber 1968).

Here, in particular, geographic proximity to Western Europe has played a vital role. Indeed, the idea of the "return to Europe" has been the single most important ideological orientation shaping Central and Eastern European politics since the collapse of communism, affecting the behavior of elites in practically every part of the political spectrum in these countries—including not only liberals, but nationalists and ex-communists as well. Where the claim of a political "return to Europe" has been most plausible, as in countries directly bordering the European Union, the consolidation of democracy has generally proceeded the furthest. Where this claim has been less plausible, as in the non-Baltic European newly independent states, enforcement by state and party officials of democratic rules has been unreliable at best. And where this claim has been altogether impossible, as in post-Soviet Central Asia, democratic procedures have hardly been enforced at all.

The material benefits available to state and party officials through the attainment of political, economic, and military integration with pan-European international institutions clearly go a long way toward explaining these officials' widespread individual decisions to behave in ways consistent with this goal. As early as 1989, the European Union began to negotiate trade and cooperation agreements with Poland and Hungary as well as to establish the PHARE assistance program, which by 1991 had already been extended as far east as the Baltic states (Gower 1999). (Significantly, the other former Soviet republics received EU support through an entirely different program, EU-TACIS, indicating the early emergence of a conceptual boundary in Western European minds between "East-Central Europe" and the non-Baltic European former Soviet republics.) Support for market reform from the International Monetary Fund, the World Bank, and the European Bank of Reconstruction and Development helped strengthen the pro-Western orientation of both neoliberals and, unexpectedly, former Communist Party elites as well. Pan-European organizations of Social Democratic, Christian Democratic, and Liberal political parties began to admit party organizations from the former communist bloc—and to train their members in norms of Western parliamentarianism. The European Union began deliberations on possible formal expansion to the east, a process accelerated by the sudden announcement by President Clinton in 1994 that NATO inclusion of new Eastern European member states was "no longer a matter of whether, but when and how" (Goldgeier 1999; Smith 1999). Finally, the NATO requirement that prospective members settle outstanding border conflicts with their neighbors played an important role in marginalizing antiliberal nationalists with possible revanchist orientations, such as Istvan Csurka in Hungary. All these factors worked to augment the dependability with which state and party bureaucrats in the new democracies of Eastern Europe enforced the formal legal rules governing the organization of national security, political competition, and citizenship rights in their countries, despite continuing problems in all three areas.

It would be a mistake, however, to see the gradual consolidation of democracy (in the sense of the term argued for here) in Central Europe as merely the product of rational utility maximization on the part of state officials seeking the standards of living typical of Western Europe. Equally important was the fact that the ideology of a "return to Europe" encapsulated genuinely heartfelt emotions and deeply held ideals among a large part of the Eastern European intelligentsia. Indeed, as Wyrda has argued, the idea that Eastern European societies were "genuinely European" had been a guiding principle for dissident politicians throughout the Leninist period (Wyrda 1999). At the same time, even Leninist Party officials in countries like Poland and Hungary could plausibly feel that the sort of state socialism they had helped to enforce in the 1970s and 1980s was far more "Westernized" than the neopatrimonial one-party rule characteristic of Leninist states farther to the east and south (Ekiert 1996; Grzymala-Busse 2000). Finally, the unsettled state of politics in the Russian Federation appeared to threaten the rise of a revanchist Russian regime, encouraging new political elites in the rest of Eastern Europe to embrace the procedural form of democracy long associated with the "West" in order to defend the nation itself. That these general political orientations were so widely shared after 1989 among politicians of both the "right" and the "left" helps to explain why the victory of former communist parties in Hungary, Poland, Lithuania, and elsewhere in the region, far from leading to destabilizing polarized politics, only further deepened democratic consolidation in these countries (Bunce 1999a).

In addition to helping us understand the general trend toward democratic consolidation at the level of rule enforcement in Eastern and Central Europe, the definition offered here also sheds light on anomalous cases poorly explained by competing approaches. The relatively undependable enforcement of democratic proceduralism in Slovakia under Mečiar, for example, is hard to explain using conventional theories; after all, Slovakia's strong economic performance, advantageous geographic position, and even its cultural background appear quite similar to its neighbors in the Visegrad group. However, Slovakia's national identity in the wake of the Czechoslovak breakup was comparatively weak and contested (Cohen 1999), which tended to undermine elite consensus concerning the proper mode of incorporation in "Europe" and thus the consistency of staff enforcement of procedural democratic rules. This, in turn, temporarily generated an environment in which principled democrats were marginalized while politicians oriented toward the short-term settling of political scores were comparatively successful—at least until Slovakia's exclusion from the first wave of both NATO and EU expansion contributed to Mečiar's defeat in the 1998 parliamentary elections (Henderson 1999). By the same token, defining democratic consolidation as reliable enforcement of democratic procedures by state staff suggests alternative hypotheses concerning anomalously successful cases of democratic institution building in the region. The relative success of the Union of Democratic Forces in Bulgaria during the 1990s, for example, appears to owe much to the UDF's consistent, staunchly pro-European stance—even in a country that suffered particularly severely from the political and economic legacies of Leninism, and with seemingly few near-term prospects for inclusion in the EU or NATO (Fish and Brooks 2000). The idea of a "return to Europe," here and elsewhere in the region, appears to have elongated decision makers' time horizons well beyond what might otherwise be expected given the general level of political and economic turbulence.

This last point brings up a final implication of the dynamic definition of democratic consolidation offered here: Institutional consolidation, from this point of view, is not necessarily irreversible. Indeed, unlike conventional definitions of consolidation that tend to overstate the degree of social acceptance of the "rules of the game" in long-established democracies, the dynamic approach suggests that once the link between principle and payoffs is challenged or broken, the predictability of staff enforcement of formal rules is likely to decline. This point is of particular importance given the complex challenges facing both the European Union and NATO in their deliberations concerning further expansion to the east in the twenty-first century. For, to the extent that state and party officials in less-well-positioned postcommunist countries have begun to orient their actions toward the maintenance of formal democratic procedures in the belief that doing so will lead to eventual inclusion in "Europe," disillusionment among them about the course of EU and NATO expansion is bound to generate serious political challenges—particularly given continuing regional problems with ethnic conflict, high unemployment, and public alienation. Countries where pro-European politicians have only recently managed to defeat incumbent demagogues, such as Slovakia and Serbia, are particularly vulnerable in this regard; indeed, the resignation of the somewhat romantically pro-Western Emil Constantinescu as president of Romania is an indication of precisely this worrisome trend.

Can Russian Democracy Consolidate?

From the point of view outlined in this essay, the Russian Federation since the adoption of the Yeltsin constitution in December 1993 through the early Putin era can usefully be classified as an unconsolidated democracy. The formal legal and procedural framework for democratic elections, citizenship, and national defense are all in place, making it reasonable for comparative purposes to categorize the regime as an electoral democracy. Indeed, the dynamics of Russian political life since 1993 would be incomprehensible without reference to the formal constitutional rules adopted at that time. While Russian democracy has arguably been of poor quality, and even marred by several instances of outright fraud, the rules of the game set out in the 1993 constitution have provided a framework for political bargaining that has been more important in practice than many analysts assume (Remington 2000).

As in the rest of postcommunist Europe, the initial establishment and maintenance during the 1990s of the formal institutional framework for Russian democracy reflects the more general regional trend to pursue a "return to Europe" through the building of procedural political institutions. Despite all of their bitter disagreements on other issues, both Gorbachev and Yeltsin saw rapprochement with the European "West" as a centerpiece of their reform programs. Indeed, the dream of building a "civic" Russian democracy—and the conviction that this could not be done, as Gorbachev proposed, within the context of Soviet institutions—was crucial to the articulation by Yeltsin and his supporters in "Democratic Russia" of the anti-Soviet, pro-Western form of Russian nationalism that ultimately broke up the Soviet Union (Dunlop 1993). Early post–Soviet Russian foreign policy subsequently made the ideal of Russian inclusion in the global democratic order an explicit priority (Kozyrev 1995).

However, Russia's geopolitical and sociological circumstances made the institutionalization of legitimate rational-legal state authority far more difficult than in postcommunist states farther west, for several reasons. First, the burden of decades of one-party rule, state-led industrialization, and collectivization of agriculture was much greater in the core of the former Soviet Union than in the Central and Eastern European states incorporated into the Soviet bloc during and after World War II; thus Russia experienced a particularly prolonged and devastating postcommunist political and economic crisis (Hanson 1995). Second, Russia's unique status as a continental power in both "Europe" and "Asia" made the country's orientation toward the "West" more controversial and contested among politicians and intellectuals than was the project of Westernization in most other European postcommunist states. Third, Yeltsin's erratic behavior vis-à-vis his own staff, and his unwillingness to directly participate in the building of democratic institutions such as political parties, played a damaging role (McFaul 1999). Finally, the end of communism symbolized for many Russians the loss of empire rather than the achievement of national independence; indeed, public opinion polls demonstrated increasing regret at the breakup of the Soviet Union in Russia throughout the 1990s (Hanson and Kopstein 1997). Thus, Russian national identity remained very much a work in progress in this period, generating high levels of uncertainty about the country's future course and encouraging rational politicians and citizens to act in terms of their short-term instrumental interests rather than to invest in the long-term institutional enforcement of procedural democracy.

All of these factors have combined to undermine any potential "feedback loops" uniting the pursuit of democratic values with the pursuit of material interests in the Russian Federation. Finding loyal, noncorrupt staff to administer state institutions is therefore extremely difficult. Given this environment, that Russian public opinion has become increasingly skeptical of the idea of "democracy" itself is hardly surprising. Indeed, this can be seen as a perfectly reasonable response by individuals to poor institutional performance—not as a reflection of some deep-seated cultural authoritarianism within the Russian "soul" (Reisinger 1998, 159–60).

If we accept the dominant definition of democratic consolidation in the literature as a situation of almost universal social support for democratic norms, there would appear to be very little hope whatsoever for the stabilization of Russia's electoral regime. From the cultural point of view expounded by many modernization theorists, a wholesale Westernization of the beliefs and values of Russian citizens would be necessary for this; obviously, given current trends, such an outcome is hardly likely. From the rational choice point of view, things look equally bleak, since instrumental power seekers in Russia today would be foolish to count on the long-term endurance of contemporary constitutional rules; instead, rational actors should simply continue to maximize their short-term gains and "defect" on anyone credulous enough to propose long-term cooperation under such uncertain conditions.

Of course, predictions by modernization theorists or rational choice analysts that Russian democracy will fail could easily turn out to be correct in the medium to long run. Yet it must be emphasized that Russia's imperfect but real observance of democratic procedures in the 1990s represents an important anomaly for unduly skeptical theorizing about postcommunist democracy. A major reason for this outcome, I would argue, lies in the fact that although the institutionalization of democratic institutions in Russia has been very weak, the ability of antidemocratic elites to attract reliable "staffs" has been equally limited. To be sure, what Sartori has termed "anti-system parties"—parties that, although they may not actively promote revolution, are programmatically committed to the overturning of the existing democratic constitution—played an important role in the Russian political system during the 1990s (Sartori 1976; Hanson 1998). Yet organizations like Gennadii Zyuganov's Communist Party of the Russian Federation and Vladimir Zhirinovsky's Liberal Democratic Party of Russia seem no more inspiring to most Russian citizens than parties claiming to support the status quo. Antiliberal groups, like those of a more pro-Western orientation, are bedeviled by corruption and free riding, and both have proven largely unable to mobilize broader social constituencies. This pattern of formally democratic politics combined with lax or corrupt enforcement of legal procedures has largely continued into the early Putin regime; intially, at least, Putin's "pragmatic patriotism" involved efforts to reassert central state power within the formal political structure bequeathed to him by Yeltsin, rather than an open break with rational-legal norms of contestation, citizenship, and state boundary enforcement. In general, the "atomization" of society engendered by Leninist rule, contrary to most analysts' expectations, has undermined the aspirations of would-be dictators as much as those of democrats (Kopstein and Hanson 1998).

From this point of view, defining democratic consolidation as a situation in which the enforcers of democratic institutions can be counted upon to behave in ways consistent with democratic rules tends to highlight the prospects for long-run democratization in Russia, despite rather threatening contemporary trends. Specifically, attention to the dynamics by which new institutions form in turbulent social environments should lead us to watch for the emergence of powerful new definitions of political leadership and membership in Russia that might reunite the pursuit of democratic values and the pursuit of material interest, and that may become the basis for effective democratic consolidation at a later date. Of course, institutional consolidation in Russia may take a profoundly antiliberal form as well, especially if new anti-Western ideologies manage to attract committed followers among alienated sectors of the populace. Alternatively, the continuing corrosion of democratic citizenship rights in the Putin era could eventually lead to a formal break with the electoral democracy imposed by Yeltsin in 1993 and its replacement by a nonideological authoritarian regime—one that would be even less legitimate than the current regime, and thus likely to be even less effective in welding together a dependable staff of state enforcers. The future, however, is more open in this respect than might be assumed by scholars with an essentialist understanding of Russian political culture or scholars who assume that Russian politicians will forever behave as short-term utility maximizers.

SIX

CONCLUSION: POSTCOMMUNISM AND
THE THEORY OF DEMOCRACY

Richard D. Anderson, Jr.,
M. Steven Fish,
Stephen E. Hanson,
and Philip G. Roeder

WE BEGAN this collaborative effort from a shared sense that in the attempt to explain developments in postcommunist countries the existing body of theory on democratization comes up short. At the same time the richness of the postcommunist experience suggests new concepts and new approaches that can improve that theory. This final chapter is itself a collaborative effort in which we draw out the themes that served as the basis for our collaboration and the complementarities that emerge from and link our separate approaches.

We draw these conclusions with some caution, however. Given the nature of the topics of our study and the questions we pose about them, we intend this volume neither as a systematic, interim "report from the front" that encompasses the entire kaleidoscope of change, nor as a definitive, retrospective statement on an established historical phenomenon. Instead, we seek to forge a bit of space for fresh thinking and debate about a remarkable set of political phenomena that have transformed the world and the academic disciplines engaged in studying it but that are still only faintly understood.

In this conclusion we address four issues. First, we make explicit our shared sense that the distinction between area studies and political science is a false dichotomy. Second, we draw out four common themes about democratization that emerge from our separate analyses. Third, we examine three major differences that define our separate approaches, but also represent either complementarities or points for further fruitful investigation. And finally, we each identify developments in the next years of postcommunist politics that might lead us to reassess our theories and conclusions.

Area Studies and Comparative Politics: A False Dichotomy

We believe that our separate projects have reinforced for us our shared sense that recent debates have overdrawn the distinction between area studies—particularly, postcommunist area studies—and comparative politics (Bates, Johnson, and Lustick 1997; Shea 1997). Our analyses have underscored for us that social science theory and knowledge of specific regions can grow only by a constant exchange of ideas that is not imprisoned by false academic boundaries. In short, each of us approaches our cases as opportunities to test, expand, and develop social science theory; we forge new syntheses from elements of existing theory or even call for novel theoretical undertakings. None of us sees the puzzles and anomalies of postcommunism as a call for rejecting the enterprise of theory building in the social sciences; nor do we see the enterprise of theory building as one that can usefully proceed in ignorance of events that occur at particular times and places.

As contributions to our knowledge of a specific set of countries, all four chapters begin from comparative theory in order to frame our questions and direct our search for answers. None is a narrow area study uninformed by theoretical development in the social sciences. Instead, each is in constant dialogue with the discipline. By the simplest standards of normal science, the new democratic and nondemocratic regimes of the postcommunist world represent a manifold increase in the number of cases for testing the chief hypotheses of the social sciences' theories of democratization. Since the original cases of successful democratization were always so few and tended to come from a very narrow range of social, economic, and cultural experience, these new cases often present tough or critical tests of these hypotheses.

None of us believes that the study of postcommunist states can stop with workmanlike application of theories from elsewhere. These chapters use the transition from communism in order to propose developments in social science theory itself. These chapters point out lacunae, anomalies, and puzzles in the corpus of theory and suggest amendments and alternatives that can move the frontiers of political science forward (Kuhn, 1970). Thus, area studies cannot be simply a laboratory for applying and testing theories derived in some abstract manner uninformed by the experience of real places. Good social science theory requires deep knowledge of empirical cases along with well-specified premises and hypotheses that are derived logically from these premises. It is precisely this sort of work, driven by knowledge of both facts and theory, that is most likely to produce insights that can push theory forward. None of us denies the value of either formal theory or rich description, but we find the points of inter-section between fact and theory the most dynamic and fruitful.

Lessons for the Theory of Democratization

The chapters of this volume focus on four different contributions to the current theory of democracy that are suggested by the transitions from communism. First, all four chapters underscore that the postcommunist experience poses a puzzle that cannot be comprehended by existing theories of democracy. While we all use and are steeped in normal social science methods and epistemologies, none of us is fully satisfied with the power of existing theories for explaining and understanding the political transformations of postcommunism. Our research leads each of us to skepticism regarding much democratization theory, whether in its classical form (e.g., Eckstein 1966; Lipset 1960; Rustow 1970), its neoclassical guise (e.g., Eckstein 1998a; Huntington 1991; Lipset 1996), or its ostensibly fully retooled contemporary form (e.g., Przeworski 1991; Przeworski and Limongi 1997).

Indeed, it is apparently possible to achieve democracy without many or most of the preconditions that the first- and second-wave theories of democracy claimed were essential. When subjected to the testing that normal science expects all hypotheses to withstand, these usual explanations for transition from authoritarianism and transitions toward democracy fail in the postcommunist cases. Thus, in attempting to find the culprit responsible for reversals of democratization, Steven Fish first considers six hypotheses that identify more distant and relatively fixed structural, cultural, and historical factors and another seven hypotheses that identify more proximate and malleable circumstantial factors. Yet, after rounding up the usual suspects and subjecting each to close scrutiny Fish finds none responsible for democratic backsliding. In the postcommunist world as a whole, Fish observes, progress or regress on the road to democracy appears to be independent of a state's economic development, equality of income distribution, size, ethnic diversity, religious tradition, or historical experience of democratic governance. Philip Roeder reviews theories that purport to find the conditions for democratization in socioeconomic modernization, civil society, specific political cultures, or elite pacts. New states such as Russia, Ukraine, and Moldova have little of the bourgeois capitalism, wealth, prosperity, civic culture, civil society, or public trust that is supposed to be necessary for democracy to emerge and to endure. Moreover, Russia has been able to achieve an imperfect democracy not by formation of the elite pacts or coalitions to which some theorists attribute democracy but by virtue of the failure of such coalitions to develop.

Richard Anderson argues that the theoretical anomalies noted by Roeder are attributable to the error of "structuralism"—that is, mistaking contingent agent behaviors for durable social conditions. Stephen Hanson explores closely the contradiction found in much extant theory that (a) ascribes a country's cultural readiness for democracy to modernization, (b) attributes Russia's democratic transition to its modernity, but (c) expresses doubt that Russia can consolidate democracy because Russians are culturally unfit. In short, given the failure of those societies to qualify for democracy by the criteria that most theories specified, authoritarianism of the Soviet type seemed natural throughout the Eastern Europe and the Soviet Union. By the standards of these theories the emergence of democracy in many postcommunist countries—as problematic as these democracies might be—poses an anomalous outcome that requires reexamination of these theories.

The rapid transition from communism to democracy in many countries stunned not only specialists on the region but the whole field of comparative politics. Thus, if such a thing is possible, our views are informed at many points by a sense of surprise at the subjects of our study. We are excited by the collapse of authoritarianism in polities that were almost universally considered the sites of the world's most steadfast and hardy authoritarian regimes and breakthroughs to the birth of an inclusive discourse in places where political communication for many decades erected towering barriers between the rulers and the ruled. We are appalled by authoritarian backsliding incited not by chest-thumping would-be dictators or "extremists" but by the former heroes of democratization themselves. We are hopeful but anxious over the prospects for democratic consolidation in turbulent polities that by the lights of many existing theories should still be sleeping soundly under fully consolidated, staunchly authoritarian partocracies.

A second theme that appears in all four chapters is that in conventional theories significant elements of the democratization processes are either ill defined, undertheorized, or simply absent. Each of the authors has tackled one aspect of these processes that needs closer attention from theory. While Roeder examines the initiation of transitions from authoritarianism, Fish analyzes regime stability once democratization begins, Anderson considers how politician and citizen behaviors change during the transition to democracy, and Hanson explains regime consolidation. Roeder's dependent variable is choices made in authoritarian regimes to retain or to change the constitution. These changes may lead to alternative forms of authoritarianism or to democracy. In order to understand the choice of democracy by authoritarian leaders, Roeder contends, the existing theory of democratization should become part of an enlarged theory of regime choice that examines the dynamics of choice in the context of authoritarianism as well as transitional regimes and democracies. Fish's dependent variable is the stability of democratic gains. He is most interested in the differences between cases in which democratic gains continue and endure, on the one hand, and those in which they erode or are reversed, on the other. Fish stresses that our theory of the success and consolidation of democracy requires fuller understanding of halted or reversed democratization. Anderson's dependent variable consists of the twin phenomena that define a transition to democracy—elite competition for popular support and citizen partisanship. Hanson addresses one of the least-well-understood aspects of the transition to democracy—the degree to which democratic institutions can be considered *consolidated*.

Each author also underscores the need for greater precision in the terminology and concepts employed in much of the literature on democratization. For example, the variety of postcommunist regimes cannot be encapsulated precisely by the prevailing terminology. Indeed, a majority of cases seem to fall outside any category and therefore beyond the explanatory powers of most theories. Hanson tackles this problem of conceptual precision directly in his discussion of democratic consolidation. As Hanson notes, the imprecision in the term "democracy" generates numerous ad hoc concepts because the existing terminology cannot distinguish cases. In proposing to fill this gap with a more precise definition of consolidated democracy, Hanson finds that cultural and rational-choice models of systemic equilibrium fail to identify the essential element of democratic stability. Through consideration of the weaknesses of Russian democracy in comparison with the more robust democracies in East-Central Europe, he proposes a new synthesis that emphasizes dependable and regularized enforcement of key institutions such as state boundaries, elections, and citizenship rights. It is the commitment of officials responsible for this enforcement that is essential to democratic consolidation. Similarly, Roeder argues that the theory of democratization lacks a careful definition of alternatives—not the alternatives *within* democracy, which are well specified, but the alternatives *to* democracy. If the theory of democratization begins from the assumption that the movement toward democracy is itself a series of choices among constitutional alternatives, the theory of democratization must define the nondemocratic alternatives. In particular, this theory must define the alternative regimes in terms that are commensurate with those used to define democracy; that is, they must represent alternatives along the dimensions that define democracy. For this reason, Roeder argues for a distinction between democracy and nondemocracies and among types of the latter based on differences in the pattern of accountability of the decision makers.

Third, despite our different approaches it is remarkable that we all come to stress that dispersion of political power is necessary for a stable democratic order. For Fish and Roeder this conclusion is explicit. Examining the full range of postcommunist cases, Fish finds that superpresidentialism is the one common characteristic distinguishing the states where democratic liberties have lost ground from those where they have gained. By concentrating power in the hands of a single person, superpresidentialism allows the executive to deprive opponents of democratic liberties—by fabricating accusations of corruption, by issuing decrees that outlaw their past behaviors (and then are used as grounds to arrest them after the fact), by denying them rights to register as candidates for office, by closing media outlets that they might use to communicate their opposition to the incumbent. Some incumbents, particularly Yeltsin in Russia, might for personal reasons avoid exploiting the full potential of superpresidential powers, but everywhere democracy is fragile where power is excessively concentrated.

Roeder finds that democracy has prevailed, however incompletely, where elites formed under Soviet rule were fragmented at the moments that Gorbachev pressed for democratization in the union republics and that the Soviet Union broke up. These Soviet-era elites chose the political procedures that could move the successor states to democracy or to a nondemocratic alternative such as exclusive republicanism, oligarchy, or autocracy. Authoritarian outcomes were likely when bureaucratic coalitions could establish their dominance without including the public—and particularly where they could expect to maintain this dominance only by continuing to exclude some or most of the public from politics. It was where divisions within the authoritarian bureaucracies of the union republic prevented cabals of bureaucrats from agreeing on pacts that would continue the exclusion of the public from the selectorate that democracy was the most likely outcome.

Anderson and Hanson implicitly reach similar conclusions. For Anderson, ordinary language lowers entry barriers to politics. That is, ordinary language enables more individuals to accumulate political followings and force their way into political bargaining, including bargaining over constitutional rules. Use of ordinary language as the medium of political expression is inconsistent with and threatens exclusive political institutions such as oligarchy, for the simple reason that oligarchy will encounter objections from would-be political contestants, whose opportunities to exercise power are limited in oligarchy, but who nevertheless possess the ability to mobilize supporters from the public. To survive, oligarchy must bar such objections; and once it bars forms of expression from political discourse, standardization begins and gradually eliminates the use of ordinary language from political life.

Hanson's argument about democratic consolidation emphasizes the importance of coherent enforcement by elites of the key institutional rules of liberal democracy. In this respect, he sees the stability of central state authority as a necessary precondition to the building of democratic state-society relationships. Yet, Hanson's viewpoint is very different from those of analysts, like Huntington (1968) or Bova (1998), who see authoritarian state building or strong presidentialism as helpful for later democratization. In fact, the emergence of a critical mass of state officials who are genuinely committed to the enforcement of rational-legal proceduralism becomes even less likely in a regime whose leaders argue for "temporary" suspensions of democracy or for the short-circuiting of duly elected legislatures. Historically, genuine ideological commitment to legal proceduralism among state staffs tends to emerge where memories of past absolutisms convince key political actors that the dispersal of political power is a public good that should be institutionalized if possible. Arguably, this means that the Russian Federation is potentially fertile ground for democratic state building in the long run (Collins 1998).

Fourth, in our approach to theory building, we do not limit ourselves to abstract processes or objective conditions, but stress processes in which there is a prominent role for human agency. That is, we draw the link between macro- and microlevels of analysis; our claims about macrolevel cause and effect demonstrate the microfoundations, be these strategic actors seeking self-interest or individuals animated by identities founded in discourse or by norms and values. Insofar as there are "objective external" constraints on human action, it must be possible to demonstrate how these are manifest through the presence of other empowered political actors. Insofar as there are "subjective constraints" such as norms or values, it must be possible to show that these are manifest in the assessments of individual actors.

In short, we are firmly agreed that "people matter" and that they matter a great deal. Not only do we all suffer from the political scientist's conceit that politics enjoys a great deal of independent force, but we all see people and the institutions they create as the prime movers in politics. We vary in our views of precisely how and what aspects of individuals' thought and action are most important, and we train our attention on different subjects of study. But as this volume shows, we collectively differ starkly from scholars who see human action as entirely scripted by cultural, economic, societal, or geographical preconditions. Thus, the analysis in each of these chapters begins by identifying the key actors and then keeps these at the center. Roeder examines the calculations of authoritarian officeholders operating under institutional constraints. Fish analyzes the choices of and constraints on chief executives in democratizing states. Anderson argues that the political elites' discursive choices influence the choices of individuals to remain passive or to take sides in politics. Hanson focuses on the purposes of elites and administrative staffs who are formally charged with enforcing democratic institutions.

Complementarities among Our Separate Approaches

Although our collaboration has been characterized by profound admiration for the work of one another, we are, nevertheless, keenly aware of our intellectual differences. These represent opportunities for intellectual growth for us as individuals much as we were schooled to believe they should in the social sciences as a whole. Moreover, we see these alternative approaches complementing rather than competing with one another. In particular, we have been impressed by three ways in which our separate analyses either help to complete the analysis of the others or define fruitful areas for further investigation.

First, we clearly state that we do not all define democracy in precisely the same way. Roeder defines the extent of democracy by the probability that half the population plus one member can remove incumbent officials (or defeat an attempt to do so). For Anderson the criterion is whether elites compete with one another and some of the citizens respond by taking sides. By this definition, not even elections are essential to democracy, although voting is the only practical way for "communities of any size" to take sides in politics (Schumpeter 1975). Fish defines democracy by the extent of rights to vote, communicate, and associate. Hanson defines democracy as "a state that formally defends institutional guarantees of electoral contestation and citizen participation."

The spare definitions of democracy used by Roeder and Anderson are complemented by the more complex definitions used by Fish and Hanson. All four chapters begin from a consensus that the core of democracy is the conventional definition of democracy found in Joseph Schumpeter's *Capitalism, Socialism, and Democracy* (1975), according to which democracy is "that institutional arrangement for arriving at political decisions in which individuals acquire the power to decide by means of a competitive struggle for the people's vote." Moreover, all use Robert Dahl's (1971) refinement of this definition, to wit, there must be both competition among those who aspire to exercise this decision-making power and accountability to the people through elections. This definition is far more parsimonious than many current in the literature on democratic theory, particularly notions that include an idea of equality of outcome (sometimes referred to as "substantive" democracy).

Yet, we differ in the extent to which we believe other elements should be added to this spare definition or distinguished as separate variables. Fish argues for including associational and communicative rights and freedoms—though *not* the *practices* of association or communication themselves—as diagnostic features of democracy. Such rights, he contends, are necessary to making electoral practice meaningful, and he shares some contemporary theorists' suspicions regarding the possible shortcomings of a strictly "electoralist" conception of democracy. His definition of democracy is therefore more inclusive, and less parsimonious, than is the basically Schumpeterian conception embraced by Roeder and Anderson, for the spare definition does not encompass the broader set of civil rights outside the electoral arena as defining features of democracy. Hanson largely concurs with Fish, but his institutional definition of democracy demands only that formal guarantees of political contestation and civic participation be in place; the extent to which these formal guarantees become dependable and predictable are for him measures of democratic consolidation rather than definitional attributes of democracy per se.

Roeder and Anderson argue for a terminological and conceptual distinction between "democracy" as a form of political accountability and "freedom," but readily agree that the former is less likely to function well or survive where there are too many restrictions on freedoms such as right of contract, property owning, and the like. Nonetheless, for them, the defining quality of democracy is the right to join in choosing leaders and policies. Whether people are denied liberties, abused by their government, forced to pay bribes to bureaucrats, or badly represented by elected officeholders matters to these people (and to all four of us), but in Anderson's and Roeder's analysis these considerations do not define a regime as democratic or authoritarian. There have been honest dictatorships and corrupt democracies. Russia has been both a corrupt dictatorship and a corrupt democracy (although the scale of corruption seems to have increased enormously in democratic Russia). It is the shift in the procedures for selecting decision makers and holding them accountable, not the quality of governance, that Anderson's and Roeder's theories explain.

The differences in definitional starting points do have consequences for our analyses—particularly, in cases in which only inclusive, fair and free elections or a broad array of civil liberties, but not both, are present. For example, these alternative definitions lead the authors to select different indicators—or operationalizations, as they are sometimes called—for measuring democratic attainment. Roeder, consistent with his Schumpeterian definition, uses the political liberties portion of the Freedom House scores as his measure of political contestation. This index includes whether the effective decision makers exercising executive and legislative powers are selected through free and fair elections with a real opposition that can displace incumbents and whether the citizens are free to organize in political parties and other political groupings for the purpose of retaining or displacing the incumbents (Freedom House 1992, 66). Fish's definition, by contrast, encompasses attention to the *quality* of democracy. True to his conceptual starting point, he uses the average of the political rights and civil liberties portions of the Freedom House ratings, which Freedom House itself dubs its "freedom rating." This adds to the political liberties index a number of other freedoms (Freedom House 1992, 67). Roeder's conceptual framework gives equal weight to political contestation and inclusiveness. This leads him to rate Estonia and Latvia as less than fully democratic, because a substantial portion of the adult population is effectively barred from electoral participation. Roeder concludes that the disfranchised minorities in the Baltic states may enjoy less sway over elected officials than do Russia's or Ukraine's universally enfranchised adult populations. Anderson is capable of joining Roeder in labeling Russia a "democracy," since post–Soviet Russia has indeed held several rounds of open, competitive elections. Alternatively, Fish concludes that disfranchised minorities in a liberal state may have more sway over their political destinies and elected officials than the enfranchised adults of an illiberal democracy. Fish argues that whatever curtails the electorate's choice—in particular, restrictions on civil liberties—compromises democracy itself and even calls into question the applicability of the term to an individual polity.

None of the definitions of democracy used by the authors may be regarded as "superior" to the others; any choice of definitions involves trade-offs. Choice is a matter of intellectual taste, as well as of the specific research question that one has posed. Early in our communications that led eventually to this book, we discussed the possibility of attempting to settle on a common definition of democracy. We agreed unanimously that such "agreement" was unnecessary and potentially counterproductive. The important thing, according to all of us, was to pick a definition and stick with it—as long as the definition was made explicit and its relationship to other definitions explained. We would maintain that polemics over the relative merits of definitions are not always worth the time that they consume in social scientific debates. But as the contributions to this volume demonstrate, it is important to set forth one's own definitions clearly and to remain acutely self-conscious of how choice of definition affects one's analytic approach and conclusions.

Second, each of the authors came to this joint undertaking with a distinctive analytic perspective on such issues as the role of interest and ideas in political action. Roeder and Fish stress interests. Roeder contends that politicians should be seen as power maximizers. Fish, despite his acknowledgment of a few exceptional leaders with the capacity to sacrifice power for the public good, sees politicians as generally motivated by an "arational" psychological drive for self-aggrandizement. While Anderson shares Roeder's assumption that politicians can be treated as power-max-imizers, he argues that discursive cues construct identities that inspire publics to active involvement in the political process on behalf of contes-tants—involvement that calculation of self-interest alone would foreclose. Hanson emphasizes the importance of principled individual action as a determinant of long-term institutional outcomes.

The difference of focus between Hanson's Weberian approach and Roeder's rational choice perspective does lead them to rather different evaluations of the conditions for regime stability. Roeder characterizes democracies, exclusive republics, oligarchies, and autocracies as perpetu-ally vulnerable to defection by elites who opt to move toward greater political openness or political closure. His approach does not call into question the theoretical utility of the concept of regime "consolidation," but he reflects the realists' skepticism that this normative unanimity is either common or enduring. The survival of democracy demands institu-tional barriers against cynical politicians and monitors who will try to play the true believers for suckers. From Roeder's perspective, consolida-tion of any regime calls for constant vigilance, monitoring, and sanc-tioning of defectors. Consolidation emerges when all major politicians and officials are confident that it is *in the interest* of one another to abide by the rules, and this occurs only when it is *in the interest* of the monitors to enforce sanctions against opportunistic politicians and officials. Han-son agrees with the first half of this formulation, but argues that monitors in an unstable institutional environment cannot be depended upon to en-force sanctions for purely self-interested purposes, because it is rarely in their self-interest to do so. At critical moments, their principles must in-spire the monitors to sacrifice their own immediate interests to long-term institutional goals.

Hanson's definition of democratic consolidation as a process by which the custodians of state agencies themselves come to behave in ways com-patible with the perpetuation of formal institutional rules resonates with Fish's findings on the supreme importance of the behavior of the chief executive. Hanson points out that democracy cannot be consolidated while enforcement of key democratic institutions remains uncertain, and Fish discovers that unconsolidated democracies are often undermined due to the intervention of power-hungry presidents. The logic connecting the two arguments seems clear: In the absence of reliable staff to enforce rules consistently, the chief executives are more likely to issue decrees and to marginalize political opponents, thereby further weakening democracy. Hanson and Fish would agree, moreover, that external support of such executives by the West in the name of "democracy" only tends to exacer-bate this problem. Still, there are also differences between their ap-proaches that merit note. Hanson, following and extending the analysis of Cirtautas and Mokrzycki (1993), draws a clear line between the consolidation or "institutionalization" of democracy, which occurs when supporters of democratic values within key state agencies are promoted ahead of relatively antidemocratic or corrupt individuals, and the nonconsolidation of democracy, which happens when this condition does not obtain. Fish, however, argues that the behavior and even ideological orientations of crucial elite actors may shift rapidly. Yesterday's democratizers, as surely as any consistently antidemocratic forces, may become today's foes of further democratization. Yeltsin, Akaev, Ter Petrosian, Nazarbaev, Kravchuk, and Berisha all served both as democratizers and, subsequently, as agents of backsliding to authoritarianism. Thus, Russia, Kyrgyzstan, Armenia, Kazakhstan, Ukraine, and Albania all suffered an erosion of earlier democratic gains—and at the hands of their own heroes of democratic revolution, not at those of openly antisystem parties or manifestly antiliberal forces.

Hanson's Weberian theory and Anderson's discursive theory have much in common. Both Hanson and Anderson are convinced that rational choice theory, taken seriously, demonstrates that no large population of purely instrumental actors should ever be able to overcome the collective action problems involved in creating stable institutions, whether democratic or authoritarian. Both draw the logical inference from this conclusion that modes of social identification are far more powerful in determining political outcomes than conventional "materialist" theories recognize, since only those who identify strongly with larger groups can be counted on to sacrifice personal interests to obtain group benefits. For Anderson identity is the solution to the paradox of participation that afflicts both enforcers of authoritarian rule and voters in a democracy when each considers only their self-interest. When a distinctive discourse cues enforcers of rules to distinguish themselves as a group from the population, they become motivated to impose the rulers' will on the population. When ordinary discourse cues the citizenry in a democracy to distinguish among candidates for office, citizens become motivated to form the partisan allegiances that motivate voting. Both undemocratic rule and democracy depend on identities, albeit of different kinds. Hanson's claim that democratic consolidation requires formation of a cadre of officials committed to the enforcement of democratic rules is an assertion that such a cadre must have a distinguishable identity separate from those on whom it enforces compliance with democratic procedure. He makes no claim that enforcement of democratic rules need benefit the officials in question more than some alternative strategy.

Where Hanson and Anderson differ is on the question of what sorts of identification matter most for institutional change. Anderson perceives a continuum of political discourse ranging from wholly inclusive (and thus democratic) to entirely invidious and closed to "outsiders" (and thus authoritarian). The condition for democracy to consolidate, in his view, is continuation over time of the condition for it to emerge—a discourse that guides production of texts in which citizens recognize sharing of political identity with politicians. Hanson instead argues that *all* political regimes require some principle of legitimation that distinguishes state enforcers from ordinary people, and that it is the *content* of these legitimating principles that distinguishes democratic from nondemocratic polities. These different theoretical positions motivate rather different sorts of research projects. Thus, Anderson finds that in 1993 ordinary citizens in Russia "connected" with liberal political discourse in Moscow and illiberal, nationalist political discourse in Voronezh. He interprets this as evidence that (at least in these two cities) Russian democracy was vibrant, not despite fundamental disagreements among Russians, but because of their political disagreements. Hanson, by contrast, would assess the degree of democratic consolidation in Russia through an examination of specific political principles promoted in Russian nationalist and liberal discourse, and the extent to which these principles consistently promote regularized, procedural enforcement of key democratic institutions. Hanson's approach produces a rather more guarded conclusion about the state of Russian democracy.

Third, the authors diverge in the extent to which they stress the role of elites or publics, yet their approaches complement one another. In particular, Anderson's analysis of the link between elites and masses in democracies naturally complements Hanson's focus on links between elites and staffs, and Fish's and Roeder's focus on elites. Fish and Roeder place elites at the center of their respective analyses, because these are the primary actors in the choice and survival of regimes. Hanson expands this with his postulate that because regime legitimacy is a quality of order giving and order taking, it necessarily also involves the enforcers of regime rules. Thus, he emphasizes the study of elite-staff relationships as the first step toward understanding regime change in unstable environments such as those typical of new democracies. Anderson expands the realm of political actors still further with his argument that we must understand how the public begins to participate as partisans of competitive politicians. Although this link between politicians and publics is central to many definitions of democracy, as Anderson points out, existing theory cannot explain the sudden willingness of previously passive publics to become active participants in the political process. Theories that focus on the fixed aspects of culture, economics, or society cannot account for this. Rational choice theories lead us to conclude that a simple change from authoritarian to democratic institutions is insufficient to elicit this change in behavior. To fill this void we must understand how discourse can cue the formation of identities that bind citizens to politicians as partisans in political competition and thereby stimulate the citizens to act on behalf of the politicians.

The Future and the Tenability of Our Approaches

In our early discussions of this volume, George Breslauer challenged us to be explicit about the conditions that might lead us to reassess our analyses. After all, social scientists commit themselves to the principle that their hypotheses must be formulated so that they are falsifiable and their support for their theories is contingent on the continuing success of the hypotheses derived from theory. Yet it often takes a challenge such as Breslauer's to remind us that we actually have a responsibility to state what developments would throw our theories into question.

In the logic of social science, theories themselves are not disconfirmed; the hypotheses they generate are. The latter are conditional expectations, not prognostications. Hypotheses are statements of the form "if . . . then . . ." Thus, hypotheses state what outcomes should appear when and where the conditions following the "if" and preceding the "then" are present, but they cannot state whether the if-conditions will, in fact, be present. Hypotheses are disconfirmed by repeated failures of the then-outcomes to occur when the if-conditions appear. We are more likely to abandon a theory when too many of the hypotheses derived from its premises fail this test, but only when there is also a better theory to replace it. That alternative theory must be able to account for more phenomena and cases than the original theory by surviving tests to falsify its own hypotheses.

A variety of real-world changes could falsify the central tenets of Fish's paper. If polities with superpresidential regimes turn out to make more progress toward democracy during the next decade or two than do polities in which power is separated and dispersed, Fish's theory is falsified. Many analysts have, in fact, argued in favor of superpresidentialism and regard it as better suited to postcommunist conditions in Russia—and perhaps elsewhere as well—than regimes that disperse power (Bova 1997; Mikheyev 1996). Many such authors hold that superexecutive power is superior from the standpoint of promoting a number of values, including democratization and democratic stability. If the weight of evidence in the region comes to favor this view, Fish will be shown to be wrong. He would be delighted to see his theory falsified and later regarded as little more than a clearly articulated, foolish, and misdirected effort to understand regime change, since the majority of inhabitants of the postcommunist world now reside in countries with a constitutionally mighty executive presidency. If this institution turns out, contrary to Fish's predictions, to facilitate democratization, several hundred million people will benefit from living in more open polities. Fish's theory will also take a beating if stronger civil societies, and in particular more vigorous opposition parties, prove to be less propitious for democratization than do weaker and more quiescent ones. Many authors have, in fact, portrayed strong civil societies as, at best, a mixed blessing for democratization, particularly in societies severely straitened by social turbulence (e.g., Hanson and Kopstein 1997; Berman 1997). If future developments show these authors to be right, then Fish's argument regarding the positive relationship between the strength of civil society and the advancement of democracy will be refuted. Again, Fish would be happy to be proven wrong, since most of the postcommunist world's citizens do not live in societies characterized by vigorous political and civil association and competition.

For Roeder the greatest challenge to his approach would be the discovery that concentrations of power promote democracy. First, if the autocrats of Belarus, Central Asia, and Azerbaijan turned out to be the George Washingtons of their respective countries, Roeder would go back to the drawing board. Indeed, over the past decade there were moments when many thought that enlightened presidents like Aleksandr Lukashenko or Nursultan Nazarbaev would, in fact, prove him wrong. These did not turn out to be particularly demanding tests. The autocracies are unlikely to evolve peacefully into democracies without crises, such as the death of the president. Second, if concentration of power in the fragile democracies, in fact, leads to an improvement in the mechanisms by which the public holds leaders accountable, Roeder would need to revisit the drawing board. (On this, the logic of Roeder's analysis is quite similar to that of Fish's.) Successful consolidation of democracy *following* the successful consolidation of control over key posts by a cohesive coalition of politicians—even if they were self-styled "democrats"—would be a major anomaly for Roeder's theory. This last may be the most important test for his theory because so many politicians in the Soviet successor states and their supporters abroad call for exactly this concentration of power. For example, the outcome of Putin's strategy to create a presidential party, win a legislative majority in the State Duma, tame the Council of the Federation, and subordinate or replace the regional governments will be an important test of the expectation that such concentrations of power normally do not lead to improvements in democratic accountability. The primary danger in such a strategy is the capture of powers that enable the president—or prime minister in other regimes—to control subsequent elections or that weaken countervailing centers of power that deter him from calling off elections. If these developments in Russia actually have the opposite effect of strengthening democratic accountability, Roeder would clearly need to rethink his analysis.

Anderson underscores that whether democracy continues to progress in Russia or suffers a reversal of the kind Fish describes is irrelevant to the validity of discursive theory. Social science is not soothsaying. Discursive theory provides explanations for a number of outcomes—the persistence of undemocratic rule (distancing political discourse), the persistence of democracy (political discourse in ordinary language), the transformation of nondemocracy into democracy (rapprochements with the vernacular), and reversal back to nondemocracy (restoration of distancing political discourse). Thus, according to the theory, any of these outcomes is possible in Russia. Discursive theory identifies the changes that must take place prior to each outcome. Discursive theory implies, among other things, that if democracy appears, then a rapprochement of political discourse with the vernacular must precede it. If any of the postcommunist states either has or does become democratic without first displaying a rapprochement of political discourse, either the theory is invalid or its domain (the set of observations to which it applies) is more limited than now appears. Discursive theory also implies that political discourse in ordinary language will always be more inclusive than political discourse in distancing language. If subsequent experiments reveal that fewer people appear likely to participate in politics (to vote, to protest, to campaign) after exposure to a political message in ordinary language than after exposure to a message preserving the semantic information in distancing language, then doubt will be cast on the theory. Discursive theory implies that undemocratic regimes require a distinctive political discourse to endure. The longer an undemocratic regime persists in the absence of a political discourse distinguishable from local vernaculars, the more invalid the theory will seem. Other hypotheses doubtless remain to be developed, but these are the ones most central to the discursive theory of regime change.

What would lead Hanson to reassess his approach to analyzing unconsolidated democracy? Definitions themselves, like the premises in theories, cannot be "falsified" by empirical evidence. Instead, we assess the fruitfulness and utility of definitions in social science by their ability to generate new, testable hypotheses—especially hypotheses left unexplored because existing social science theories and associated definitions failed to highlight their potential importance. If such new hypotheses fail to find empirical support, however, then eventually the definition that generated them may reasonably be rejected as unfruitful and untenable. If we accept that Russia today is an "unconsolidated democracy," three testable hypotheses concerning the future of the Russian Federation suggest themselves—although given the Weberian emphasis on the probabilistic rather than deterministic nature of social change, these should be understood as statements concerning the likelihood of trends rather than "point predictions" about a remarkably fluid situation. First, and most critically, the Weberian approach suggests that Russian democracy cannot become stable until a critical mass of state officials begins to accept the formal legal principles of the regime as legitimate—that is, they must see enforcement of such principles as a duty and not merely as expedient for their own personal advancement. Until this happens, one should expect the current regime to be subject to perpetual challenges from within and without. Second, it suggests that unless some specific alternative form of nondemocratic rule becomes legitimate for a critical mass of key enforcers, movements to establish authoritarianism in Russia will also suffer from problems of free-riding, corruption, and instability. Indeed, the formal framework of Russian electoral democracy may endure for much longer than one might ordinarily expect due to the programmatic incoherence and uncharismatic personalities of the majority of leading antiliberal Russian politicians. Third, if this approach is right, the most powerful factor influencing the direction of long-term institutional change in Russia will not be the material interests of unorganized social groups or the formal rules governing political contestation, but rather the nature of the political ideologies that find social support in the vast, turbulent post-Soviet space.

Of course, at this juncture none of us foresees developments in the next decade that are likely to lead us to reassess our findings drawn from the first decade of postcommunism. Still, just as the first decade filled us with a sense of surprise and wonderment, each of us has a healthy respect for the power of events to challenge theories and so we realize that we must continue to test and question our own judgments. If we are to be proved wrong by future events, we all hope—for the sake of the peoples of these lands—that we learn that establishing, deepening, and consolidating democracy, and avoiding authoritarianism, are less problematic undertakings than we have explained here.

NOTES

CHAPTER ONE
INTRODUCTION

1. For stimulating, recent contributions to the literature on defining democracy, see Comisso (1997) and Collier and Levitsky (1997).

2. There are innumerable works that could be cited; many of them are mentioned in the chapters that follow. For purposes of an "Introduction," I will not repeat those citations. The concept of "Third Wave," however, comes from Huntington (1991).

CHAPTER TWO
THE REJECTION OF AUTHORITARIANISM

1. In most instances these four categories also correspond to increasing proportionate size of the selectorate; that is, autocracy, oligarchy, exclusive republics, and democracies, in that order, represent regimes in which an increasingly larger share of the adult population constitutes the selectorate. Yet, some exclusive republics, such as plutocracies, can have smaller selectorates than bureaucratic oligarchies.

2. In both of the latter two groups, relative levels of participation by the public in elections are unimportant for the classification of regimes.

3. Of course, in any of these successor states one can point to isolated elements that might be interpreted as the seeds of a democratic tradition (Petro 1995; Critchlow 1992). Yet, the national cultures *taken as a whole* and viewed in comparison with other cultures show little evidence that they are as congruent with the institutions of democracy as cultures found in countries where democracy has flourished. Indeed, when viewed comparatively, the political culture of the Russian Empire and the Soviet Union seems to represent a rather extreme example of noncongruence with democracy.

4. Even in a very stable democracy such as the United States there will be minor jockeying among political forces that seek to tailor the selectorate by manipulating census-taking methods, voter registration procedures, or barriers to citizenship. Yet, these do not change the nature of the selectorate.

5. Of course, not every intra-elite power struggle threatens the stability of an autocratic constitution—only those that threaten to expand the selectorate. Challenges from aspiring autocrats, particularly during a succession, are normal politics in autocracy.

6. For example, a junta representing different military branches may delegate decision making to executives, but it retains the power to select and remove the president and other key officials.

7. I am particularly in debt to Barbara Ann Chotiner for several discussions about rural control structures.

8. Data on indigenization from Hodnett (1978: 101–103, 377–78); Jones and Grupp (1984, 174); Helf (1988); USSR (1984). For long-term trends in indigenization within specific republics, see Armstrong (1959, 15–17); Burg (1979, 43–59); Lubin (1981, 283); Olcott (1987, 199–246); Parsons (1982, 554); Suny (1988, 209–318); USSR (1972–73, II,12–75, IV, 365–82).

9. This figure (32.6 percent) is calculated from the report of Latvian officials that as of 26 May 1993, the eligible electorate stood at 1,245,530, while the adult population at that time was estimated to have been 1,848,514 (Bungs 1993, 8–49).

10. While richer definitions may correspond more closely to a complex reality, the inevitable trap of such compound or multidimensional definitions is that they quickly overtax the explanatory power of any theory. Even in the simplest of worlds, where each dimension is simply a dichotomy, the number of discrete outcomes (that is, categorical values of the dependent variable) rises exponentially. It rises from 2 to 4 (that is, 2^2) to 8 (that is, 2^3) and so forth with each additional dimension. For example, Linz (1975, 278) emphasizes at least three dimensions of authoritarian regimes—limits on pluralism, degree and type of participation, and ideologization. Linz's dimensions are not simply dichotomous and so there are at least $5 \times 4 \times 2 = 40$ possible discrete outcomes or types of authoritarian regimes that need explanation. This exceeds the explanatory power of most social science theories. If the number of regime-types is actually less because these dimensions are collinear, then Linz's distinction is actually unidimensional. (This possibility is suggested by Linz's [1975, figure 1] typology in which all regimes fall on a single diagonal line that runs from one to the opposite extreme on all three dimensions.) In this latter case one must either define the "factor" on which all three dimensions are "loaded" or identify the one dimension that trumps the other two. This is what a spare definition provides. My claim is that accountability is this dimension.

CHAPTER THREE
THE DYNAMICS OF DEMOCRATIC EROSION

1. Tajikistan, which experienced a very short-lived opening and received a score of 3 in 1991–92, but quickly moved back to hard authoritarianism and never scored better than 6 from 1992–93 to 1999–2000, is classified in this category.

2. Bulgaria, which is located in Category III, represents an exception; it developed fairly strong programmatic parties during the 1990s. As discussed below, Bulgaria is exceptional in several respects.

3. Bulgaria achieved an impressive Freedom House score of 2 in the 1993–94 survey and held this level until 1996–97, when it was downgraded to a 2.5 due to "increasing restraints on the media" (Freedom House 1996–97). Its score subsequently remained at that level. While the hapless Zhan Videnov, the prime minister at the time, presided over the growth of restrictions on the media, one cannot attribute the change mainly to him. The Bulgarian Socialist Party, the governing party at the time, was itself largely to blame. In early 1997, massive street demonstrations forced the paralyzed and inept Socialist government to hold new elections, and the Socialists were subsequently drubbed by the main center-right party,

the Union of Democratic Forces. Bulgaria's score slipped from a relatively high level, and even after the change, which was modest, the country still enjoyed a rating that was far better than any other country in the backsliders category and as good or better than some countries in the democratizers category.

4. Information here and elsewhere on elections and referenda are drawn from Freedom House, various volumes; *Europa World Yearbook*, various volumes; Radio Free Europe/Radio Liberty Newsline reports; and various press and World Wide Web sources.

CHAPTER FOUR
THE DISCURSIVE ORIGINS OF RUSSIAN DEMOCRATIC POLITICS

1. A discursive theory breaks with its predecessors by rejecting the conception of democracy as an institution. While democracies do feature distinctive institutions, Schumpeter's (1975) concept of the electoral method implies that this is to be understood as a resultant or product of the opportunity to take sides. Given the opportunity to take sides, people demand institutions that make this opportunity easier to exercise—it takes less time and effort to vote than to assemble, to demonstrate or to fight, and it is easier to determine the winner in a vote than in, say, competitive demonstrations.

2. A discursive theory derives its propositions about these inferences of self, these identities, from the assumption of individuality, not that of individualism. Individualism is the assumption that each person has a fixed identity peculiar to himself or herself. Individuality is the assumption that people are biological individuals, observably distinguishable from each other but possibly bearing some common traits. It is readily observable that the organic traits common to biological individuals do not include any fixed identity. Identities are mental constructs, not organic traits. People assume that their identities are stable only to the degree that they forget what their identities have been in the past.

3. When the effect of partisanship on voting is decomposed, its correspondence with the implications of social identity theory becomes even more evident. Partisanship predicts voting if the background condition is present that campaigning by candidates supplies discursive cues reminding partisans of their party identifications. When this background condition is present, those who identify with either party are more likely to pay the cost of voting than those who do not identify. When this background condition is absent, for instance, at the early stage of a campaign before most partisans have been exposed to discursive cues reminding them of their political identity, many partisans are undecided—that is, are not ready to make the choice between candidates that is the act of voting. Moreover, the relationship of partisanship to voting holds more strongly when the office at stake is more important and when the candidate of the voter's own party is more likely to win. In other words, when the office makes less difference to the perceptual spread between the voter's own party and the other party, or when the contribution of a vote to the candidate seems less likely to increase the advantage for the voter's own party over the other party, partisan identity has less impact on voting. Finally, that anyone is observed to vote when not identifying with a political party appears to be a consequence of the failure of questions about party

identification to correctly classify persons who claim to be independents (Keith et al. 1992).

4. In general a personal self is definable only with some social self, by the individual contrasting the self against other individuals bearing that same social identity, and multiple social selves are nested within some overarching category.

5. The Hungarian constitution of 1514 (Kann 1950, 116) supplies another example: "Under the name and designation of the people one comprehends here only the bishops, lords, the other aristocrats, and all the nobles, but not the commoners. . . . Under the name of plebs only the commoners are comprehended." "People" are defined, while "plebs" are a residual category, those "not" comprehended among the people.

6. It has been persuasively argued that an unexpectedly large demonstration, if it is not too large, may signal people to revise their estimates of the probability of overthrowing the regime, with the result that for enough demonstrators, the expected disutility of action becomes smaller than the expected utility of overthrowing of the regime (Lohmann 1994). If the size of the demonstration is sufficiently uncertain, however, its capacity to signal dissolves in the uncertainty about whether it is large enough or too large. And the size of any given demonstration is highly uncertain (for variance in estimates of Russian demonstrations, see Beissinger 1997).

7. Definition of political identity by a privative opposition, assigning no identity to the majority, also generates antipathy among the people.

8. In discursive theory, partisan identification results from distinguishing between individual contestants for power. In the absence of cues to opposed identities, social identity theory predicts that people will become more attentive to differences among individuals. In contrast to nondemocracy, where rulers with quite distinctive political identities may be seen as indistinguishable by people cued by discourse to attend to group rather than individual traits, in democracy the absence of these cues allows perceived difference between individual candidates to become the criterion by which people arrange themselves on either side of the vertical, partisan cleavage that defines a democratic order. John Petrocik and Shanto Iyengar (1998) have recently argued that U.S. presidential campaigns align voters according to a simple rule that applies to a tripartite division of the electorate. First, partisan voters vote for the candidate of their own party. Second, independents vote for the incumbent if they approve his performance and vote for the challenger if they disapprove. Third, some partisan voters defect. They defect if their approval for the candidate of the opposing party exceeds their approval for the candidate of their own party.

9. Such partisan identities are independent of, and prior to, stable parties, which is why Russia can be democratic despite its remarkably unstable party system (as can, for instance, France). A voter can identify with "right" or "left" even if the parties contending for those labels are kaleidoscopic in their shifting configurations.

10. In a two-oligarch model the result of playing "expel" can be represented as "succeed with some probability."

11. More generally, in a similar analysis Geddes (1994) has shown how political reforms of various kinds can become more likely when the opposing sides to a political conflict are close in relative power.

12. A particular merit of this model is its ability to explain why Soviet specialists could not have anticipated democratization in Russia. This event depended on a variable that was highly labile in the short term—the precise configuration of power within the Politburo. Of course, Soviet specialists did make a mistake, but it was to attend to the wrong variables—economic and social conditions.

13. To test for the effect of education, we deliberately oversampled respondents with higher education. This variable turned out to be insignificant and is omitted below.

14. The experiment was also conducted in Pskov by a local team, but I omit the Pskov data here because incomplete recording of responses by local interviewers renders the data not precisely comparable to the Moscow and Voronezh results. For this reason discussion of the Pskov data requires more space than is available here.

15. A discursive theory begins with the assumption that human action responds to environmental cues. Some cues are linguistic, some extralinguistic, e.g., social or physical. Because decisions to take sides will depend on the social and physical context as well as on the linguistic cues encountered by the individual, no experiment confined to varying the linguistic cues alone can possibly reproduce the behavior of taking sides. Moreover, not only is it infeasible, but it obviously would be highly unethical for an experimenter to assume such control of the individual's social and physical environment as to manipulate behavior. Finally, in the experiment we exposed each respondent to one text, but discursive theory holds that individuals' behavioral choices depend on the stream of texts they encounter. Each of our respondents had previously encountered, directly or indirectly, many other political texts, and discursive theory assumes that behavior depends on the sum of those encounters, not merely on the latest cue.

16. Voting is known to vary with political affiliation. In established democracies political affiliation has been measured in survey research by asking respondents about partisanship and about membership in organizations with political agendas. In a new democracy where partisanship will inevitably be nascent and organizations with political agendas scarce, the appropriateness of such measures is doubtful.

17. Another objection may contend that the experiment is tapping ideological attitudes rather than responses to linguistic cues. This objection rests on a misunderstanding of attitude formation. There is nothing innate about ideological attitudes. People encounter political communications, process them, and form attitudes. It may well be that there are congenital dispositions that affect the processing of political communications, with the result that a person is born with or develops personality traits that influence the reception of political texts. This possibility, while plausible, remains unproven. It is clear that people's life experience—for example, their position in the economy—does bear on their processing of political communications. But in the absence of encounters with textual cues, people's life experience and their predispositions would not suffice to enable them to converge on a coherent set of ideological attitudes. The Russian participants

in the experiment had frequently—to the point of "nausea," as more than one remarked—encountered authoritarian communist texts. Coupled with their experience, those encounters led them, on average, to develop a negative or indifferent attitude toward the communist texts. Over a shorter, more recent period, they had also encountered "democratic," "centrist," and "patriotic" texts. Despite the overwhelmingly negative experiences associated with the more recent encounters—2,000 percent inflation during 1992, mass insecurity about employment, difficulties finding affordable food—encounters with electoral texts had led the respondents, on average, to form positive attitudes. To say that the experiment taps ideological attitudes expressed in response to texts of various kinds is to confirm the theoretical prediction that electoral texts cue people to take sides while authoritarian texts cue people to recognize difference of social identity.

REFERENCES

Almond, Gabriel A., and Sidney Verba. 1963. *The Civic Culture: Political Attitudes and Democracy in Five Nations*. Princeton, N.J.: Princeton University Press.

"And the Winner Is?" 2000. *Moscow Times* (September 9), 1–2.

Anderson, Richard D., Jr. 1993. *Public Politics in an Authoritarian State: Making Foreign Policy During the Brezhnev Years*. Ithaca, N.Y.: Cornell University Press.

———. 1997. "Speech and Democracy in Russia: Responses to Political Texts in Three Russian Cities," *British Journal of Political Science* 27 (January):23–45.

Armstrong, John A. 1959. *The Soviet Bureaucratic Elite: A Case Study of the Ukrainian Apparatus*. New York: Frederick A. Praeger.

Bahry, Donna. 1993. "Society Transformed: Rethinking the Social Roots of Perestroika," *Slavic Review* 52 (Fall):512–54.

Bahry, Donna, and Lucan Way. 1994. "Citizen Activism in the Russian Transition," *Post-Soviet Affairs* 10(October–December):330–66.

Banfield, Edward C., and Laura Fasano Banfield. 1958. *The Moral Basis of a Backward Society*. Glencoe, Ill.: Free Press.

Barany, Zoltan. 1995. "The Return of the Left in East-Central Europe," *Problems of Post-Communism* 42 (January–February):41–45.

Barnard, Chester Irving. 1938. *The Functions of the Executive*. Cambridge: Harvard University Press.

Barrington, Lowell. 1995. "The Domestic and International Consequences of Citizenship in the Soviet Successor States," *Europe-Asia Studies* 47 (July):731–63.

Basom, Kenneth E. 1996. "Prospects for Democracy in Serbia and Croatia," *East European Quarterly* 29, 4 (Winter):509–28.

Bates, Robert H., Chalmers Johnson, and Ian Lustick. 1997. "Controversy in the Discipline: Area Studies and Comparative Politics," *PS: Political Science and Politics* 30 (June): 166–79.

Beaugrande, Robert de. 1985. "Text Linguistics in Discourse Studies." In *Disciplines of Discourse*, edited by Teun A. van Dijk. London: Academic Press, vol. 1, pp. 41–70.

Beissinger, Mark. 1997. "Event Analysis in Transitional Societies: Protest Mobilization in the Former Soviet Union." In *Acts of Dissent: New Developments in the Study of Protest*, edited by Dieter Rucht, Friedhelm Neidhardt, and Ruud Koopmans. Berlin: Sigma Press.

Berezovskii, V. N., and N. I. Krotov. 1990. *Neformal'naia Rossiia: O Neformal'-nykh politizirovannykh dvizheniiakh i gruppakh v RSFSR (opyt spravochnika)*. Moscow: Molodaia gvardiia.

Berman, Sheri. 1997. "Civil Society and the Collapse of the Weimar Republic," *World Politics* 49, 3 (April):401–29.

Bermeo, Nancy. 1992. "Democracy and the Lessons of Dictatorship," *Comparative Politics* 24(April):273–91.

Bermeo, Nancy. 1997. "Getting Mad or Going Mad? Citizens, Scarcity and the Breakdown of Democracy in Interwar Europe." Research Monograph Series no. 10, University of California, Irvine.

Bernhard, Michael. 1999. "Institutional Choice and the Failure of Democracy: The Case of Interwar Poland," *East European Politics and Societies* 13, (Winter):34–70.

Bojcun, Marko. 1995. "The Ukrainian Parliamentary Elections in March–April 1994," *Europe-Asia Studies* 47 (March):229–49.

Bollen, Kenneth A. 1979. "Political Democracy and the Timing of Development, *American Sociological Review* 44 (August):572–87.

Bova, Russell. 1997. "Democracy and Liberty: The Cultural Connection," *Journal of Democracy* 8, 1 (January):112–26.

———. 1998. "Political Culture, Authority Patterns, and the Architecture of the New Russian Democracy." In *Can Democracy Take Root in Post–Soviet Russia?: Explorations in State-Society Relations*, edited by Harry Eckstein et al. Lanham, Md.: Rowman and Littlefield, pp. 177–200.

Breslauer, George W. 1989. "Evaluating Gorbachev As Leader," *Soviet Economy* 5 (October–December):299–340.

———. 2000. "Evaluating Gorbachev and Yeltsin As Leaders." University of California, Berkeley.

Bresser Pereira, Luiz Carlos, José Maria Maravall, and Adam Przeworski. 1993. *Economic Reforms in New Democracies*. Cambridge: Cambridge University Press.

Brovkin, Vladimir. 1990. "First Party Secretaries: An Endangered Species?" *Problems of Communism* 39 (January–February): 15–27.

———. 1996. "The Emperor's New Clothes: Continuity of Soviet Political Culture in Contemporary Russia," *Problems of Post-Communism* 43, 2 (March–April):21–28.

Brown, Bess. 1992a. "The Presidential Election in Uzbekistan," *RFE/RL Research Report* 1 (24 January): 23–25.

———. 1992b. "Whither Tajikistan?" *RFE/RL Research Report* 1 (12 June): 1–6.

———. 1993. "Central Asia: The First Year of Unexpected Statehood," *RFE/RL Research Report* 2 (1 January): 25–36.

Brown, Gillian, and George Yule. 1983. *Discourse Analysis*. Cambridge University Press.

Brzezinski, Zbigniew, and Samuel P. Huntington. 1964. *Political Power: USA/ USSR*. New York: Viking Press.

Bunce, Valerie. 1994. "Sequencing of Political and Economic Reforms." In *East-Central European Economies in Transition*, edited by John P. Hardt and Richard Kaufman. Washington, D.C.: U.S. GPO.

———. 1995. "Comparing East and South," *Journal of Democracy* 6, 3 (July):87–100.

———. 1998. "Regional Differences in Democratization: The East Versus the South," *Post-Soviet Affairs* 14, 3 (July–September):187–211.

———. 1999a. "The Return of the Left and the Future of Democracy in Eastern and Central Europe." In Birol A Yeilada, ed. *Comparative Political Parties and*

Party Elites: Essays in Honor of Samuel J. Eldersveld. Ann Arbor: University of Michigan Press, pp. 151–76.

———. 1999b. *Subversive Institutions.* Cambridge: Cambridge University Press.

Bungs, Dzintra. 1993. "Twenty-three Groups Vie for Seats in the Latvian Parliament," *RFE/RL Research Bulletin* 2 (4 June): 48–49.

Burg, Steven L. 1979. "Russians, Natives, and Jews in the Soviet Scientific Elite: Cadre Competition in Central Asia," *Cahiers du Monde Russe et Sovietique* 20 (January–March): 43–59.

Burkhart, Ross E., and Michael S. Lewis-Beck. 1994. "Comparative Democracy: The Economic Development Thesis," *American Political Science Review* 88 (December):903–10.

Burton, Michael, Richard Gunther, and John Higley. 1992a. "Introduction: Elite Transformations and Democratic Regimes." In *Elites and Democratic Consolidation in Latin America and Southern Europe*, edited by Higley and Gunther. Cambridge: Cambridge University Press, pp. 1–37.

———. 1992b. "Elites and Democratic Consolidation in Latin America and Southern Europe: An Overview." In *Elites and Democratic Consolidation in Latin America and Southern Europe*, edited by Higley and Gunther. Cambridge: Cambridge University Press, pp. 323–48.

Calinescu, Matei, and Vladimir Tismaneanu. 1991. "The 1989 Revolution and Romania's Future," *Problems of Communism* 40 (January–April):42–59.

Callaghy, Thomas M. 1994. "Africa: Back to the Future?" *Journal of Democracy* 5, 4 (October):133–45.

Carey, Henry F. 1996. "From Big Lie to Small Lies," *East European Politics and Societies* 10, 1 (Winter):16–45.

Carothers, Thomas. 1996. "Romania: Projecting the Positive," *Current History* (March):118–23.

Chernov, V. A. 1984. *Russkii iazyk v XVII veke.* Krasnoyarsk: Izdatel'stvo Krasnoiarskogo universiteta.

Cirtautas, Arista Maria, and Edmund Mokrzycki. 1993. "The Articulation and Institutionalization of Democracy in Poland," *Social Research* 60 (Winter):787–810.

Clark, Terry D. 1995. "The Lithuanian Political Party System: A Case Study of Democratic Consolidation," *East European Politics and Societies* 9 (Winter): 41–62.

Cmiel, Kenneth. 1990. *Democratic Eloquence: The Fight over Popular Speech in Nineteenth-Century America.* Berkeley: University of California Press.

Cohen, Lenard J. 1997. "Embattled Democracy." In *Politics, Power, and the Struggle for Democracy in South-East Europe*, edited by Karen Dawisha and Bruce Parrott. Cambridge: Cambridge University Press, pp. 69–121.

Cohen, Shari. 1999. *Politics Without a Past: The Absence of History in Postcommunist Nationalism.* Durham, N.C.: Duke University Press.

Cohen, Youssef. 1994. *Radicals, Reformers, and Reactionaries.* Chicago, Ill.: University of Chicago Press.

Collier, David, and Steven Levitsky. 1997. "Democracy with Adjectives: Conceptual Innovation in Comparative Research," *World Politics* 49, 3 (April):430–51.

Collier, Ruth Berins, and James Mahoney. 1997. "Adding Collective Actors to Collective Outcomes: Labor and Recent Democratization in South America and Southern Europe," *Comparative Politics* 29(3):285–303.

Collins, Kathleen. 1997. "Clans, Parties, and Politics: The Failure of Political Parties in 'Democratic' Kyrgyzstan." Stanford University, Stanford.

Collins, Randall. 1998. "Democratization in World-Historical Perspective." In *Democracy and Modernization*, edited by Ralph Schroeder. New York: St. Martin's, pp. 14–31.

Comisso, Ellen. 1997. "Is the Glass Half Full or Half Empty? Reflections on Five years of Competitive Politics in Eastern Europe," *Communist and Post-Communist Studies* 30, 1 (March): 1–23.

Cotteret, Jean-Marie et al. 1976. *Giscard d'Estaing, Mitterand: 54774 mots pour convaincre*. Paris: Presses universitaires de France.

Craumer, Peter R., and James I. Clem. 1999. "Ukraine's Emerging Electoral Geography: A Regional Analysis of the 1998 Parliamentary Elections," *Post-Soviet Geography* 40 (January): 1–26.

Critchlow, James. 1992. "Democratization in Kazakhstan," *RFE/RL Research Report* 1 (24 July): 12–14.

Crowther, William. 1994. "Moldova After Independence," *Current History* 93 (October): 342–47.

———. 1997. "The Politics of Democratization in Postcommunist Moldova." In *Democratic Changes and Authoritarian Reactions in Russia, Ukraine, Belarus, and Moldova*, edited by Karen Dawisha and Bruce Parrott. Cambridge: Cambridge University Press, pp. 282–329.

Curry, Jane L. 1995. "Elected Communists in Poland," *Problems of Post-Communism* 42 (January–February):46–50.

Dahl, Robert A. 1971. *Polyarchy: Participation and Opposition*. New Haven, Conn.: Yale University Press.

———. 1982. *Dilemmas of Pluralist Democracy*. New Haven, Conn.: Yale University Press.

———. 1989. *Democracy and Its Critics*. New Haven, Conn.: Yale University Press.

Dahl, Robert A., and Edward R. Tufte. 1983. *Size and Democracy*. Stanford, Calif.: Stanford University Press.

Davies, Philip John, and Andrejs Valdis Ozolins. 1994. "The Latvian Parliamentary Election of 1993," *Electoral Studies* 13, 1.

Deletant, Dennis. 1995. "The Securitate Legacy in Romania," *Problems of Post-Communism* 42 (November–December):23–28.

Di Palma, Giuseppe. 1977. *Surviving Without Governing*. Berkeley: University of California Press.

———. 1990. *To Craft Democracies: An Essay on Democratic Transitions*. Berkeley and Los Angeles: University of California Press.

Diamond, Larry. 1996. "Toward Democratic Consolidation." In *The Global Resurgence of Democracy*, edited by Larry Diamond and Marc F. Plattner, 2d. ed. Baltimore, Md.: Johns Hopkins University Press, pp. 227–40.

Diez, Mary E. 1986. "Negotiation Competence: A Conceptualization of the Rules of Negotiation Interaction." In *Contemporary Issues in Language and Dis-*

course Processes, edited by Donald G. Ellis and William A. Donahue. Hillsdale, N.J.: Lawrence Erlbaum, pp. 223–37.

Downs, Anthony. 1957. *An Economic Theory of Democracy*. New York: Harper.

Dudwick, Nora. 1997. "Political Transformations in Postcommunist Armenia." In *Conflict, Cleavage, and Change in Central Asia and the Caucasus*, edited by Karen Dawisha and Bruce Parrott. Cambridge: Cambridge University Press, pp. 69–109.

Dunlop, John. 1993. *The Rise of Russia and the Fall of the Soviet Empire*. Princeton, N.J.: Princeton University Press.

Easter, Gerald M. 1997. "Preference for Presidentialism: Postcommunist Regime Change in Russia and the NIS," *World Politics* 49, 2 (January): 184–211.

Eckstein, Harry. 1961. *The Theory of Stable Democracy* (Research Monograph 10). Princeton, N.J.: Princeton University, Center of International Studies.

———. 1966. *Division and Cohesion in Democracy: A Study of Norway*. Princeton, N.J.: Princeton University Press.

———. 1998a. "Congruence Theory Explained." In *Can Democracy Take Root in Post–Soviet Russia?: Explorations in State-Society Relations*, edited by Harry Eckstein et al. Lanham, M.D.: Rowman and Littlefield, pp. 3–33.

———. 1998b. "Russia and the Conditions of Democracy." In *Can Democracy Take Root in Post–Soviet Russia?: Explorations in State-Society Relations*, edited by Harry Eckstein et al. Lanham, M.D.: Rowman and Littlefield, pp. 349–81.

Economou, Konstantin. 1997. "Representing Politics—Politicizing Journalism; Exploring Communicative Dilemmas in the Collegial Relationship between Swedish Journalists and Politicians." Paper presented to a conference on "Analysing Political Discourse," Birmingham, UK, July 17–19, 1997.

Edelman, Murray. 1988. *Constructing the Political Spectacle*. Chicago: University of Chicago Press.

Ekiert, Grzegorz. 1996. *The State Against Society*. Princeton, N.J.: Princeton University Press.

Elster, Jon. 1989. *The Cement of Society*. Cambridge: Cambridge University Press.

Errington, James Joseph. 1985. *Language and Social Change in Java: Linguistic Reflexes of Modernization in a Traditional Royal Polity*. Athens: Ohio University, Center for International Studies.

Ertman, Thomas. 1998. "Democracy and Dictatorship in Interwar Western Europe Revisited," *World Politics* 50, 3 (April):475–505.

Europa World Yearbook. Various volumes.

Faundez, Julio. 1997. "In Defense of Presidentialism: The Case of Chile, 1932–70." In *Presidentialism and Democracy in Latin America*, edited by Scott Mainwaring and Matthew Soberg Shugart. Baltimore, Md.: Johns Hopkins University Press, pp. 300–320.

Finer, S. E. 1971. *Comparative Government*. New York: Basic Books.

Fiorina, Morris P., and Kenneth A. Shepsle. 1989. "Formal Theories of Leadership." In *Leadership and Politics: New Perspectives in Political Science*, edited by Bryan D. Jones. Lawrence: University Press of Kansas, pp. 17–40.

Fish, M. Steven. 1995. *Democracy from Scratch: Opposition and Regime in the New Russian Revolution*. Princeton, N.J.: Princeton University Press.

Fish, M. Steven. 1997a. "The Pitfalls of Russian Superpresidentialism," *Current History* 96, 612 (October):326–30.

———. 1997b. "The Predicament of Russian Liberalism," *Europe-Asia Studies* 49 (March):191–220.

———. 1998a. "Democratization's Requisites," *Post-Soviet Affairs* 14, (July–September):212–47.

———. 1998b. "The Determinants of Economic Reform in the Post-Communist World," *East European Politics and Societies* 12, 1 (Winter):31–78.

———. 1998c. "Mongolia: Democracy Without Prerequisites," *Journal of Democracy* 9, 3 (July):127–41.

———. 1999. "The End of Meciarism," *East European Constitutional Review* 8, 1/2 (Winter–Spring):47–55.

Fish, M. Steven, and Robin S. Brooks. 2000. "Bulgarian Democracy's Organizational Weapon," *East European Constitutional Review* 9 (Summer): 63–71.

Fleron, Frederic J., Jr., and Richard Ahl. 1998. "Does the Public Matter for Democratization in Russia? What We Have Learned from Third Wave Transitions and Public Opinion Surveys." In *Can Democracy Take Root in Post–Soviet Russia?: Explorations in State-Society Relations*, edited by Harry Eckstein et al. Lanham, Md.: Rowman and Littlefield, pp. 287–327

Forsyth, J. 1970. *A Grammar of Aspect: Usage and Meaning in the Russian Verb.* Cambridge: Cambridge University Press.

Frangoudaki, Anna. 1992. "Diglossia and the Present Language Situation in Greece: A Sociological Approach to the Interpretation of Diglossia and Some Hypotheses on Today's Linguistic Reality." *Language and Society* 21 (September):365–81.

Freedom House. Various years. *Freedom in the World.* New York: Freedom House.

Friedgut, Theodore H. 1979. *Political Participation in the USSR.* Princeton, N.J.: Princeton University Press.

Frye, Timothy. 1997. "A Politics of Institutional Choice: Post-Communist Presidencies," *Comparative Political Studies* 30 (October): 523–52.

Fukuyama, Francis. 1993. "The Modernizing Imperative: The USSR As an Ordinary Country," *National Interest* 31 (Spring):10–19.

———. 1995. "The Primacy of Culture," *Journal of Democracy* 6, 1 (January):7–14.

Fuller, Elizabeth. 1992a. "Georgian President Flees, Opposition Seizes Power," *RFE/RL Research Report* 1 (17 January): 4–7.

———. 1992b. "The Ongoing Political Power Struggle in Azerbaijan," *RFE/RL Research Report* 1 (1 May): 11–13.

———. 1992c. "Azerbaijan After the Presidential Elections," *RFE/RL Research Bulletin* 1 (26 June): 1–7.

———. 1992d. "The Georgian Parliamentary Elections," *RFE/RL Research Bulletin* 1 (27 November): 1–4.

———. 1992e. "Armenia, Azerbaijan, and Georgia," *RFE/RL Research Bulletin* 1 (2 October): 74–76.

———. 1996. "The Fall from Democratic Grace," *Transition* 2 (15 November):41–45.

Gati, Charles. 1996. "If Not Democracy, What? Leaders, Laggards, and Losers in the Postcommunist World." In *Postcommunism: Four Views*, edited by Michael Mandelbaum. New York: Council in Foreign Relations, pp. 168–98.

Geddes, Barbara. 1994. *Politician's Dilemma: Building State Capacity in Latin America*. Berkeley: University of California Press.

Geis, Michael L. 1987. *The Language of Politics*. New York: Springer-Verlag.

Gelman, Harry. 1990. *Gorbachev's First Five Years in the Soviet Leadership*. Santa Monica, Calif.: Rand Corporation.

Gibson, Edward L. 1996. *Class and Conservative Parties*. Baltimore, Md.: Johns Hopkins University Press.

———. 1997. "Social Networks and Civil Society in Processes of Democratization." Paper presented to Annual Meeting of the American Political Science Association, Washington, D.C.

Goldgeier, James. 1999. *Not Whether but When: The U.S. Decision to Enlarge NATO*. Washington, D.C.: Brookings Institution Press.

Gorbachev, M. S. 1990. "Krepit' kliuchevoe zveno ekonomiki," *Pravda* (10 December).

Gorchinskaya, Katya. 1998. "Ukraine Joins the Party," *Transitions* 5 (May): 54–61.

Gower, Jackie. 1999. "EU Policy to Central and Eastern Europe." In *Back to Europe: Central and Eastern Europe and the European Union*, edited by Karen Henderson. London: University College London Press, pp. 3–19.

Grillo, R. D. 1989. *Dominant Languages: Language and Hierarchy in Britain and France*. New York : Cambridge University Press.

Grzymala-Busse, Anna. 2000. "Redeeming the Past: Communist Successor Parties After 1989." Paper presented at the Twelfth International Conference of Europeanists, Chicago, Ill.

Gumperz, John J., and Jenny Cook-Gumperz. 1982. "Language and the Communication of Social Identity." In *Language and Social Identity*, edited by John J. Gumperz. Cambridge: Cambridge University Press, pp. 1–15.

Gunther, Richard, P. Nikiforos Diamandouros, and Hans-Jurgen Puhle, eds. 1995. *The Politics of Democratic Consolidation: Southern Europe in Comparative Perspective*. Baltimore, Md. and London: Johns Hopkins University Press.

Gyimah-Boadi, E. 1997. "The Challenges Ahead," *Journal of Democracy* 8, 2 (April):78–91.

Hadenius, Axel. 1992. *Democracy and Development*. Cambridge: Cambridge University Press.

Haggard, Stephan, and Robert R. Kaufman. 1994. "The Challenges of Consolidation," *Journal of Democracy* 5, 4 (October):5–16.

———. 1997. "The Political Economy of Democratic Transitions," *Comparative Politics* 29 (April):263–83.

Haiman, John. 1985. *Natural Syntax: Iconicity and Erosion*. New York: Cambridge University Press.

Hanson, Philip. 1993. "Estonia's Narva Problem," *RFE/RL Research Bulletin* (20 April): 17–23.

Hanson, Stephen E. 1995. "The Leninist Legacy and Institutional Change," *Comparative Political Studies* 28, 2 (July): 306–14.

Hanson, Stephen E. 1997. *Time and Revolution: Marxism and the Design of Soviet Institutions.* Chapel Hill: University of North Carolina Press.

———. 1998. "Ideology, Uncertainty, and the Rise of Anti-System Parties in Postcommunist Russia," *Journal of Communist Studies and Transition Politics* 14, 1–2 (March/June):98–127.

Hanson, Stephen E., and Jeffrey S. Kopstein. 1997. "The Weimar/Russia Comparison," *Post-Soviet Affairs* 13, 3 (July–September):252–83.

Helf, Gavin, compiler. 1988. *A Biographical Directory of Soviet Regional Party Leaders*, 2d ed. Munich: Radio Free Europe/Radio Liberty.

Hellman, Joel S. 1998. "Winners Take All: The Politics of Partial Reform in Postcommunist Transitions," *World Politics* 50, 2 (January):203–34.

Henderson, Karen. 1999. "Slovakia and the Democratic Criteria for EU Accession." In *Back to Europe: Central and Eastern Europe and the European Union*, edited by Karen Henderson. London: University College London Press, pp. 221–40.

Hermens, Ferdinand A. 1941. *Democracy or Anarchy?* Notre Dame, Ind.: Notre Dame University Press.

Higley, John, Jan Pakulski, and Wlodimierz Wesolowski. 1998. "Introduction: Elite Change and Democratic Regimes in Eastern Europe." In *Postcommunist Elites and Democracy in Eastern Europe*, edited by John Higley, Jan Pakulski, and Wlodimierz Wesolowski. New York: St. Martin's Press, pp. 1–33.

Hirschman, Albert. 1970. "The Search for Paradigms As a Hindrance to Understanding," *World Politics* 22, 3(April): 329–43.

Hodnett, Grey. 1978. *Leadership in the Soviet National Republics.* Oakville, Ontario: Mosaic Press.

Horowitz, Donald L. 1985. *Ethnic Groups in Conflict.* Berkeley: University of California Press.

———. 1996. "Comparing Democratic Systems." In *The Global Resurgence of Democracy*, edited by Larry Diamond and Marc F. Plattner, 2d. ed. Baltimore, Md.: Johns Hopkins University Press, pp. 143–49.

———. 1993. "Democracy in Divided Societies," *Journal of Democracy* 4, 4 (October):18–38.

Hosking, Geoffrey. 1991. *The Awakening of the Soviet Union*, enlarged edition. Cambridge, Mass.: Harvard University Press.

Howard, Marc Morjé. 2000. "Free Not to Participate: The Weakness of Civil Society in Post-Communist Europe." Studies in Public Policy No. 325, Centre for the Study of Public Policy, University of Strathclyde, Glasgow, Scotland.

Huntington, Samuel P. 1968. *Political Order in Changing Societies.* New Haven, Ct.: Yale University Press.

———. 1970. "Social and Institutional Dynamics of One-Party Systems." In *Authoritarian Politics in Modern Society*, edited by Samuel P. Huntington and Clement H. Moore. New York: Basic Books, pp. 3–47.

———. 1984. "Will More Countries Become Democratic?" *Political Science Quarterly* 99, 2 (Summer);193–218.

———. 1991. *The Third Wave: Democratization in the Late Twentieth Century.* Norman: University of Oklahoma Press.

———. 1996. *The Clash of Civilizations and the Remaking of World Order.* New York: Simon and Schuster.

———. 1997. "After Twenty Years: The Future of the Third Wave," *Journal of Democracy* 8, 4 (October):3–12.

Huskey, Eugene. 1993. "Kyrgyzstan Leaves the Ruble Zone," *RFE/RL Research Report*, 2 (3 September):38–43.

———. 1995. "The Rise of Contested Politics in Central Asia: Elections in Kyrgyzstan, 1989–90," *Europe-Asia Studies* 47 (July):813–33.

———. 1997. "Kyrgyzstan: The Fate of Political Liberalization." In *Conflict, Cleavage, and Change in Central Asia and the Caucasus,* edited by Karen Dawisha and Bruce Parrott. Cambridge: Cambridge University Press, pp. 242–76.

Huttenbach, Henry R. 1995. "Post-Soviet Crisis and Disorder in Transcausasia." In *Political Culture and Civil Society in Russia and the New States of Eurasia,* edited by Vladimir Tismaneanu. Armonk, N.Y.: M. E. Sharpe.

Inglehart, Ronald. 1988. "The Renaissance of Political Culture," *American Political Science Review* 82 (December):1203–30.

International Institute for Democracy and Electoral Assistance. 1998. *Voter Turnout from 1945 to 1997: A Global Report on Political Participation.* Stockholm: IDEA.

Irvine, Jill A. 1997. "Ultranationalist Ideology and State-Building in Croatia, 1990–1996," *Problems of Post-Communism* 44, 4 (July–August):30–43.

Ishiyama, John T. 1993. "Founding Elections and the Development of Transitional Parties: The Cases of Estonia and Latvia, 1990–1992," *Communist and Post-Communist Studies* 26 (September): 277–99.

Jones, Ellen, and Fred W. Grupp. 1984. "Modernisation and Ethnic Equalisation in the USSR," *Soviet Studies* 36 (April):159–84.

Jones, Stephen F. 1996. "Georgia's Return from Chaos," *Current History* 95 (October): 340–45.

Jowitt, Ken. 1992a. "The Leninist Legacy." In *Eastern Europe in Revolution,* edited by Ivo Banac. Ithaca, N.Y.: Cornell University Press pp. 207–24.

———. 1992b. *New World Disorder: The Leninist Extinction.* Berkeley and Los Angeles: University of California Press.

———. 1996a. "Dizzy with Democracy," *Problems of Post-Communism* 43, 1 (January-February):3–8.

———. 1996b. "The New World Disorder." In *The Global Resurgence of Democracy,* edited by Larry Diamond and Marc F. Plattner, 2d. ed. Baltimore, Md.: Johns Hopkins University Press, pp. 26–35.

———. 1998. "Russia Disconnected," *Irish Slavonic Studies* 19.

Kangas, Roger D. 1994. "Uzbekistan: Evolving Authoritarianism," *Current History* 93 (April): 178–82.

Kann, Robert A. 1950. *The Multinational Empire: Nationalism and National Reform in the Habsburg Monarchy 1848–1918.* Vol. 1: Empire and Nationalities. New York: Columbia University Press.

Karatnycky, Adrian. 1995. "Ukraine at the Crossroads," *Journal of Democracy* 6 (January): 117–30.

Karl, Terry Lynn, and Philippe C. Schmitter. 1991. "Modes of Transition in Latin America, Southern and Eastern Europe," *International Social Science Journal* 43 (May): 269–84.

Karmanov, Yuras. 1995. "Belarus: Lukashenko Wins Referendum," *Nezavisimaia gazeta* May 16, p. 1; translated in *The Current Digest of the Post-Soviet Press* 47 (June 14): 18.

Karpov, Aleksandr. 1992. "Tadzhikistan: Prizyv k miru ne uslyshan," *Izvestiia* 12 November, p. 1.

Kechichian, Joseph A., and Theodore W. Karasik. 1995. "The Crisis in Azerbaijan: How Clans Influence the Politics of an Emerging Republic," *Middle East Policy* 4 (September): 57–71.

Keith, Bruce E., et al. 1992. *The Myth of the Independent Voter.* Berkeley: University of California Press.

Kiewiet, Roderick, and Mathew McCubbins. 1991. *The Logic of Delegation: Congressional Parties and the Appropriations Process.* Chicago, Ill.: University of Chicago Press.

Kionka, Riina. 1992. "Estonian Political Struggle Centers on Voting Rights," *RFE/RL Research Report* 1 (12 June): 15–17.

Kitschelt, Herbert. 1999. "Accounting for Outcomes of Post-Communist Regime Change: Casual Depth or Shallowness in Rival Explanations." Paper presented at the 1999 Annual Meeting of the American Political Science Association, Atlanta, Georgia. September 1–5.

Kohli, Atul. 1997. "On Sources of Social and Political Conflicts in Follower Democracies." In *Democracy's Victory and Crisis*, edited by Axel Hadenius. Cambridge: Cambridge University Press, pp. 71–80.

Kopstein, Jeffrey S., and Stephen E. Hanson. 1998. "Paths to Uncivil Societies and Anti-Liberal States: A Reply to Shenfield," *Post-Soviet Affairs* 14, 4 (October–December): 369–75.

Kopstein, Jeffrey S., and David A. Reilly. 2000. "Geographic Diffusion and the Transformation of Postcommunist Europe," *World Politics* 52 (October):1–37.

Kozyrev, Andrei. 1995. *Preobrazhenie.* Moskva: Mezhdunarodnye Otnosheniia.

Kubicek, Paul. 1994. "Delegative Democracy in Russia and Ukraine," *Communist and Post-Communist Studies* 27 (December): 423–41.

Kuhn, Thomas S. 1970. *The Structure of Scientific Revolutions.* Chicago, Ill.: University of Chicago Press.

Kuzio, Taras. 1995. "The 1994 Parliamentary Elections in Ukraine," *Journal of Communist Studies and Transition Politics* 11 (December): 335–61.

———. 1996. "Kravchuk to Kuchma: The Ukrainian Presidential Elections of 1994," *Journal of Communist Studies and Transition Politics* 12 (June): 117–44.

Laitin, David, D. 1992. *Language Repertoires and State Construction in Africa.* Cambridge: Cambridge University Press.

Lardeyret, Guy. 1996. "The Problem with PR." In *The Global Resurgence of Democracy*, edited by Larry Diamond and Marc F. Plattner, 2d. ed. Baltimore, Md.: Johns Hopkins University Press, pp. 175–80.

Lasswell, Harold D., and Abraham Kaplan. 1950. *Power and Society: A Framework for Political Inquiry.* New Haven, Conn.: Yale University Press.

Lebedeva, Marina. 1993. "Uzbekskogo pravozashchitnika Abdumannnova Pulatova khotiat upriatat' v tiurmu na 6 let, xotia vina ego ne dokazana," *Izvestiia* 28 November, p. 2.

Leff, Carol Skalnik. 1996. "Dysfunctional Democratization?" *Problems of Post-Communism* 43 (September–October):36–50.

Levi, Margaret. 1997. *Consent, Dissent and Patriotism*. Cambridge: Cambridge University Press.

Levitskii, Leonid. 1992. "Vybory v Estonii: Delaia ustupniki radikalam, umerennye proigryvaiut," *Izvestiia* 21 September, pp. 1–2.

Lewin, Moshe. 1988. *The Gorbachev Phenomenon*. Berkeley and Los Angeles: University of California Press.

———. 1991. *The Gorbachev Phenomenon: A Historical Interpretation*, expanded edition. Berkeley: University of California Press.

Lewis, Bernard. 1968. *The Emergence of Modern Turkey*, 2d. ed. London: Oxford University Press.

Lieven, Anatol. 1998. "History Is Not Bunk," *Perspective* (October). (From website: www.prospect-magazine.co.uk/highlights/lieven/index.html)

Lijphart, Arend. 1984. *Democracies*. New Haven, Conn.: Yale University Press.

———. 1996. "Constitutional Choices for New Democracies." In *The Global Resurgence of Democracy*, edited by Larry Diamond and Marc F. Plattner, 2d. ed. Baltimore, Md.: Johns Hopkins University Press, pp. 162–74.

Linz, Juan J. 1964. "An Authoritarian Regime: Spain." In *Cleavages, Ideologies, and Party Systems*, edited by Erik Allart and Yrjo Littunen. Helsinki: Academic Bookstore, pp. 291–341.

———. 1975. "Totalitarianism and Authoritarian Regimes." In *Macropolitical Theory (Handbook of Political Science*, vol. 3), edited by Fred I. Greenstein and Nelson W. Polsby. Reading, Mass.: Addison-Wesley, pp. 175–411.

———. 1978. *The Breakdown of Democratic Regimes*. Baltimore, Md.: Johns Hopkins University Press.

———. 1990. "The Perils of Presidentialism," *Journal of Democracy* 1, (Winter):51–69.

———. 1996. "The Perils of Presidentialism." In *The Global Resurgence of Democracy*, edited by Larry Diamond and Marc F. Plattner, 2d. ed. Baltimore, Md.: Johns Hopkins University Press, pp. 124–42.

Linz, Juan J., and Alfred C. Stepan. 1996a. "Toward Consolidated Democracies," *Journal of Democracy* 7 (April):14–33.

———. 1996b. *Problems of Democratic Transition and Consolidation: Southern Europe, South America, and Post-Communist Europe*. Baltimore, Md. and London: Johns Hopkins University Press.

Linz, Juan J., and Arturo Valenzuela, eds. 1994. *The Failure of Presidential Democracy*. Baltimore, Md.: Johns Hopkins University Press.

Lipset, Seymour Martin. 1960. *Political Man: The Social Bases of Politics*. Garden City, N.Y.: Doubleday.

———. 1994. "The Social Requisites of Democracy Revisited," *American Sociological Review* 59 (February):1–22.

Lipset, Seymour Martin. 1996. "The Centrality of Culture." In *The Global Resurgence of Democracy*, edited by Larry Diamond and Marc F. Plattner, 2d. ed. Baltimore, Md.: Johns Hopkins University Press, pp. 150–53.

Lohmann, Susanne. 1994. "The Dynamics of Informational Cascades: The Monday Demonstrations in Leipzig, East Germany, 1989–91," *World Politics* 47 (October):42–101.

Lubarksii, Kronid, and Aleksandr Sobyanin. 1995. "Falsifikatsiia-3," *Novoe vremia*, no. 15 (April), pp. 6–12.

Lubin, Nancy. 1981. "Assimilation and Retention of Ethnic Identity in Uzbekistan," *Asian Affairs* 12 (October):277–85.

Lukashuk, Alexander. 1992. "Belarus," *RFE/RL Research Report* 1 (2 October): 18–21.

———. 1998. "Yesterday As Tomorrow: Why It Works in Belarus," *East European Constitutional Review* 7, 3 (Summer):43–49.

Luong, Pauline Jones. 2000. "After the Break-up: Institutional Design in Transitional States," *Comparative Political Studies* 33 (June): 563–92.

Lyons, Terrence. 1997. "A Major Step Forward," *Journal of Democracy* 8, 2 (April):65–77.

Maddox, Graham. 1982. "A Note on the Meaning of 'Constitution,'" *American Political Science Review* 76 (December): 805–809.

Mahr, Alison, and John Nagle. 1995. "Resurrection of the Successor Parties and Democratization in East-Central Europe," *Communist and Post-Communist Studies* 28, (December):393–409.

Mann, Michael. 1970. "The Social Cohesion of Liberal Democracy," *American Sociological Review* 35 (June):423–39.

Martin, Keith. 1993. "Tajikistan: Civil War Without End?" *REF/RL Research Report* 2 (20 August): 18–29.

Marx, Karl. 1869. *The Eighteenth Brumaire of Louis Bonaparte*. New York: International Publishers.

McAuley, Mary. 1992. "Politics, Economics, and Elite Realignment in Russia: A Regional Perspective," *Soviet Economy* 8 (January–March): 46–88.

McDaniel, Tim. 1997. *The Agony of the Russian Idea*. Princeton, N.J.: Princeton University Press.

McFaul, Michael. 1997. *Russia's 1996 Presidential Election*. Stanford, Calif.: Hoover Institution Press.

———. 1999. "The Perils of a Protracted Transition," *Journal of Democracy* 10 (April): 4–18.

Mekhtiyev, Aidyn. 1993. "Azerbaijan: Insurgents Seize Five Districts in the Republic," *Nezavisimaia gazeta* 15 June, p. 1; translated in *The Current Digest of the Post-Soviet Press* 45 (14 July 1993): 1–2.

Melvin, Neil J. 1998. "The Consolidation of a New Regional Elite: The Case of Omsk, 1987–1995," *Europe-Asia Studies* 50 (June):619–50.

Michta, Andrew A. 1997. "Democratic Consolidation in Poland After 1989." In *The Consolidation of Democracy in East-Central Europe*, edited by Karen Dawisha and Bruce Parrott. Cambridge: Cambridge University Press, pp. 66–108.

Migdal, Joel S. 1988. *Strong Societies and Weak States: State-Society Relations and State Capabilities in the Third World.* Princeton, N.J.: Princeton University Press.

Mihalisko, Kathleen J. 1993. "Belarus: Neutrality Gives Way to 'Collective Security,'" *RFE/RL Research Report* 2 (23 April): 24–32.

———. 1997. "Belarus: Retreat to Authoritarianism." In *Democratic Changes and Authoritarian Reactions in Russia, Ukraine, Belarus, and Moldova,* edited by Karen Dawisha and Bruce Parrott. Cambridge: Cambridge University Press, pp. 223–81.

Mikheyev, Dmitry. 1996. *Russia Transformed.* Indianapolis, Ind.: Hudson Institute.

Montesquieu, C. L. de Secondat. 1995. *The Spirit of the Laws.* Cambridge: Cambridge University Press.

Moore, Barrington. 1966. *Social Origins of Dictatorship and Democracy: Lord and Peasant in the Making of the Modern World.* Boston, Mass.: Beacon Press.

Moreira Alves, Maria Helena. 1985. *State and Opposition in Military Brazil.* Austin: University of Texas Press.

Morgenthau, Hans J. 1948 [1967]. *Politics Among Nations: The Struggle for Power and Peace.* New York: Alfred A. Knopf.

Murphy, James Bernard. 1996. "Rational Choice Theory As Social Physics." In *The Rational Choice Controversy: Economic Models of Politics Reconsidered,* edited by Jeffrey Friedman. New Haven, Conn.: Yale University Press, pp. 155–74.

Natalyin, Vladimir. 1995. "Belorussia: Aleksandr Lukashenko Insists on Holding Referendum," *Segodnia* April 14, p. 5; translated in *The Current Digest of the Post-Soviet Press* 47 (May 10): 19–20.

Nelson, Daniel N. 1996. "Civil Society Endangered," *Social Research* 63, 2 (Summer): 345–68.

Nelson, Lynn D., and Paata Amonashvili. 1992. "Voting and Political Attitudes in Soviet Georgia," *Soviet Studies* 44:687–97.

Nissman, David. 1994. "Turkmenistan (Un)transformed," *Current History* 93 (April): 183–86.

Nist, John A. 1966. *A Structural History of English.* New York: St. Martin's Press.

North, Douglass. 1991. *Institutions, Institutional Change, and Economic Performance.* Cambridge: Cambridge University Press.

Nourzhanov, Kirill, and Amin Saikal. 1994. "The New Kazakhstan: Has Something Gone Wrong?" *The World Today* 50 (December): 225–29.

Nove, Alex. 1986. *The Soviet Economic System,* 3d. ed. Boston, Mass.: Allen and Unwin.

O'Donnell, Guillermo A. 1973. *Modernization and Bureaucratic Authoritarianism.* Berkeley: University of California Institute of International Studies.

———. 1988. *Bureaucratic Authoritarianism: Argentina, 1966–1973, in Comparative Perspective.* Translated by James McGuire in collaboration with Rae Flory. Berkeley: University of California Press.

———. 1994. "Delegative Democracy," *Journal of Democracy* 5 (January):55–70.

O'Donnell, Guillermo A. 1996. "Illusions About Consolidation," *Journal of Democracy* 7 (April):34–52.

O'Donnell, Guillermo, and Phillipe C. Schmitter. 1986. *Transitions from Authoritarianism: Tentative Conclusions and Uncertain Democracies*. Baltimore, Md.: Johns Hopkins University Press.

Olcott, Martha Brill. 1987. *The Kazakhs*. Stanford, Calif.: Hoover Institutions Press.

———. 1997a. "Democratization and the Growth of Political Participation in Kazakstan." In *Conflict, Cleavage, and Change in Central Asia and the Caucasus*, edited by Karen Dawisha and Bruce Parrott. Cambridge: Cambridge University Press, pp. 201–241.

———. 1997b. "Kazakstan: Nursultan Nazarbaev As a Strong President." In *Postcommunist Presidents*, edited by Ray Taras. Cambridge: Cambridge University Press, pp. 106–29.

Olson, Mancur. 1965. *The Logic of Collective Action*. Cambridge, Mass.: Harvard University Press.

O'Neil, Patrick H. 1997. "Hungary: Political Transition and Executive Conflict." In *Postcommunist Presidents*, edited by Ray Taras. Cambridge: Cambridge University Press, pp. 195–224.

Ordeshook, Peter J. 1995. "Russia's Party System: Is Russian Federalism Viable?" *Post-Soviet Affairs* 12, 3 (July–September): 195–217.

Ordeshook, Peter, and Olga Shvetsova. 1997. "Federalism and Constitutional Design," *Journal of Democracy* 8, 1 (January): 27–43.

Orenstein, Mitchell. 1998. "Lawlessness from Above and Below," *SAIS Review* 18, 1 (Winter–Spring):35–50.

Orlik, Iurii. 1992. "Tsenzura v Uzbekistane suverena," *Izvestiia* 13 November. Pp. 1–2.

Ostrom, Elinor. 1990. *Governing the Commons: The Evolution of Institutions for Collective Action*. Cambridge and New York: Cambridge University Press.

Parrott, Bruce. 1997. "Perspectives on Postcommunist Democratization." In *The Consolidation of Democracy in East-Central Europe*, edited by Karen Dawisha and Bruce Parrott. Cambridge: Cambridge University Press, pp. 1–39.

Parsons, J.W.R. 1982. "National Integration in Soviet Georgia," *Soviet Studies* 34 (October):547–69.

Parsons, Talcott. 1951. *The Social System*. Toronto: MacMillan.

Petro, Nicolai. 1995. *The Rebirth of Russian Democracy: An Interpretation of Political Culture*. Cambridge: Harvard University Press.

Petrocik, John, and Shanto Iyengar. 1998. " 'Basic Rule' Voting: The Impact of Campaigns on Party and Approval-Based Voting." Los Angeles: Department of Political Science, UCLA. Typescript.

Pion-Berlin, David. 1983. "Political Repression and Economic Doctrines," *Comparative Political Studies* 16, 1 (April):37–66.

Plakans, Andrejs. 1997. "Democratization and Political Participation in Postcommunist Societies." In *The Consolidation of Democracy in East-Central Europe*, edited by Karen Dawisha and Bruce Parrott. Cambridge: Cambridge University Press, pp. 245–89.

Prizel, Ilya. 1997. "Ukraine Between Proto-Democracy and 'Soft' Authoritarianism." In *Democratic Changes and Authoritarian Reactions in Russia, Ukraine, Belarus, and Moldova*, edited by Karen Dawisha and Bruce Parrott. Cambridge: Cambridge University Press, pp. 330–69.

Pryde, Ian. 1995. "Kyrgyzstan's Slow Progress to Reform," *World Today* 51 (June): 115–18.

Przeworski, Adam. 1991. *Democracy and the Market: Political and Economic Reforms in Eastern Europe and Latin America*. Cambridge: Cambridge University Press.

Przeworski, Adam, et al. 1996. "What Makes Democracies Endure?" *Journal of Democracy* 7 (January): 39–55.

Przeworski, Adam, and Fernando Limongi. 1997. "Modernization: 'Theories and Facts,'" *World Politics* 49 (January): 155–83.

Pusic, Vesna. 1998. "Croatia at the Crossroads," *Journal of Democracy* 9, 1 (January):111–24.

Putnam, Robert D., with Robert Leonardi and Raffaella Y. Nanetti. 1993. *Making Democracy Work: Civic Traditions in Modern Italy*. Princeton, N.J.: Princeton University Press.

Pye, Lucian W. 1990. "Political Science and the Crisis of Authoritarianism," *American Political Science Review* 84 (March):3–20.

Rabushka, Alvin, and Kenneth A. Shepsle. 1972. *Politics in Plural Societies*. Columbus, Ohio: Merrill.

Rae, Douglas W. 1971. *The Political Consequences of Electoral Laws*. New Haven, Conn.: Yale University Press.

Ramseyer, J. Mark, and Frances M. Rosenbluth. 1996. *The Politics of Oligarchy: Institutional Choice in Imperial Japan*. New York: Cambridge University Press.

Random House Geographical Dictionary, The. 1992. New York: Random House.

Reisinger, William M. 1998. "Congruence Theory As a Perspective on Russian Politics." In *Can Democracy Take Root in Post–Soviet Russia? Explorations in State-Society Relations*, edited by Harry Eckstein et al.. Lanham, Md.: Rowman and Littlefield, pp. 151–62.

Reisinger, William M., et al. 1994. "Political Values in Russia, Ukraine and Lithuania: Sources and Implications for Democracy," *British Journal of Political Science* 24, (April):183–223.

Remington, Thomas. 2000. "The Evolution of Executive-Legislative Relations in Russia Since 1993," *Slavic Review* 59 (Fall): 499–520.

Remmer, Karen L. 1996. "The Sustainability of Political Democracy: Lessons from South America," *Comparative Political Studies* 29, 6 (December):611–34.

Riker, William. 1962. *The Theory of Political Coalitions*. New Haven, Conn.: Yale University Press.

Roberts, Kenneth M. 1995. "Neoliberalism and the Transformation of Populism in Latin America," *World Politics* 48, 1 (October):82–116.

Roeder, Philip G. 1989. "Modernization and Participation in the Leninist Developmental Strategy," *American Political Science Review* 83 (September): 859–84.

Roeder, Philip G. 1993. *Red Sunset: The Failure of Soviet Politics.* Princeton, N.J.: Princeton University Press.

———. 1994. "Varieties of Post-Soviet Authoritarian Regimes," *Post-Soviet Affairs* 10, 1 (January–March):61–101.

Romania, Constitution of. 1991. Bucharest: Monitorul Oficial.

Rose, Richard, and Do Chull Shin. 1998. "Qualities of Incomplete Democracies: Russia, the Czech Republic, and Korea Compared." *Studies in Public Policy,* no. 302. Glasgow: University of Strathclyde, Center for the Study of Public Policy.

Rosenstone, Steven J., and John Mark Hansen. 1993. *Mobilization, Participation, and Democracy in America.* New York: Macmillan Publishing Co.

Rowen, Henry S. 1995. "The Tide Underneath the 'Third Wave,'" *Journal of Democracy* 6: 1 (January):52–64.

Rueschemeyer, Dietrich, Evelyn Huber Stephens, and John D. Stephens. 1992. *Capitalist Development and Democracy.* Chicago, Ill.: University of Chicago Press.

Rupnik, Jacques. 1999. "The Postcommunist Divide," *Journal of Democracy* 10 (January): 57–62.

Russell, John. 2000. "Yeltsin vs. Gorbachev: January to June 1991—Key Turning Points in the Struggle for Power and Legitimacy in Russia and the USSR." Paper presented to the ICCEES VI World Congress, Tampere, Finland.

Rustow, Dankwart. 1970. "Transitions to Democracy: Toward a Dynamic Model," *Comparative Politics* 2 (April): 337–63.

Rutland, Peter. 1994. "Democracy and Nationalism in Armenia," *Europe-Asia Studies* 46:839–61.

Sakwa, Richard. 1993. *Russian Politics and Society.* New York: Routledge.

Sartori, Giovanni. 1966. "European Political Parties: The Case of Polarized Pluralism." In *Political Parties and Political Development,* edited by Joseph LaPalombara and Myron Weiner. Princeton, N.J.: Princeton University Press, pp. 137–76.

———. 1976. *Parties and Party Systems: A Framework for Analysis.* Cambridge: Cambridge University Press.

Sautman, Barry. 1995. "The Devil to Pay: The 1989 Debate and the Intellectual Origins of Yeltsin's 'Soft Authoritarianism,'" *Communist and Post-Communist Studies* 28 (March): 131–51.

Schattschneider, E. E. 1975. *The Semi-Sovereign People: A Realist's View of Democracy in America.* Hinsdale, Ill.: Dryden Press.

Schedler, Andreas. 1998. "What Is Democratic Consolidation?" *Journal of Democracy* 9, 2 (April):91–107.

Schiffrin, Deborah. 1987. *Discourse Markers.* Cambridge: Cambridge University Press.

———. 1996. "Narrative As Self-Portrait: Sociolinguistic Constructions of Identity." *Language in Society* 25(June):167–203.

Schmitter, Philippe C., and Terry Lynn Karl. 1996. "What Democracy Is . . . and Is Not." In *The Global Resurgence of Democracy,* edited by Larry Diamond and Marc F. Plattner, 2d. ed. Baltimore, Md.: Johns Hopkins University Press, pp. 49–62.

Schumpeter, Joseph. 1975 [1947]. *Capitalism, Socialism, and Democracy.* New York: Harper and Row.

Selznick, Philip. 1949. *TVA and the Grass Roots: A Study in the Sociology of Formal Organization.* Berkeley: University of California Press.

———. 1957. *Leadership in Administration.* New York: Harper and Row.

Shea, Christopher. 1997. "Political Scientists Clash over the Value of Area Studies," *Chronicle of Higher Education* 58 (10 January), A13–A14.

Shevtsova, Lilia. 1996. "Parliament and the Political Crisis in Russia, 1991–1993." In *Democratization in Russia: The Development of Legislative Institutions,* edited by Jeffrey W. Hahn. Armonk, N.Y.: M. E. Sharpe.

Shevtsova, Lilia, and Scott A. Bruckner. 1997. "Toward Stability of Crisis?" *Journal of Democracy* 8 (January): 12–26.

Shugart, Matthew S., and John M. Carey. 1992. *Presidents and Assemblies: Constitutional Design and Electoral Dynamics.* New York: Cambridge University Press.

Shugart, Matthew Soberg, and Scott Mainwaring. 1997. "Presidentialism and Democracy in Latin America: Rethinking the Terms of the Debate." In *Presidentialism and Democracy in Latin America,* edited by Scott Mainwaring and Matthew Soberg Shugart. Baltimore, Md.: Johns Hopkins University Press, pp. 12–54.

Singer, J. David. 1961. "The Level-of-Analysis Problem in International Relations." In *The International System: Theoretical Essays,* edited by Klaus Knorr and Sidney Verba. Princeton, N.J.: Princeton University Press, pp. 77–92.

Smith, Martin A. 1999. "The NATO Factor: A Spanner in the Works of EU and WEU Enlargement?" In *Back to Europe: Central and Eastern Europe and the European Union,* edited by Karen Henderson. London: University College London Press, pp. 53–67.

Smith, Olivia. 1984. *The Politics of Language 1791–1819.* Oxford: Oxford University Press.

Socor, Valdimir. 1992. "Moldova's New 'Government of National Consensus,'" *RFE/RL Research Report* 1 (27 November): 5–10.

———. 1993. "Moldova: Another Major Setback for Pro-Romanian Forces," *RFE/RL Research Report* 2 (26 February): 15–21.

Stanchev, Krassen. 1997. "Bulgaria's Caretaker Cabinet," *Institute for Market Economic Newsletter* (Sofia) 4, 1 (January–February).

Starikevich, Aleksandr, and Besik Urigashvili. 1996. "Za kompromiss v Belorussii zaplacheno konstitutsiei," *Izvestiia* 23 November, p. 2.

Starr, S. Frederick. 1988. "The Soviet Union: A Civil Society," *Foreign Policy* 70 (Spring):26–41.

Steele, Jonathan. 1994. *Eternal Russia: Gorbachev, Yeltsin, and the Mirage of Democracy.* London: Faber.

Stepan, Alfred. 1978. "Political Leadership and Regime Breakdown." In *The Breakdown of Democratic Regimes,* edited by Juan J. Linz and Alfred Stepan. Baltimore, Md.: Johns Hopkins University Press. Part 3, pp. 110–37.

———. 1988. *Rethinking Military Politics: Brazil and the Southern Cone.* Princeton, N.J.: Princeton University Press.

Stepan, Alfred, and Cindy Skach. 1993. "Constitutional Frameworks and Democratic Consolidation," *World Politics* 46, 1 (October):1–22.

Stinchcombe, Arthur. 1997. "On the Virtues of the Old Institutionalism," *Annual Review of Sociology* 23:1–19.

Sukhanov, Lev. 1992. *Tri goda s El'tsinym: Zapiski pervogo pomoshchnika.* Riga: "Vaga."

Suny, Ronald Grigor. 1988. *The Making of the Georgian Nation.* Bloomington: Indiana University Press.

Svensson, Christian. 1997. "The Commonalization of Politics—Political Roles and Ordinariness in TV Debates." Paper presented to a conference on "Analysing Political Discourse," Birmingham, UK, 17–19 July 1997.

Szomolanyi, Sona, and John A. Gould (eds.). 1997. *Slovakia: Problems of Democratic Consolidation.* Bratislava: Friedrich Ebert Foundation.

Taylor, Michael. 1976. *Anarchy and Cooperation.* London: Wiley.

———. 1987. *The Possibility of Cooperation.* Cambridge: Cambridge University Press.

Taylor, Michael, and Sara Singleton. 1993. "The Communal Resource: Transaction Costs and the Solution of Collective Action Problems," *Politics and Society* 21, 2 (June): 195–215.

Tilly, Charles. 1990. *Capital, Coercion, and European States, A.D. 990–1990.* Oxford: Oxford University Press.

Tismaneanu, Vladimir. 1997. "Romanian Exceptionalism?" In *Politics, Power, and the Struggle for Democracy in South-East Europe*, edited by Karen Dawisha and Bruce Parrott. Cambridge: Cambridge University Press, pp. 403–451.

Tocqueville, Alexis de. 1966. *Democracy in America.* New York: Harper and Row.

Todres, Vladimir. 1993. "Rebellion: Local Soviets Present an Ultimatum to Yeltsin," *Segodnia* October 2, p. 2: translated in *The Current Digest of the Post-Soviet Press* 39 (October 27): 16.

Tregubova, Yelena. 1995. "Unity: Most Regional Chiefs Support the 'Chernomyrdin Bloc,'" *Segodnia* May 4, p. 2; translated in *The Current Digest of the Post-Soviet Press* 47 (May 31): 1–2.

Tucker, Robert C. 1971. *The Soviet Political Mind: Stalinism and Post-Stalin Change*, rev. ed. New York: W. W. Norton.

———. 1992. "Sovietology and Russian History," *Post-Soviet Affairs* 8 (July–September):175–96.

Tulis, Jeffrey. 1987. *The Rhetorical Presidency.* Princeton: Princeton University Press.

Turner, John C., et al. 1987. *Rediscovering the Social Group: A Self-Categorization Theory.* New York: Basil Blackwell.

United States. Commission on Security and Cooperation in Europe. 1990. *Elections in the Baltic States and Soviet Republics: A Compendium of Reports on Parliamentary Elections Held in 1990.* Washington, D.C.: Commission on Security and Cooperation in Europe.

———. 1993a. *Human Rights and Democratization in Estonia.* Washington, D.C.: Commission on Security and Cooperation in Europe.

———. 1993b. *Human Rights and Democratization in Latvia*. Washington, D.C.: Commission on Security and Cooperation in Europe.

———. 1994a. *Report on the March 7, 1994 Parliamentary Election in Kazakhstan*. Washington, D.C.: Commission on Security and Cooperation in Europe.

———. 1994b. *Report on the Moldovan Parliamentary Elections, February 27, 1994*. Washington, D.C.: Commission on Security and Cooperation in Europe.

———. 1994c. *Russia's Parliamentary Election and Constitutional Referendum, December 12, 1993*. Washington, D.C.: Commission on Security and Cooperation in Europe.

———. 1994d. *Ukraine's Parliamentary Elections, March 27, 1994, April 10, 1994*. Washington, D.C.: Commission on Security and Cooperation in Europe.

United States. 1995a. *Report on Armenia's Parliamentary Elections and Constitutional Referendum, July 5, 1995*. Washington, D.C.: Commission on Security and Cooperation in Europe.

———. 1995b. *Report on the Parliamentary Election in Kyrgyzstan, February 5, 1995*. Washington, D.C.: Commission on Security and Cooperation in Europe.

———. 1995c. *Report on the Parliamentary Election in Turkmenistan, December 11, 1994*. Washington, D.C.: Commission on Security and Cooperation in Europe.

———. 1996a. *Report on Azerbaijan's November 1995 Parliamentary Election*. Washington, D.C.: Commission on Security and Cooperation in Europe.

———. 1996b. *Report on the Russian Duma Elections of December 1995*. Washington, D.C.: Commission on Security and Cooperation in Europe.

———. 1996c. *Report on the U.S. Helsinki Commission Delegation to Georgia and Azerbaijan, April 22–29, 1996*. Washington, D.C.: Commission on Security and Cooperation in Europe.

———. 1998a. *Political Reform and Human Rights in Uzbekistan, Kyrgyzstan, and Kazakstan*. Washington, D.C.: Commission on Security and Cooperation in Europe.

———. 1998b. *Report on Armenia's Presidential Election, March 16 and 30, 1998*. Washington, D.C.: Commission on Security and Cooperation in Europe.

———. 1998c. *Report on the Moldovan Parliamentary Elections: Southern Moldova, the "Security Zone," and Gagauzia, March 22, 1998*. Washington, D.C.: Commission on Security and Cooperation in Europe.

———. 1998d. *Ukrainian Parliamentary Election, March 29, 1998*. Washington, D.C.: Commission on Security and Cooperation in Europe.

———. 1999a. *Georgia's Parliamentary Elections, October 31, 1999*. Washington, D.C.: Commission on Security and Cooperation in Europe.

———. 1999b. *Kazakhstan's Parliamentary Election, October 10, 1999*. Washington, D.C.: Commission on Security and Cooperation in Europe.

———. 1999c. *Report on Armenia's Parliamentary Election, May 30, 1999*. Washington, D.C.: Commission on Security and Cooperation in Europe.

———. 1999d. *Report on Kazakhstan's Presidential Election, January 10, 1999*. Washington, D.C.: Commission on Security and Cooperation in Europe.

———. 1999e. *Ukraine's Presidential Election, October 31 and November 14, 1999*. Washington, D.C.: Commission on Security and Cooperation in Europe.

United States. 2000a. *Report on the Parliamentary Election in Kyrgyzstan, February–March 2000*. Washington, D.C.: Commission on Security and Cooperation in Europe.

———. 2000b. *Report on the Presidential Election in Georgia, April 9, 2000*. Washington, D.C.: Commission on Security and Cooperation in Europe.

———. State Department official. Anonymous interview, 1997.

Urban, Michael. 1997. *The Rebirth of Politics in Russia*. Cambridge: Cambridge University Press.

USSR Facts and Figures Annual. Various. Gulf Breeze, Fl.: Academic International Press.

USSR. 1972–73. Tsentral'noe Statisticheskoe Upravlenie. *Itogi vsesoiuznoe perepisi naseleniia, 1970 goda*. Moscow: Statistika.

———. 1984. Prezidium Verkhovnogo Soveta SSSR. *Deputaty verkhovnogo soveta SSSR, odinadtsatyi sozyv*. Moscow: Izvestiia.

———. 1990. Gosudarstvennyi Komitet SSSR po Statistike. *Demograficheskii ezhegodnik SSSR, 1990 g*. Moscow: Finansy i statistika.

Valdman, Albert. 1988. "Diglossia and Language Conflict in Haiti." *International Journal of the Sociology of Language* 71:67–80.

Valenzuela, Arturo. 1991. "The Military in Power: The Consolidation of One-Man Rule in Chile." In *The Struggle for Democracy in Chile, 1982–1990*, edited by Paul Drake and Ivan Jaksic. Lincoln: University of Nebraska Press, pp. 21–72.

Varshney, Ashutosh. 1998. "Why Democracy Survives," *Journal of Democracy* 9, 3 (July):36–50.

Wallerstein, Michael. 1980. "The Collapse of Democracy in Brazil," *Latin American Research Review* 15, 3:3–40.

Wasilewski, Jacek. 1998. "Elite Circulation and Consolidation of Democracy in Poland." In *Postcommunist Elites and Democracy in Eastern Europe*, edited by John Higley, Jan Pakulski, and Wlodimierz Wesolowski. New York: St. Martin's Press, pp. 163–87.

Waterbury, John. 1994. "Democracy Without Democrats?" In *Democracy Without Democrats?* edited by Ghassan Salamé. London: I. B. Tauris, pp. 23–47.

Weber, Max. 1968. *Economy and Society*, vols. I and II, edited by Guenther Roth and Claus Wittich. Berkeley and Los Angeles: University of California Press.

White, Stephen. 1995. "The Presidency and Political Leadership in Post-Communist Russia." In *Elections and Political Order in Russia*, edited by Peter Lentini. Budapest: Central University Press.

White, Stephen, Richard Rose, and Ian McAllister. 1997. *How Russia Votes*. Chatham: Chatham House.

Widmer, Urs. 1966. *1945 oder die "neue Sprache."* Duesseldorf: Pedagogischer Verlag Schwann.

Wilson, Andrew, and Sarah Birch. 1999. "Voting Stability, Political Gridlock: Ukraine's 1998 Parliamentary Elections," *Europe-Asia Studies* 51 (September):1039–68.

Wolchik, Sharon L. 1997a. "The Czech Republic: Havel and the Evolution of the Presidency Since 1989." In *Postcommunist Presidents*, edited by Ray Taras. Cambridge: Cambridge University Press, pp. 168–94.

———. 1997b. "Democratization and Political Participation in Slovakia." In *The Consolidation of Democracy in East-Central Europe*, edited by Karen Dawisha and Bruce Parrott. Cambridge: Cambridge University Press, pp. 197–244.

World Bank. 1995. *World Tables 1995*. Baltimore, Md.: Johns Hopkins University Press, 1995.

———. 1996. *From Plan to Market*. New York: Oxford University Press.

———. 1997. *World Development Indicators 1997*. Washington, D.C.: The World Bank.

Wolchik, Sharon L. 1998. *World Development Indicators 1998*. Washington, D.C.: World Bank.

Wyrda, Harald. 1999. "Democracy in Eastern Europe As a Civilizing Process." In *Whose Europe?: The Turn Toward Democracy*. Oxford: Blackwell, pp. 288–310.

Yashar, Deborah J. 1997. "The Quetzal Is Red." In *The New Politics of Inequality in Latin America*, edited by Douglas A. Chalmers et al. New York: Oxford University Press, pp. 239–60.

Yuryev, Yevgeny. 1995. "Party Life in Russia: Ivan Rybkin in Search of Allies," *Kommersant-Daily* May 5, p. 3; translated in *The Current Digest of the Post-Soviet Press* 47 (May 31): 2–3.

Zakaria, Fareed. 1997. "The Rise of Illiberal Democracy," *Foreign Affairs* 76, 6 (November–December): 22–44.

Zhdanko, Valentin. 1994a. "Belorussia: Vyacheslav Kebich Resigns," *Segodnia* July 13, p. 5; translated in *The Current Digest of the Post-Soviet Press* 46 (August 10): 14–15.

———. 1994b. "Belorussia: President Calls His New Powers 'Regal,'" *Segodnia* October 12, p. 4; translated in *The Current Digest of the Post-Soviet Press* 46 (November 9): 22.

INDEX

Akaev, Askar, 66, 71, 73, 74, 87
Albania: chief executive as agent of de-democratization, 68; constitutional structure, 69–70; decline in freedom rating, 68; external financial support for, 73; parliamentary system of, 69
Aliev, Geidar, 41
Anderson, Richard D., Jr., 5–6, 52–53, 154–65, 167. *See also* Fish, M. Steven; Hanson, Stephen E.; Roeder, Philip G.
Antall, Jozsef, 85
Armenia: chief executive as agent of de-democratization, 68; constitutional structure, 69–70; decline in freedom rating, 68; external financial support for, 73–74; selectorate in postcommunist, 15–16, 19
Atatürk, Kemal, 112
authoritarianism: bargaining model of regime choice, 23–29; communicated by use of language, 114–15; conditions for failure of, 6–7, 12, 40–49; conditions in postcommunist Europe for, 140; constitutional instability in, 41–42; defined, 13; fixed conditions for reversal to, 57–58; influence of pre-1990 power on creation of, 33–35; proximate circumstances for reversal to, 58–60; survival in postcommunist countries, 11; without privative opposition, 105
autocracy: dilemmas of authority and accountability in design; of, 27; influence of pre-1990 power on creation of, 33, 36–37; political order in, 14; in Soviet successor states, 15–16
Azerbaijan: autocracy maintained in, 40–41; selectorate in postcommunist, 15–16

Barnard, Chester, 143
Belarus: autocracy in, 41–42; chief executive as agent of de-democratization, 66–67; external financial support for, 74; selectorate in postcommunist, 15–16
Berisha, Sali, 68, 69, 70–73, 87–89
Bollen, Kenneth A., 130
Bova, Russell, 130, 131, 158
Bruckner, Scott, 49

Bunce, Valerie, 52, 63
Burbulis, Gennadi, 47

Central Europe, consolidation of democracy in, 146–47
Chernomyrdin, Viktor, 47
choice: of constitutions in postcommunist countries, 89–93; to make transition to democracy, 11; of regime within authoritarianism, 11–12, 155–56
Cirtautas, Arista Maria, 141–42
competition: as incentive for institution building, 84–85; incentives among politicians for, 96–97
Constantinescu, Emil, 79, 148
constitutions: autocratic, 14, 17–19; of Belarus (1996), 42; choice of, 89–93; of countries with reversal of democracy, 69; democratic, 14, 17–19; differences in former Soviet republics', 14–19; dilemma of accountability and authority in design; of, 25–27; exclusively republican, 14, 17–19; oligarchic, 14, 17–19; post-1991 authoritarian, 34–36; Russian (1993), 148–49; Uzbekistan, 37. *See also* autocracy; democracy; exclusive republics; oligarchy
Croatia: chief executive as agent of de-democratization, 68; constitutional provisions and structure, 69; decline in freedom rating, 68; external financial support for, 74
Czechoslovakia: parliamentarism of, 90
Czech Republic: parliamentary system of, 76; ties with Western countries, 77

Dahl, Robert, 17, 55, 141, 159
democracy: accountability and authority under, 14–15, 25–27; choices under, 160; conditions for emergence of procedural, 2; consolidation of, 139; contestation as manifestation of, 49; defined, 13; defined in institutional terms, 135–36; discursive theory of, 97–98; distinct from nondemocracy, 106–7, 156; in modernization theory, 129; Oligarch's